The Bank of Lebanon

The Bank of Lebanon

Central Banking in a Financial Centre and Entrepôt

Abdul-Amir Badrud-Din

Frances Pinter (Publishers)
London and Dover N.H.

First edition published in Great Britain in 1984 by
Frances Pinter (Publishers) Limited
5 Dryden Street, London WC2E 9NW

Published in the United States of America in 1984 by
Frances Pinter (Publishers), 31 Washington Street,
Dover, New Hampshire

British Library Cataloguing in Publication Data
Badrud-Din, Abdul-Amir
1. The Bank of Lebanon
I. Title
332.1'1'095692 HG3259
ISBN 0-86187-461-7

Library of Congress Catalog Card Number 83-043270
US CIP applied for

Typeset by Joshua Associates, Oxford
Printed by SRP, Ltd., Exeter

To Lord Bullock of Leafield, formerly Founding Master of St. Catherine's College, Oxford, and Vice-Chancellor of the University of Oxford

Contents

List of Tables

List of Figures

Abbreviations

BSL Banque de Syrie et du Liban
CMC Conseil de la Monnaie et du Credit
BL Bank of Lebanon
SNB Swiss National Bank
FX Foreign Exchange
LL Lebanese Pounds
LP Lebanese Piastres

Foreword

The Rt. Hon. Lord Bullock, FBA, formerly Founding Master of St. Catherine's College, and Vice-Chancellor of the University of Oxford.

The destruction of Lebanon has become one of the major tragedies of the later twentieth century. Yet it is only a short time ago that it was universally regarded as the Switzerland of the Middle East, an oasis of sanity in the middle of an area of endemic instability. This reputation was due not to luck but to the skill with which the Lebanese had managed to construct and preserve a balance between the different religious and political groups within their country. How this remarkable system worked, what part was played in it by the Bank of Lebanon and how, even as Lebanon's only surviving national institution, is the subject of this unique study by Abdul-Amir Badrud-Din.

It is unique for two reasons. The first is because, among all the financial institutions of the world there is nothing quite like the Bank of Lebanon, and surely no other which has been called on to continue its role in such impossible circumstances. The second reason is because its author writes with the inside knowledge and authority of one who has been for many years the Deputy-Governor of the Bank. Such a study cannot fail to be of interest to anyone interested in the role of central banking in the modern world.

It was primarily undertaken as a research project at Oxford under the supervision of the late Sir Roy Harrod. It was then I came to know Mr Badrud-Din as a graduate student of my own college, St. Catherine's. Since then the original study has been rewritten, enlarged and brought up to date, using material to which no other writer has had access. I have followed with admiration the determination with which my friend Abdul-Amir Badrud-Din has remained at his post and the courage he and his wife have shown in bringing up a young family in a Beirut which for seven long years has been racked with violence, the scene of war, civil war, invasion and counter-invasion.

In such circumstances, it is an act of faith to publish this account of how Lebanon has managed its finances. I believe, however, that the author is quite right to believe that, even in the circumstances—indeed, because of these circumstances—it is important to make clear the role

Lebanon formerly played, and could yet play again, in the Middle East. It is an act of faith in the future which those who have seen with horror what has happened to Lebanon can only applaud.

It is in reponse to that act of faith as well as to the claims of friendship with a valued old member of St. Catherine's College that I am glad to introduce this book to the public.

Preface

This work originated in a thesis written while the author was at Oxford, reading for the degree of Doctor of Philosophy under the supervision of Sir Roy Harrod. It is an attempt not only to deal with central banking in general, but also to expose and analyse central banking in a financial centre and a financial entrepôt.

The Bank of Lebanon came into being to meet a particular need. It was created by the Money and Credit Board, on which the author served for nearly three years. The legislation establishing the Central Bank roused determined opposition from the Bankers' Association, who were apprehensive about regulation. For twenty years the author has been one of the Deputy-Governors of the bank. For about twenty-three years, therefore, he has been concerned daily with central banking problems. This study of a central bank in a country that is a financial centre and a financial entrepôt is an analysis of a special field of central banking, an assessment of the past few years and a basis for the years to come.

The study begins by surveying economic, social and political conditions in modern Lebanon. It then turns to monetary and banking developments in the period 1920–64, which led to the establishment of the Bank of Lebanon. The prime need of the years 1948–64 was to free the system from dependence on the French franc, and to set a pattern of free money and exchange markets. Added to this was the Banking Secrecy Law, which indicated the intention of the nation to establish a financial centre and entrepôt for those who wanted a safeguard.

The entrepôt character is not alien to the principles of banking: here the whole country acts as a bank. It uses to a great extent the money of others. As in Switzerland, the centre and the entrepôt principle in Lebanon is central. These two nations have many challenges and many problems in common.

April 1981 A. A. B.

Acknowledgements

There are eight authorities to whom the author is deeply grateful for vital help on many points. They have given generously of their time and attention to the author notwithstanding heavy ties and responsibilities when this study was undertaken, particularly in the 1960s. They are: the former Founding Master of St. Catherine's, Oxford; the late Sir Roy Harrod; Mr R. I. Hallows, adviser to the Governors of the Bank of England; Mr Alexander Hay, Vice-President of the Swiss National Bank; Dr Pierre Fluckinger, General Director of the Swiss National Bank; HE the Prime Minister Dr Salim Al-Hoss, when Chairman of the Banking Control Commission; Mr Michel Tasso, Director of the Department of Statistics and Economic Studies (BL); and Mr K Schattmeier of the Swiss Bank Corporation.

Also, the Hon. Paul A. Volcker, Chairman of the Board of Governors of the Federal Reserve System, when President of the Federal Reserve Bank of New York, was most kind to supply the author with the material on monetary aggregate targeting procedures.

A special word of thanks is also due to my secretary Mrs S. R. Moukheiber who has performed her task with kindness, patience and efficiency.

1 Lebanon's economy and currency

INTRODUCTION

The Lebanese banking system has grown out of an exceptional environment. The Republic has about three million people living in an area of about 10,380 square kilometres, but despite this relatively high density of population (285 people to the square kilometre) they enjoy a higher standard of living than most countries in Asia or Africa. Neighbouring Arab countries, however, have more oil and other natural resources. Hence it is by their own skill that the Lebanese people have built up their high standards. Indeed, the Lebanese are among the most literate (80 per cent), sophisticated, shrewd and adventurous of Arab peoples.

The Lebanese became independent only in 1943 and soon began to realise the potential of their country as a commercial and a banking centre. History provided them with many encouragements. Lebanon, with its beautiful countryside and favourable climate, has proved from earliest times an ideal situation for the development of human ingenuity. The city of Beirut was a commercial centre long before any of the present world centres. It was first settled by the Phoenicians prior to 1500 BC[1] and became one of the city-states which, after 1200 BC, developed the great Phoenician trading empire.[2] The earliest authentic records available from Beirut are the Tel-el-Amarna tablets[3] discovered in Egypt in 1886. Beyond a doubt, as Porter states, Beirut was involved in the commercial activity of the Phoenicians. From its coins it appears that Poseidon, the god of the sea, was its tutelary deity. The Beirut Phoenicians made a point of honouring him as they were extensively engaged in trade by sea.[4] Some historical sources estimate the Phoenician merchant fleet at over two thousand ships.[5]

Peaceful coexistence contributed to the import–export trade of Phoenician Beirut. Besides its sea traffic, trading caravans explored inland Asia through Syria and Iraq.[6] Phoenician sailors and traders sailed from Tyre, Sidon and other Phoenician cities carrying goods from the Near East to Greece, Italy, Spain and the Mediterranean islands. They ventured as far as Cape Verde, the Azores and even Britain. They established trading posts, they founded Carthage and Utica in North Africa and Gades (now Cadiz) in Spain. They were manufacturers as well as traders. Glass, metalwork, pottery and dyestuffs were produced in their cities. And they were important bearers of culture: it was the Phoenicians who introduced the alphabet to the Greeks, contributing to the growth of civilisation in those once-backward areas of the western Mediterranean.[7]

Beirut was also a leading centre of Roman civilisation in Syria. Its coins reveal that it advanced to high status in the days of Augustus. Its Law School was perhaps the most famous in the Roman Empire.

In more recent times the city of Beirut became the export–import centre to most Ottoman states.[8] It increased in importance, becoming a provincial capital after the Vilayet of Beirut was separated from that of Damascus in 1888.[9] Its commerce, stagnant during the First World War, revived after its occupation by the Allies in 1918.[10]

Many cultures and traits have influenced the Lebanese way of life. Besides the Phoenician heritage of trade and adventure, there was the Arab business acumen and temperament and, most important, the recent impact of Western culture and education. The country is the gateway to the East, and its mountain recesses have welcomed refugees of all kinds, who have taught the Lebanese a high degree of tolerance. The friendly atmosphere of Lebanon attracted Western missionaries: Jesuit and other Catholic schools have existed since the seventeenth century, and other missionary schools came later. In 1866 the Syrian Protestant College, which became the American University of Beirut, was created and in 1875 the Université Saint Joseph. German, Russian and other schools were also established towards the end of the nineteenth century. A nation speaking French, English and other European languages came into existence.[11]

The patriarchal pattern of family life is passing, thanks to the change in the status of women, particularly in the urban class. Women are found in an ever-increasing number of occupations, including the liberal professions.[12]

Although social cohesion is growing, religious groups play an essential role in politics.[13] There are many sects, none of which can claim an overall majority of the population. The Lebanese Constitution guarantees religious freedom and equality of opportunity, and provides for the equitable representation of the communities in the cabinet and in public employment.[14] The political party system in the Western sense, has not yet fully developed.

THE ECONOMY

In 1948 a Belgian economist, invited by the Government to advise on development, said 'I don't know what makes the economy work, but it seems to do pretty well. I suggest, therefore, that you leave it alone.'[15] Thus, there has been an impression that the economy is mysterious, functioning as a result of luck and extraordinary forces. A closer look reveals that there is nothing mysterious, but that the economy is indeed unique.

The apparent mystery arose from the fact that there was not enough data to reveal what was going on. One reason for this was that figures for Lebanon and Syria were not separated in the early and rather crude statistical material.[16] Another was a tradition of extreme economic liberalism among authorities and people, involving smuggling and other unauthorized activities not recorded in official statistics.

Lebanon's prosperity, contrasting with most Asian and African countries, is due mainly to the special qualities of its people, who are known for their aptitude for business; and to the country's geographical position, climate and topography which, together with its large customs-free zone, have combined to make it a crossroads for commerce, tourism and politics.[17] About 42 per cent of Lebanon's land is cultivable (including pastures), 8 per cent consists of forest, and the remaining part is either wasteland or built-up areas. Of the total area only 22 per cent is actually cultivated.[18] A wide variety of fruits and vegetables can be grown, ranging from tropical and sub-tropical on the coast, such as bananas, to apples in the higher altitudes. Lebanon as a summer resort offers beautiful scenery and many historical sites.

National income

Until June 1962 there was no Central Directorate for Statistics at the Ministry of Planning, but the Economic Research Institute of the American University of Beirut did some pioneer work, conducting in 1953 a study on the national income for 1948–50, and using the 1950 figures as the basis for a projection up to 1958. This series has been used by the Lebanese Government, the United Nations and the International Monetary Fund. The Economic Section of the American Embassy in Lebanon prepared another series of estimates for 1954–7, on the same principles. Official government statistics, compiled by the Central Directorate, have been available since 1965. A simplified presentation of the French system of national accounting is employed.

Table 1.1 shows the main national income aggregates for the years 1965–70. The great involvement of the Lebanese economy in foreign trade, and especially its reliance on imported goods is clear. In 1970, for example, the ratio of gross imports to total sources of supply was 30 per cent. Net imports (imports minus re-exports) represented about 15 per cent of total sources of supply. Lebanese manufacturing industry depends on imports for equipment and most raw materials. The country also depends heavily on importing consumer goods.

Table 1.1. Gross Domestic Product and overall equilibrium in the Lebanese economy (current prices) (LL Millions)

	1965	1966	1967	1968	1969	1970	Percentage changes 66/65	67/66	68/67	69/68	70/69
Sources											
Gross Domestic Product	3,239.6	3,547.5	3,483.3	3,915.7	4,171.6	4,442.1	109.50	98.19	112.41	106.54	106.48
Imports	1,402.2	1,587.5	1,448.9	1,615.8	1,761.6	1,896.8	113.21	91.27	111.52	109.02	107.67
Total	4,641.8	5,135.0	4,932.2	5,531.5	5,933.2	6,338.9	110.63	96.05	112.41	107.26	106.84
Uses											
Private consumption	3,110.7	3,393.4	3,299.4	3,666.6	3,934.2	4,196.9	109.09	97.23	111.13	107.30	106.68
Government consumption	70.8	81.9	82.1	81.2	85.0	88.2	115.68	100.24	98.90	104.68	103.76
Sub-total	3,181.5	3,475.3	3,381.5	3,747.8	4,019.2	4,285.1	109.23	97.30	110.83	107.24	106.62
Gross fixed capital formation by enterprises	649.4	761.3	627.0	640.6	703.7	765.9	117.23	82.36	102.17	109.85	108.84
Gross fixed capital formation by government	129.8	127.8	131.8	146.1	173.2	172.0	98.46	103.13	110.85	118.55	99.31
Sub-total	779.2	889.1	758.8	786.7	876.9	937.9	114.10	85.34	103.68	111.47	106.96
Variations of stock	13.3	43.7	11.0	−11.5	4.8	−32.9					
Exports	667.8	726.9	780.3	1,008.5	1,032.3	1,148.8	108.85	107.35	129.25	102.36	111.29
Total	4,641.8	5,135.0	4,932.2	5,531.5	5,933.2	6,338.9	110.63	96.05	112.15	107.26	106.84

Source: Direction Centrale de la Statistique, *Recueil de Statistiques Libanaises*, No. 6 (1970), p. 401.

Table 1.1 also shows fluctuations in Gross Domestic Product and imports. Both decreased in 1967 because of the Intra Bank crisis and because of the June war. They decreased also in 1969 and 1970 due, among other things, to the international monetary situation. The percentages suggest that a crisis in the domestic economy has a multiple effect on imports. When for example, in 1967 Gross Domestic Product decreased by about 2 per cent, this led to a 9 per cent decrease in imports. Private-sector fixed capital formation was also greatly affected at that time, decreasing by about 18 per cent.

Table 1.2 shows the Gross Domestic Product (GDP) divided into ten branches of activity. It is clear from this table that tertiary branches such as finance, commerce, and other services represent the largest portion of GDP. These three items alone accounted for 44.68 per cent of total GDP in 1970. Including housing, transport and communications among services brings the ratio to 61.76 per cent. Including Government as well, raises it to 70.5 per cent. Moreover, this high ratio of services to GDP has been maintained right through the development of the economy since 1965, as the following data indicate: 1965, 67 per cent: 1966, 67 per cent; 1967, 68.40 per cent; 1968, 70 per cent; 1969, 70.2 per cent; 1970, 70.5 per cent.

The ratio of services to the other branches (agriculture, power, construction, industry, etc.) works out at 233 per cent, which may be the highest in the world. Table 1.2 also reveals that services were less influenced by the Intra crisis than the other branches. This was basically because a large part of such services were related to Lebanese external economic activities and therefore less affected by the crisis than internal activity.

In 1971 national income (Table 1.3) was about 60 per cent above the 1965 level, giving an average increase of 10 per cent per year at current prices. The real growth in that period may be estimated at 8.4 per cent per annum. Allowing for population growth of about 3.2 per cent leaves an increase of 5 per cent per annum in average income per capita.[19] Per capita national income in 1971 was about LL1754, or $585.[20]

The same table also shows an increase in national income of 25 per cent in 1972 and 11 per cent in 1974. But the picture changed when the Lebanese War started in 1975 and national income started to decrease by 12 per cent and to 33 per cent in 1976, which was the most difficult of the war years.[21]

In 1977 there was a relative peace and national income went up again to the 1974 level at current prices, but in real terms it was equal to two-thirds of the 1974 level. In 1978 the increase continued to 6 per cent over the previous year.

Table 1.2. Composition of Gross Domestic Product by branches of activity* (LL Millions at current prices)

Branches of activity	1965	1966	1967	1968	1969	1970	Percentage of total					
							1965	1966	1967	1968	1969	1970
1. Agriculture, cattle breeding, fishing	409.2	441.7	426.1	436.0	431.5	445.0	11.61	11.47	11.15	10.20	9.45	9.14
2. Power and water	77.8	87.5	93.3	98.8	104.2	112.6	2.21	2.26	2.44	2.31	2.28	2.31
3. Industry and handicrafts	462.4	511.9	492.6	552.4	609.2	661.2	13.12	13.24	12.90	12.93	13.35	13.59
4. Construction	200.4	231.2	195.5	193.7	216.2	218.5	5.69	5.98	5.12	4.53	4.74	4.49
5. Transport and communication	290.8	309.5	329.4	379.8	382.9	400.8	8.25	8.00	8.62	8.89	8.39	8.24
6. Housing	269.1	284.0	300.0	335.0	385.0	430.0	7.64	7.34	7.85	7.84	8.43	8.84
7. Services (financial)	124.5	141.0	149.2	164.1	146.9	165.0	3.53	3.65	3.91	3.84	3.22	3.39
8. Other services	320.2	357.3	336.7	396.9	460.8	482.3	9.09	9.24	8.81	9.29	10.10	9.91
9. Commerce	1,085.2	1,183.4	1,160.5	1,359.0	1,434.9	1,526.7	30.80	30.61	30.38	31.80	31.43	31.38
10. Government	283.8	319.2	336.8	357.5	393.0	423.7	8.06	8.26	8.82	8.37	8.61	8.71
Total	3,523.4	3,866.7	3,820.1	4,273.2	4,564.6	4,865.8	100	100	100	100	100	100

*Gross Domestic Product *minus* government wages and rent (item 10 above) equals Gross Domestic Product, as in Table 1.1.
Source: Direction Centrale de la Statistique, *Recueil de Statistiques Libanaises*, No. 6 (1970), p. 401.

Table 1.3 National income, 1965–78*† (LL Millions)

Year	National income	Each year as a percentage of the previous year
1965	3,154.2	109
1966	3,460.0	109
1967	3,442.9	98
1968	3,861.7	118
1969	4,112.2	107
1970	4,411.0	106
1971	5,035.0	114
1972	6,285.0	125
1973	6,930.0	110
1974	7,700.0	111
1975	6,750.0	88
1976	4,500.0	67
1977	7,800 0	173
1978	8,300.0	106

* Provisional estimate.

† GDP (Table 1.2) + net property income from abroad = gross national product (GNP). GNP − indirect taxes + subsidies = GNP at factor cost. GNP at factor cost — depreciation = net national product or national income (as above).

Source: Direction Centrale de la Statistique, *Recueil de Statistique Libanaise*, No. 6 (1970), p. 400.

The balance of payments

As with national income, the first systematic balance of payments study was undertaken by the Economic Research Institute of the American University of Beirut and the American Embassy in Beirut. The former started with 1951 and 1952,[22] projecting results to 1957, and the latter with the period after 1957.[23] The Economic Research Institute continued to produce figures annually from 1961 to 1965. This section, however, draws on the more recent balance of payments estimates of the Central Directorate of Statistics for the years 1960–70.

The balance of payments, 1960–1970

Lebanon's balance of payments as illustrated in Table 1.4 reflects the structural characteristics of the economy, notably its heavy dependence

Table 1.4. Lebanon's balance of payments, 1960–1970 (LL Millions)

	1960	1961	1962	1963	1964	1965	1966	1967	1968	1969	1970*
A. *Goods and services*											
1. Imports and exports of goods	−675.0	−812.2	−682.9	−755.5	−896.6	−1,061.8	−1,153.3	−922.0	−1,065.1	−1,033.9	−1,088.8
2. Non-monetary gold (net)	−6.5	−6.5	−5.9	−7.2	−6.8	−7.1	−11.0	−9.0	−10.7	−10.0	−12.0
3. Imports and exports of services	+482.3	−509.0	+555.8	+575.5	+651.0	+717.0	+753.6	+722.0	+891.8	+908.1	+960.1
4. Total (1, 2, 3)	−199.2	−309.7	−133.0	−187.2	−252.4	−351.9	−410.7	−209.0	−184.0	−135.8	−140.7
5. Donations and transfers	+105.0	+110.8	+89.5	+95.4	+82.5	+78.3	+68.7	+85.4	+82.4	+85.0	+90.0
6. Total (4, 5)	−94.2	−198.9	−43.5	−92.1	−169.9	−273.6	−342.0	−123.6	−101.6	−50.8	−50.7
B. *Capital movement*											
7. Private long-term	+51.4	+48.3	+45.6	+40.4	+50.9	+52.4	+44.7	+14.5	+32.5	+35.7	+20.0
8. Private short-term	+84.2	+103.7	+67.0	+58.0	+107.8	+147.2	+264.4	+117.6	+260.6	+103.8	+156.0
9. Government long-term	+14.0	+18.3	+11.0	+7.2	+20.5	+4.8	+12.2	+15.7	+13.0	+12.0	+10.0
10. Total capital movement (7, 8, 9)	+149.6	+170.3	+123.6	+105.6	+179.2	+204.4	+321.3	+147.8	+306.1	+151.5	+186.0
11. Errors and omissions	+18.5	+79.5	+65.2	−9.7	+71.7	+124.0	+143.1	−25.6	−28.2	−27.4	−10.2
C. *Balance of current and capital accounts*	+36.9	+50.9	+145.3	+3.8	+81.0	+54.8	+122.4	−1.4	+176.3	+73.3	+125.1

* Provisional estimates.
Source: Direction Centrale de la Statistique.

Table 1.5. Eleven years' summary of the balance of payments of Lebanon, 1960–1970 (LL Millions)

Main accounts	Total 11 years	Annual average
Current account	−1,541	−140
Private long-term capital	+436	+40
Government long-term capital	+139	+13
Government short-term capital	+1,470	+134
Errors and omissions	+364	+33
Official reserves (increase represented by minus)	−868	−79
	0	0

Note: Official reserves increased during the 11-year period by over LL860 million, i.e., by an annual average of about LL80 million. This measures the surplus in the balance of payments according to the international liquidity concept.

on tertiary activities. Despite a substantial and chronic trade deficit, the overall balance was almost continuously in surplus during the 1960s. The gap between the growth rates of merchandise exports and imports narrowed, with the result that the trade deficit grew but at a decreasing rate. In 1970 imports of goods amounted to twice the value of exports, compared to four times in 1960. In absolute terms, the trade deficit almost doubled, reaching LL1.1 billion pounds in 1970, an annual rate of increase of 5 per cent. The trade deficit has been mostly covered by net earnings from invisibles such as foreign travel and tourism, transportation, and miscellaneous services, including transit and triangular trade and allied services such as banking. Other elements which help to meet the trade deficit are donations and transfers, which contributed a net annual surplus of about LL90 million during the 1960s. Nevertheless, the surplus contributed by invisibles and transfers has remained short of the trade deficit so that Lebanon has had a persistent deficit on current account; this, however, has been more than met by capital movements. Long-term capital inflows, private and government-financed, covered on average about 40 per cent of the current account deficit, and the remaining 60 per cent was amply met by inflow of private short-term capital.

The year 1971 witnessed a considerable increase in the payments surplus. The net gain in official reserves was LL543 million,[24] more than six times as great as the average annual increase in the period 1960–70.

Taking the rise in the net foreign assets of the Central Bank and the banking system[25] together, the reserve gain amounted to LL471 million in 1970 and LL919 million in 1971, of which LL741 was short-term capital, reflecting to a large extent the flight from the dollar at this time and the prosperity in the Middle East oil-producing countries.

Capital inflow reached LL968.9 millions in 1971 and LL813.4 millions in 1972, leading to an excess in the monetary movements equal to LL919 millions in 1971 and to LL766 millions in 1972. Errors and ommissions are included with the capital flows for the period 1973–8. The overall balance of payments remained in surplus even during the war years.

Whereas the inflow of capital in the 1950s was predominantly long-term, this was replaced in the 1960s by private short-term funds of which a good part was suspected to belong to Lebanese emigrants who were repatriating their capital from West Africa and Latin America. Generally, repatriated emigrants' capital comes to stay in Lebanon, while foreign capital may be withdrawn at relatively short notice. Foreign capital continued to be attracted into Lebanon, particularly from the oil-rich states of the Arabian Gulf area. It was, and still is, attracted into Lebanon by institutional and political factors, among them (a) a free enterprise system of the economy; (b) absence of exchange control; (c) a developing banking system with facilities and privileges not existing elsewhere in the area; and (d) relative economic and political stability until 1975. These factors together have made Lebanon a kind of regional financial centre and an entrepôt for capital.

MONETARY CONDITIONS 1918–1964

The French exchange standard

Before the French Mandate Lebanon's monetary system and unit of account were those of the Ottoman Empire (1560–1918). Currencies were predominantly metallic (of gold, silver, nickel and copper), of various denominations and values.[26] The Allies occupied Lebanon and Syria in 1918 and the Turkish paper currency introduced during the war was demonetised by the Franco-British authorities and temporarily replaced by Egyptian banknotes as official legal tender, alongside the Turkish gold pound. However, the people were very reluctant to accept Egyptian currency after their wartime experiences with Turkish inconvertible notes, and the Egyptian pound was never exchanged at the official rate (87.75 Egyptian piastres to one Turkish pound).

At San Remo in April 1920, the Allies put Lebanon and Syria under French mandate. The French High Commissioner suspended the use of

Table 1.6. Balance of payments, 1971–1978 (LL Millions)

	1971	1972	1973	1974	1975	1976	1977	1978^E
A. Total balance	−1,284.9	−1,401.4	−1,912	−2,123.0	−2,228.0	−370.0	−2,326.0	−2,751.0
Exports, f.o.b.	(1,149.7)	(+1,551.3)	(+2,186)	(+3,462.0)	(+2,589.0)	(+1,441.0)	(+1,978.0)	(+1,849.0)
Imports, c.i.f.	(−2,434.6)	(−2,952.7)	(−4,098)	(−5,585.0)	(−4,817.0)	(−1,811.0)	(−4,304.0)	(−4,600.0)
B. Services	1,140.0	1,249.0	1,249.0	1,490.8	1,400.0	800.0	1,310.0	1,280.0
C. Unrequited transfers, capital flows (including errors and omissions)	1,063.9	918.4	833.1	2,125.3	1,179.0	78.5	3,425.0	1,994.5
D. Total (A, B, C)	919.0	766.0	216.0	1,493.0	351.0	508.5	2,409.0	523.5
E. Monetary movements (increase in assets)	−919.0	−766.0	−216.0	−1,493.0	−351.0	−508.5	−2,409.0	−523.5
Official reserves	(−543.0)	(−317.0)	(−118.0)	(−1,644.7)	(−54.3)	(−1,040.1)	(−913.9)	(−795.0)
Private institutions	(−376.0)	(−449.0)	(−98.0)	(+151.7)	(−296.7)	(+531.5)	(−1,495.1)	(+271.6)

E: Preliminary estimates.
Sources: 1971 and 1972, Bank of Lebanon. The rest are those of IMF (SM/79/188, 12 July 1979).

the Egyptian pound note. He established (arrêté No. 129, 2 April 1920)[27] a new Lebano–Syrian currency based on the French franc and redeemable in cheques on Paris or Marseilles.[28] The note-cover was to consist of French Treasury bonds, foreign exchange and eligible commercial paper. The pound was divisible into 100 piastres and equivalent to 20 francs. By the same decree, the right of note-issue was granted to a newly incorporated Anglo–French bank, La Banque de Syrie, which replaced the local agencies of the Ottoman Bank. Its name was changed in 1924 to 'Banque de Syrie et du Grand Liban' and in 1938, to 'Banque de Syrie et du Liban' (BSL). For the first time in modern history, Lebanon and Syria had their own currency.

The Syrian and Lebanese-mandated governments negotiated with the Banque de Syrie et du Liban, and on 23 January 1924, a convention was signed. This sanctioned the French exchange standard, giving exclusive right of note-issue to the BSL for fifteen years (i.e., till 1 April 1939). The BSL was also made the custodian of government funds, while remaining a profit-making bank in ordinary commercial business.

Negotiations took place between Lebanon and the BSL on the one hand, and the Syrian Government and the BSL on the other, before the 1924 Convention ran out, and on 29 May 1937 a new convention was signed between Lebanon and the BSL for a period of twenty-five years, operative from 1 April 1939. A similar convention was signed between the BSL and Syria on 25 March 1938.[29]

The 1937 Convention renewed the concessions of the BSL as the bank of issue and fiscal agent of the government for twenty-five years, until 31 March 1964. No ceiling was set on the note-issue. There were minor differences from the previous convention as regarded note-cover.

From its introduction in 1920 until 1941, the Lebano–Syrian pound was rigidly pegged to the French franc, and until 1948 it was backed almost completely by French franc assets. From June 1926 until September 1949 there were eleven devaluations of the franc, causing continuous instability of the Lebanese pound. In June 1941, when the Allies (British and Free French), invaded Syria and Lebanon, one of the declared aims of liberation was to allow Syria and Lebanon to join the sterling bloc and facilitate their trade with sterling-area countries. This was made good, and the link between the Lebanese pound and sterling was established at the pre-war rate of LL8.83 to the sterling pound and 20 French francs to the Lebanese pound. On 25 January 1944 a monetary agreement (the Catroux Accord) was signed between the British Government and the French Committee of National Liberation. It was followed by a similar Franco–Lebano–Syrian agreement, signed in Damascus on 9 February 1944. This separated the Lebanese–Syrian currency from the French exchange standard and linked it directly with the sterling pound. It stipulated, among other things, that 'the Committee also pledged itself to replenish the franc assets of the note-cover and the Exchange Office at existing rates, to maintain their value in sterling, should the franc be devalued.[30]

In accordance with the 1944 agreement on the devaluation of the franc, on 26 December 1945, the franc assets of note-cover and of the exchange office were increased, to maintain parity of LL8.83 to the sterling pound. The franc was devalued at that time from 22.65 francs to 54.35 francs to the Lebanese pound (and from 200 to 480 francs to the sterling pound). A month later (10 January 1946), however, the French Government withdrew its undertaking and declared that it could no longer be responsible for losses in the value of the francs in the note-cover and deposits with the BSL arising from any new devaluation. The Lebanese and Syrian Governments denounced this declaration as a violation of the 1944 agreement.

The French subsequently invited the Lebanese and Syrian Governments to Paris for negotiations. In 1948 an agreement between France and Lebanon was concluded, despite Syrian opposition, and this difference of opinion broke the monetary unity of the Lebano–Syrian currency, thus hastening the economic rupture of 1950.

INDEPENDENCE AND THE MONETARY LAW OF 1949

On 24 May 1949 Lebanon promulgated a monetary law declaring the sovereignty of its currency, with a Lebanese pound of 405.512 milligrams of pure gold, as already declared at the IMF, and changed the 1937 Convention in four respects:

1. The pound was divisible into 100 piastres.
2. Legal-tender currency in circulation was to comprise: notes of one pound and above, issued by the BSL department of issue; and coins of less than one pound, to be issued by the Treasury.
3. Banknotes in circulation issued by the Department of Issue were to have 100 per cent note-cover—50 per cent in gold and foreign exchange and 50 per cent in government loans or government-guaranteed loans (particularly Treasury bills)—and other securities accepted by the government, or trade bills.
4. The execution of this law was entrusted to the Council of Ministers, with authority to regulate by decree, upon the recommendation of the Minister of Finance, the proportions of each element in the note-cover, and the conditions for issuing Treasury bills.

The firm step towards sovereignty represented by this new law brought about a certain degree of elasticity in the money supply by permitting 50 per cent of the cover to be held in the form of domestic paper money. This elasticity, however, was limited in scope in so far as it regulated on the note-issue, without provision for other important central banking functions. There was at this time neither a central bank nor a money and credit board to regulate the volume of money and general credit structure of the country.

Admittedly, the BSL—the bank of issue and the largest commercial bank—was given a certain degree of operational flexibility. It could move eligible trade bills from its commercial banking department to the issue department, against the issue of additional notes, increasing its private liquidity at a time when this might have been inadvisable. The BSL was basically a commercial bank, seeking to maximise profits, and so might pursue a discount and a credit policy inappropriate to the objective of exercising overall monetary control.

THE EXCHANGE SYSTEM

A further step taken by independent Lebanon was the liberalisation of the foreign exchange system. A common exchange office within the Lebano–Syrian customs union was jointly controlled, until the separation of their currencies in 1948. Lebanon then established its independent general exchange control within the Ministry of Finance (Law of 7 September 1948). Control was limited to specific hard currencies which included Belgian francs, Canadian dollars, Egyptian pounds, French francs, Iraqi dinars, sterling pounds, Swiss francs, and United States dollars. For other currencies, a free market was authorised (Decree No. 13532/K, 5 November 1948).[31] Restrictions were gradually removed, and finally abolished on 17 May 1952 (Decree No. 8300). Private foreign exchange transactions since then have been made at current free-market rates, and movements of funds have been unrestricted.[32]

The official exchange rate, after 1952, was of little practical significance. It was used mainly as a basis for the calculation of *ad valorem* import duties, as well as for government income and expenditure in foreign currencies. This practice, on balance, had increased the budgetary burden (see also Chapter 3). The exchange office operated within the BSL, handling government receipts in foreign exchange (mainly from oil-transit royalties) as well as government expenditures (largely for diplomatic services abroad).

The removal of exchange control necessitated the stabilisation of the

Lebanese pound in the free market *vis-à-vis* foreign currencies. Accordingly, an Exchange Stabilisation Fund was set up alongside the exchange office and the control department, its directorate comprising:[33] Minister of Finance (President), Director-General of Finance (Member), Controller-General of Exchange (Member), Director of the Issue Department (Member), Official delegated by Minister of Finance (Member).

The Fund's functions were left to the discretion of the Minister of Finance. Its reserves included the 'free' official reserves of gold and foreign exchange, i.e., government deposits not earmarked for currency-cover. It did not operate until 1953, when the Minister of Finance instructed it to intervene in the exchange market, buying US dollars to hold the downward trend in the dollar rate at the end of the Korean War. The government aim has been to stabilise the foreign exchange cost of Lebanese goods and services. The fund acted to prevent appreciation of the Lebanese pound in 1963–4 and 1966.

Table 1.7 records average annual foreign exchange rates for leading currencies quoted in the Beirut market. Figures for the dollar reflect a depreciation of the Lebanese currency which started during the Second World War and continued up to 1951. Thereafter, the Lebanese currency was firmer, its rate *vis-à-vis* the dollar appreciated from LL3.73 = $1 to LL3.00 = $1 in 1962. In 1963 the rate fell slightly to LL3.10 = $1.

Figure 1.1 and Table 1.8 show the fluctuations in the dollar rate in the Beirut market, as influenced by the intervention of the Stabilisation Fund. A brief survey of trends on the exchange market and the factors that prompted the operations of the Stablisation Fund is in order.

The year 1954 was characterised by much greater activity—commercial as well as speculative—than the previous year, and by irregular tendencies in the rate of exchange. Various opposing factors were at work. The liquidation of substantial foreign exchange balances by credit institutions towards the end of 1953 involved large dollar sales by these institutions; on the other hand, the Lebanese Government was buying wheat from abroad, which provoked speculative dollar purchases by the market in anticipation of a falling Lebanese pound. Overall, the balance of payments recorded a surplus which was absorbed by the Stablisation Fund, and the dollar rate reached a peak of LL326 in December.

In 1955 foreign currencies were somewhat stronger relative to the Lebanese pound, since their supply in the Beirut market was relatively reduced. *This could be attributed to the expansion of economic activity in North America as well as in Europe*, and to restrictions by the Saudi financial authorities on their capital outflows which had been invested in Lebanon.

Table 1.7. Free exchange rates: average rates in the Beirut market (Lebanese Piastres)

Year (annual average)	1,000 old French francs	US dollars	Sterling pounds
1949	808.40	326.00	975.25
1950	944.00	347.10	906.50
1951	949.00	373.33	941.65
1952	915.00	366.25	937.25
1953	909.33	342.00	931.17
1954	877.50	321.58	888.08
1955	906.00	324.00	895.00
1956	903.00	322.00	891.00
1957	827.08	318.42	822.42
1958	920.04	318.33	888.17
1959	642.83	315.50	886.17
1960	641.70	316.96	887.92
1961	609.70	307.86	862.67
1962	614.76	300.90	845.00
1963		310.50	

Source: Central Office of Statistics, Beirut.

Table 1.8. Fluctuations in dollar rates in the Beirut market, 1954–1964 (Lebanese Piastres)

Date	Average rate	Maximum rate	Minimum rate
1954	320.50	326.00	307.00
1955	323.85	326.00	322.75
1956	321.75	324.50	318.00
1957	318.20	320.50	311.50
1958	318.00	330.00	316.00
1959	315.25	318.25	313.75
1960	316.84	319.125	314.30
1961	307.75	314.50	300.50
1962	300.68	308.25	299.00
1963	309.77	317.00	305.00
1964	307.48	312.25	303.75

Source: Banque de Syrie et du Liban.

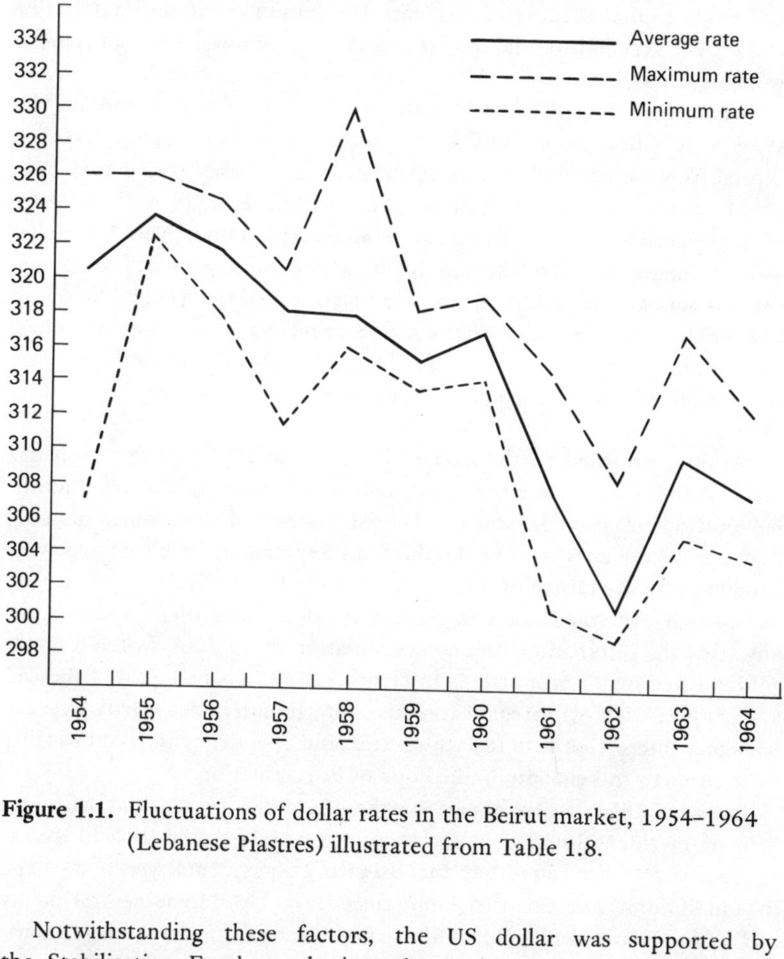

Figure 1.1. Fluctuations of dollar rates in the Beirut market, 1954–1964 (Lebanese Piastres) illustrated from Table 1.8.

Notwithstanding these factors, the US dollar was supported by the Stabilisation Fund merely in order to iron out sharp fluctuations in the foreign exchange rate of the Lebanese pound. A new factor contributing to a favourable balance of payments in Lebanon in 1956 was the introduction of the Banking Secrecy Law, which attracted Arab capital. In 1957 there was greater activity, a larger volume of operations, and larger profits in the foreign exchange market. This could have been attributed to the favourable performance of the Lebanese economy and the concomitant general confidence—at home as well as abroad—in the country's economic prospects, which encouraged foreign firms to use Beirut as their centre of activities for the whole Middle East region, and attracted Arab capital seeking refuge, as well as foreign capital seeking investment. The purchases of the Stablisation Fund were very substantial and the dollar rate showed little movement, averaging LL318.20.

Between 1956 and 1958 a political crisis was brewing and in May 1958 a rebellion broke out in Lebanon which lasted until October. Capital flowed out and foreign investment in Lebanon came to a halt. The Lebanese currency weathered this difficult episode with the help of intervention by the Exchange Stabilisation Fund. The US dollar was no longer in abundant supply, since the balance of payments was less favourable. In addition to American assistance (Point Four) of $12,500,00, the Exchange Stabilisation Fund made net sales of dollars for the first time since it began operating. The dollar exchange rate also oscillated quite sharply, with the average rate slightly below that of 1957.

Stability returned to the exchange market in 1959 and the Exchange Stabilisation Fund was again a substantial purchaser of dollars. Increasing outflow of capital from the United States had occasioned rumours that the US dollar was to be devalued. In September these rumours were dampened by the raising of interest rates in the United States.

Concern over the deficit in the American balance of payments again unsettled the international monetary situation in 1960. A switch towards gold reached major proportions in October. The Lebanese pound showed a slight weakness with regard to major foreign currencies, partly because of higher interest rates in foreign centres, and a tendency to gold hoarding by individuals in Lebanon, in the hope of its revaluation.

Early in 1961 the weakness of the US dollar was halted with the help of President Kennedy's declaration that gold would be held steady at $35 per ounce, and that the balance of payments would be kept in equilibrium. For the first time since July 1959 some central banks and governments sold gold to the United States. In March the D-Mark and the Dutch florin were revalued by 5 per cent, and in June the Canadian dollar was devalued in an effort to reduce the excessive deficit in Canada's trade balance. The American economy's difficulties at the start of 1962 occasioned a heavy outflow of gold, as many governments, fearing devaluation, asked for the conversion of their dollars into gold. President Kennedy intervened again with an assurance that there would be no devaluation, and was able to point out that the balance of payments deficit had shrunk during the year from $2.5 billion to $1.5 billion.[34]

In 1963 the Lebanese Stabilisation Fund felt obliged to sell large quantities of dollars for the first time since 1958. The Lebanese pound weakened, largely due to higher money rates overseas (in Japan, for instance, they were 5–6 per cent, as against 2 per cent in the Lebanon), and to capital outflows, due in turn to Middle East troubles. In May speculation pushed the dollar rate up to a peak of 3.17.

THE LEBANESE CURRENCY SYSTEM AND THE GOLD STANDARD

How far did the semi-automatic working of the Lebanese currency system resemble the gold standard—the earliest international monetary and financial system? At first sight the two are dramatically opposed since the gold standard was a fixed-rate system *par excellence*, whereas the Lebanese system was characterised by a floating exchange rate. Nevertheless, there is a basic resemblance between the two, in that inflows of foreign currency into Lebanon were completely free and created money in the same way as inflows of gold. And not only did purchases by the Stabilisation Fund create money but accruals of foreign exchange induced banks to expand credit directly.

As regards official purchases, the Lebanese consider any sort of management or control undesirable, and even after the establishment of the Bank of Lebanon there was little intereference by the monetary authorities, especially in its early years. However, there was the desire on the part of the authorities to prevent an undue appreciation of the Lebanese pound in relation to the dollar. Between 1953 and 1966 the rate was not permitted to appreciate beyond quite narrow limits. This meant that, in one direction, the flexible exchange system came close to the automatic gold standard. The spread between the high and low rates was, although greater than the gold export and import points, not large; between 1953 and 1966 it amounted to LL41, or about 13 per cent of the average rate for the whole period.[35] When the inflow of foreign capital became excessive, and depressed the dollar rate to the limits set, the authorities went into the market and absorbed the surplus with newly-created Lebanese currencies. Thus, large inflows of capital tended to give rise to increases in the money supply.

The dangers in such a system are clear: on several occasions the exchange authorities were compelled, temporarily, to stop pegging the dollar rate, or to think again about the limit to which the rate was to be permitted to depreciate, so as to hold off the threat of inflation. Obviously, sales of local securities instead of currency could have reduced these dangers, but this device was never used.

Aside from the intervention policy of the Central Bank, it has been the practice of Lebanese commercial banks to make use of their foreign assets as a reserve of liquid resources for the creation of credit. This practice has never been challenged by the monetary authorities of the country. In these circumstances the net inflow of funds into Lebanon, whether dollar assets, European assets or others, would normally offer the banking system an opportunity to increase lending in the domestic market, whereas a reduction in the commercial bank's foreign assets would act in the opposite direction by reducing the capacity and willingness of commercial banks to lend or to create credit.

The underlying reason for this practice is that commercial banks can, in the free money market of Lebanon, convert the foreign assets into Lebanese assets. So, by lending on the basis of liquid dollar reserves, they can meet the claims of depositors by converting some of their dollar assets into Lebanese pounds, should their liquid reserves be inadequate. However, this practice of using foreign assets internally for lending purposes is not completely free from constraints. In fact, commercial banks fear exchange fluctuation, and in the presence of wide fluctuation they are reluctant to resort to lending on the basis of foreign assets on a large scale, lest they should incur losses in the possible conversion of their foreign assets to and from Lebanese pounds. Hence, a sizeable proportion of funds received from abroad tend to be retained abroad.

One may conclude by re-emphasising that the Lebanese realised the potential of their country as a financial centre and entrepôt, especially after funds had begun to accrue in neighbouring oil-producing countries. The Government contributed directly to the evolution of the entrepôt character by introducing the free foreign exchange system (in 1952), and the Banking Secrecy Law of 3 September 1956. But it is the banking system itself which has largely handled the business of a financial centre. The next chapter outlines the structure and scope of the operations of Lebanese banks.

NOTES

1. *Collier's Encyclopedia*, Vol. 4, p. 5. Some human remains found in Antelias to the north of Beirut seem to belong to the third millennium BC—Kanaan, Daoud, Khalil, *Beirut in History* (Arabic), 1963, Beirut, pp. 56–7.
2. *Collier's Encyclopedia*, Vol. 18, pp. 7–8.
3. These are letters from the governors of various cities and districts of Palestine and Syria to the King of Egypt who appointed them. Porter, Harvey, *The History of Beirut*, Syria, 1912. Originally reprinted from *Al-Kulliyah*, The journal of the Syrian Protestant College of Beirut, Syria, pp. 5–6.
4. Ibid.
5. Those ships were about 81m long and 27m wide, and of three to five storeys. Kanaan, op. cit., p. 73.

6. Ibid.
7. *Collier's Encyclopedia*, Vol. 18, pp. 7–8.
8. Kanaan, op. cit., p. 178.
9. Porter, op. cit., p. 44.
10. Kanaan, op. cit., p. 178.
11. Hourani, A. F., *Syria and Lebanon*, London, Oxford University Press, 1954, p. 93.
12. Hourani, op. cit., p. 93.
13. The various religious communities, listed in order of numerical importance are: Maronites, Sunnis, Shi'is, Greek Orthodox, Druse, Greek Catholics, Armenian Orthodox, Protestant, Armenian Catholics, Jews, Syrian Catholics, Syrian Orthodox, Latins (Roman Catholics of Latin rite), Chaldean Catholics and Others (Alawis, Nestorians, Bahai's, etc.). Hourani, A. F., *Minorities in the Arab World*, London, Oxford University Press, 1947, p. 63.
14. Articles 12 and 22 of the Lebanese Constitution.
15. Quoted by A. J. Meyer, 'Economic Thought and its Application and Methodology in the Middle East', *Middle East Economic Papers*, 1956, p. 74.

    According to Professor Klat of the American University of Beirut, P. Van Zeeland told the Government, 'It is a miracle; I can't understand it. But my advice to you, since things are going so well . . . don't ask too many questions or try to do anything about it . . . Let it go on'. Klat, P. J., 'Lebanese Prosperity: Myth or Miracle', *Middle East Forum*, February, 1961, p. 11.
16. Fei, Edward and Klat, Paul, *The Balance of Payments of Lebanon, 1951 and 1952*, Beirut, Dar El-Kitab, 1954, p. 2.
17. Ibid.
18. Central Directorate of Statistics.
19. 1963 = 100. The wholesale price index rose from 103 in 1965, to 122 in 1971. IFS, Vol. 25, No. 12, December 1972, p. 228.
20. Assuming the population in 1971 to be 2.87 million. IFS, ibid. There are those who believe that the figures of national income and per capita national income are both underestimated.
21. See Chapter 7 for war damage to the economy.
22. Fei and Klat, op. cit.
23. The IMF Consultations with the Government of Lebanon (1961 and 1962). The complete series is in the *IFS Balance of Payments Yearbook*, Vol. 10, 1956–1957, Lebanon's Table, Washington, DC, 1958.
24. BL Annual Reports 1971 and 1972: foreign assets of the BL were LL1,725 million in 1971 and LL2,041 million in 1972, as compared to LL1,186 million in 1970. Foreign liabilities were LL10 million in 1970 and dropped to LL6 million in 1971 and to LL5 million in 1972.
25. Ibid., Table 27.
26. See Himadeh, Said, *Monetary and Banking System of Syria*, Beirut, American Press, 1935, pp. 24–33.
27. It should be noted, however, that the lowest specimen of the banknotes in the photograph carries the date of 1 August 1919—probably the date of the first note-issue by the BSL.
28. Himadeh, op. cit., pp. 50–7. (It was even thought feasible at the beginning to introduce the French franc itself as the currency for Lebanon and Syria. Fou'ad, Marsi, *Lectures on money and banking in the Arab countries (Syria and Lebanon)*, Arab League Institute of Arab Higher Studies (in Arabic) 1958. p. 15.
29. The former convention was ratified by the Lebanese parliament shortly after its signature. The latter was not presented to the Syrian parliament, for political reasons, on account of which the parliament had been dissolved by the French High Commissioner.
30. Article 5 of Franco–Lebano–Syrian agreement, 1944.

31. Saba, E. S., *The Foreign Exchange System of Lebanon and Syria, 1939–1957*, Beirut, American University of Beirut, 1961, p. 105.
32. Ibid., pp. 115–21.
33. Decree No. 8, 6 October, 1949.
34. In fact the adjusted deficit in the balance of payments in 1961 has been \$2.370 billion and in 1962 \$2.186 billion.
35. In fact the spread was 7.36 per cent on the basis of average annual rates seasonally adjusted.

2 The Lebanese banking system, 1920–1964

During the first half of the nineteenth century there were no real banking institutions in Lebanon. The main obstacles to these, under Turkish rule, were religion, improvidence and lack of confidence in the state.[1] Even after 1850 few banks were established, and most loans and discounts were provided by money-lenders. Between 1900 and 1914 several banks, and branches of foreign banks, were set up.[2] The main activity of the Imperial Ottoman Bank, founded in 1856, was to issue currency to finance foreign trade. There were also national banks and discount houses.

THE COMMERCIAL BANKING INSTITUTIONS

Of late years, commercial banking establishments have been predominant in Lebanon. Of all the first-class banks operating in Lebanon, even to this day, there have been only four non-commercial banks.

It seems that until 1929 only three commercial banks had been established: one French, one Italian and one Lebanese.[3] There was also one non-commercial French bank established in 1919, and another two set up in the period 1929–39. No other banking institutions were established during that period.

By 1950 there were eleven commercial banks. Of these, five were Lebanese, two French, and one of each of the following nationalities: Italian, Jordanian, Iraqi and British. Since then, until 1964, commercial banks have been established every year. It is worth noting that in 1963, on the eve of the establishment of the Central Bank, sixteen commercial banks were already established.

By the end of March 1964 the number of agreed banks was seventy-nine. Of these, nineteen were non-Lebanese: four French,[4] three American, two British, two Jordanian, and one from each of the following countries: Holland, Italy, Iran, Syria, Saudi Arabia, Iraq, Tunisia and Pakistan. 'Agreed' banks are those banks whose guarantee is accepted by the Lebanese Government, and are as such considered first-class banks. At the same time there were thirty-five non-agreed banking institutions; like agreed banks, they had corporate status, but they were considered second-class banks in view of their size.

Evidence of the development of the banking habit in Lebanon is also shown by the statistics of the clearing house of Beirut. Cheques cleared by the commercial banks of Beirut increased in value from LL92.4 million in 1943 to LL3,617 million in 1963, an increase of about seventy times within twenty-one years. The number of cheques increased from 5.061 million in 1943 to 802.646 million in 1962.

Commercial bank operations in Lebanon were, and still are limited, in general, to the finance of short-term mercantile transactions, although some were (in 1956) authorised to lend on mortgages.[5]

Non-commercial banks

The four non-commercial banks established before 1964 were: Société de Crédit Agricole et Industriel du Liban (SCAIL), Banque de Crédit Agricole Industriel et Foncier (BCAIF), the Compagnie Méditerranéenne de Placement et de Gestion, which in December 1967 merged with two other companies, forming the Société Centrale de Participations et d'Etudes (SAF) and the Monts de Piété Egyptiens. The first two gave medium- and long-term loans to agriculture, industry and real estate against mortgages on real property. SCAIL charged 8 to 9 per cent annum on loans, except on government-guaranteed loans and BCAIF charged 5 per cent.[6] In 1954 the Government guaranteed a BSL loan of LL55 million to BCAIF for forty years at 2 per cent. The other two non-commercial banks were French companies. The Compagnie Méditerranéenne was an investment bank, a subsidiary of the Crédit Foncier d'Algérie et de Tunisie. It bought shares in corporations in Lebanon and abroad. The Monts de Piété Egyptiens was a small French company giving advances on the security of movable goods and merchandise, including precious metals and jewellery. BCAIF overshadowed the other three non-commercial banks due to government help. It was decided to liquidate SCAIL in 1964; the Compagnie Méditerranéenne de Placement et de Gestion was finally liquidated in 1971; and the Monts de Piété Egyptiens was liquidated in 1957.

The Government's objective in encouraging and helping BCAIF was to enable it to acquire enough resources and facilities to help farmers and industrialists whom Lebanese and foreign banks might not be prepared to help. Since half the Lebanese lived by farming and the country's industries were still in the early stages of development, this proved a worthwhile service.

Characteristics of the Lebanese banking system

Banking in Lebanon was almost unregulated, owing to the absence of any commercial banking law, or any requirements regarding management, reserve ratios, investments or annual reports. On 17 December 1932, Decree No. 1245 was passed. It stipulated (Article 2) that:

> an agreed credit establishment must be in the form of an anonymous company (*société anonyme*), having its headquarters or branch in Lebanon, and with a capital of at least four hundred thousand Lebano-Syrian pounds or its equivalent: at least a quarter of this capital must be effectively paid up.

This was amended on 14 January 1955, by Decree No. 8004, to require the minimum capital to be one million Lebanese pounds, with half of this amount paid up.[7]

An important regulation was the Banking Secrecy Law of 3 September 1956, under which the funds of customers could not be disclosed except by their consent.[8] Further, Decree No. 9860 of 25 June 1962, amended by Decree No. 10412 of 24 August 1962, demanded that no bank could be considered an agreed institution unless it joined the credit risk office. A few rules were also given in the Lebanese Code of Commerce[9] with regard to bank deposits and credit.

The banking system reflected the economic liberalism of the country and it enjoyed a high reputation, particularly between 1950 and 1957 when its services to a growing population and expanding business led to major developments.

Unlike in more developed banking systems, there was a marked lack of the co-ordination needed by the country's financial and economic conditions.[10] Many banks considered the Banque de Syrie et du Liban a strong competitor and were reluctant to reveal to it the names of their customers.[11] They had a strong sense of being at a disadvantage compared with BSL, and resented its status and concessionary privileges. However, whenever they encountered serious difficulties they had to turn to the BSL. Foreign banks preferred to ask their head offices for short-term accommodation. The BSL established two forms of operation: the clearing service (1943), and the credit risk office, Centrale de Risques (1953).

The only forms of short-term investment available to the banks were self-liquidating loans such as discounts, advances on securities and overdrafts for less than a year, usually against property or signature endorsement. There was thus a lack of highly liquid investments, easily marketable and rediscountable.

Gold and foreign exchange business came readily since Beirut was the door to the Mediterranean and the link between the West and the Middle and Far East. Between 1950 and 1960 Lebanese banks did well on gold and arbitrage transactions; subsequently profits on this type of business decreased.

Table 2.1 shows deposits and major assets of commercial banks in Lebanon in Lebanese currency. In a period of twelve years, i.e., from 1951 to 1963, deposits increased six times (from LL259 million to LL1,585 million) while advances and discounts rose by close to 4.5 times (from LL318 million to LL1,333 million).

Table 2.1. Bank deposits and advances, 1951-1963 (LL Millions)

Year	Deposits	Advances and discounted bills
1951	259	318
1952	313	356
1953	343	357
1954	389	402
1955	483	492
1956	483	564
1957	602	601
1958	613	622
1959	856	744
1960	1,069	966
1961	1,220	1,108
1962	1,452	1,159
1963	1,585	1,333

Source: Central Office of Statistics.

As the number of banks increased in the early 1950s profits fell, and there was also a decline in gold and foreign exchange transactions in the Beirut market and the diversion of some bank and trade operations to Syria. The system was faced with liquidity and safety problems; banks were tempted to increase loans, keeping smaller reserves, i.e., reducing liquidity; or to invest in speculative assets, offering higher returns.

Information about the overall position of Lebanese banks was inadequate, and certain factors in the system tended to lessen liquidity. Deposit withdrawals were substantial, for example, in the 1956 Suez crisis and in the 1958 internal crisis, causing difficulties for several banks. The BSL relieved this, however, mainly by re-discounting bills.

LA BANQUE DE SYRIE ET DU LIBAN

After the First World War the Banque de Syrie et du Liban (BSL) took over the functions of the Ottoman Bank, and provided monetary and banking services to the governments of Syria and Lebanon. The 1937 Convention extended its monopoly of note-issue and confirmed it as sole custodian of government funds. The Franco–Lebanese Monetary Agreement of 1948 reaffirmed its privileges, and as no real central bank existed in Lebanon at that time, the BSL enjoyed *de facto* many central banking prerogatives.

The commercial activities of the bank were defined in its statute, while the note-issue department was governed by the Conventions of 1925 and 1937 and the Monetary Law of 1949. Its paid-up capital was 10 million francs in 1919, increased to 57 million francs in 1940 and to 300 million francs in 1949.[12] French and English shareholders owned most of the shares: only about 15 per cent were owned by Syrians and Lebanese. Its eighteen directors appointed a president, a vice-president and a general managing director (administrateur directeur-général), who was given wide powers, since the president and most of the directors did not live in Lebanon. The head office was in Beirut, and there were twelve branches in Syria and six in Lebanon.[13]

The issue department

The BSL's note-issue department managed the currency-cover under the Monetary Law of 1949, and was nominally distinct from the banking department.[14] But it had power to transfer assets for note-cover purposes from the banking department to the issue department, as defined in the 1949 Law in the case of a net increase of notes in circulation. A government commissioner ensured compliance with government policy.

The BSL was the ultimate source of liquidity for the whole economy:

1. The Stabilisation Fund, which was in direct contact with the issue and the banking departments, created liquidity, which tended to flow outside the BSL.
2. Deposits created through BSL discounts and re-discounts to business firms and to banks resulted in net claims on its currency reserves.
3. Drafts by the Government on its deposits with the BSL resulted in currency transfers to the public. Loans granted to government agencies resulted in the same kind of drafts on the BSL. On the other hand, the BSL's liquidity benefited from the deposit of government revenues with the banking department, from maturing public loans and other claims. The BSL banking department maintained a certain stock of

currency to the account of the issue department, which represented the likely day-to-day need for currency payment in any commercial bank. In normal conditions, when inflows were equal to outflows, this currency stock was kept at its optimum level. When outflows exceeded inflows, the stock was reduced and the BSL responded, moving currency from the issue department to the banking department; and vice versa in the case of excess inflow.

The Law of 1949 empowered the issue department to exercise flexibility in expanding currency. For every increase of one unit in its reserve of gold and foreign exchange, two units of currency could be issued, since the other half could be covered easily by government bonds and guaranteed loans, or by moving qualified commercial paper from the banking department to the issue department. Purchases of gold and foreign exchange did not, however, lead to an immediate or automatic increase in currency circulation; part of the proceeds tended to be kept, at least temporarily, to the credit of the banks concerned with the BSL.

Under the 1937 Convention, earnings on the note-cover were to be divided between the BSL and the Lebanese Government. Such earnings, however, decreased considerably, owing to the increase in gold and other non-earning assets for which the Government was responsible. The Government found that the issue department was not covering the cost of the issuing operations, and so relinquished its right to shares in any earnings therefrom.

The banking department

The BSL banking department performed banking operations both for the public and for private enterprise, commanding the largest volume of business deposits and extending to business the largest volume of loans and discounts, besides being the government's banker and fiscal and financial agent. The BSL also assumed, with the passage of time, other central banking functions, such as bank clearing and bankers' banking.

The government bank

Besides the exclusive privilege of note-issue, the BSL acted as the government bank and as fiscal agent, and kept the deposits of all public administrations, paying interest at a rate equal to the discount rate of the Banque de France, less 2 per cent for demand deposits, and less 1.25 per cent for time deposits with three months' notice. Almost all government deposits with the BSL were on demand. The discount rate of the Banque de France averaged around 3 per cent. The government earned, therefore 1 per cent on its deposits.

It is interesting to note that government deposits reached high levels during the two recession years of 1949 and 1953. This had a deflationary effect, since these balances consisted of money taken from the public in tax. Note-circulation declined from LL184 million at the end of January 1949 to LL164.5 million at the end of November 1949. The decline was less sharp in 1953, mainly because it was mitigated by the operations of the Exchange Stabilisation Fund. Note-circulation fell from LL203 million at the end of October 1952 to LL196 million at the end of July 1953. Thus, the BSL did not counteract the deflationary effects of the increase in government deposits and it did not try to stabilise the volume of money supply by increasing the amount of its private deposits during recessions.

The BSL was to provide all advances to the government or to public agencies, unless better terms were offered by other banks. But other banks were unable to compete with the BSL as long as it enjoyed this privileged position. Besides keeping government deposits and granting loans to the government, the BSL fulfilled many other functions as the government bank; it organised free of charge, and on request, payments to public departments, movements of funds in the country or between Lebanon and the outside world, and the custody of securities.

The BSL was the government's financial agent for all credit operations. Further, the director of the issue department acted as a member of the Exchange Stabilisation Fund, whose operations were conducted by the BSL. It managed the Office des Changes until 1952 by which time this office no longer had a function. After that, it kept the assets of the office in its banking department.

The bankers' bank

Aside from its position as the government bank and the bank of issue, the BSL acted as the bankers' bank and lender of last resort. It had free access to the issue department and had authority to shift trade bills totalling up to 15 per cent of the note-cover and/or government obligations totalling up to 50 per cent of the note-cover. Further, the large amount of government deposits at its disposal increased its capacity to create credit.

The BSL granted accommodation to banks in various ways. First, it allowed them unsecured open accounts, subject to overdrafts up to a certain maximum. Repayment was usually agreed upon by contract for one year. However, general practice was that the BSL could call in a loan on forty-five days' notice, and other banks, therefore, had to lend for shorter periods. The BSL did not encourage this method of borrowing, since it wanted shorter lending periods and secured loans.

A safer method of accommodation was the re-discounting of trade bills. These had to have two signatures and a banker's acceptance, and their maturity period was not to exceed ninety days. Lebanese bankers were often reluctant to use these re-discounting facilities, since the BSL was considered to be a competitor, to whom they were unwilling to communicate clients' names. Further, it was considered a loss of prestige to let clients pay at the BSL desks and to know that their banks had resorted to it for accommodation.

To alleviate such fears, the BSL adopted a new device: this was not a re-discount proper, but a sale of trade bills under a re-purchase agreement. A bank could sell bills[15] and buy them again three or four days before maturity, without the knowledge of its customers, who would thus pay at their own banks.

Another device adopted was known as borrowing *en pension*. Again, these bills had to have three signatures and ninety days' maturity, but the BSL added the interest due at maturity, instead of deducting it in advance, as in re-discount. A further difference from the discount was that the time limit varied from seven days to fourteen, or thirty at the most. While in re-discount the whole amount was given, the BSL here deducted 1 per cent of the total value and kept it blocked until the advance had been paid back. Another difference was in the 3.25 per cent charge as against 3 per cent.

These facilities were on a purely commercial basis, which meant that during periods of high economic activity the BSL increased its discounts, and during periods of recession it decreased them, contrary to the policy of a central bank which, to mitigate fluctuations in the economy, would lower discount rates in the periods of low economic activity and raise them in periods of high activity.

Among other functions performed by the BSL in its capacity as a bankers' bank was the management of the clearing house and, after 1948 of the Centrale des Risques—a French innovation—banks kept the BSL informed on credits authorised (over LL20,000), and the extent to which these had been used. In turn, the banks were advised of the aggregate figure recorded for customers' credits with all institutions. No bank's individual credits to a customer were divulged to its competitors, but each institution knew the extent of a borrower's total indebtedness to the banking system and, consequently, its own share of total borrowings. This information was not allowed to be communicated to third parties. It was of great value to individual banks in cases where a customer attempted to buttress an untenable position by increasing his borrowing from other banks.

The commercial bank

In addition to being the banker and fiscal agent of the government, and the bankers' bank, the BSL was authorised to carry out all banking and financial operations pertaining to Lebanon and Syria, except in real estate and mortgage loans. Except for its Paris branch, however, the BSL was not allowed any branches outside Lebanon and Syria. The BSL's credit activities were almost exclusively concentrated on financing short-term mercantile credit in the form of direct loans, overdrafts or discounts. Its general credit policy was profit-maximising, since it was basically a commercial bank. It was entirely proper for it to increase facilities in expansion periods and to decrease them during recessions, if it was to maintain a competitive position.

EVALUATION OF BSL ACTIVITIES

The role of the BSL as stated by its president was 'to see to the safety of money, so that no abuse of credit leads to inflation'.[16] Its directors believed that the best security against inflation was one hundred per cent gold-cover for the note-issue. Nothing was said about regulating the volume of credit (or of demand deposits) to prevent inflation and deflation. It contended that it was well aware of its duty to the nation and would spare neither diligence nor energy in its service.[17]

It has been alleged that the BSL was primarily concerned with the interests of its stockholders. This was a natural result of the 1937 Convention, to which there were some basic objections. First, its provisions were still those of 1924, without adaptation to the new conditions. The authorisation of the BSL to carry out ordinary banking operations in addition to its functions as a central bank was necessary and desirable at a time when there was no other banking institution in Lebanon. But when commercial banks opened branches, the need for ordinary banking operations by the BSL was removed. Yet the BSL was allowed to compete at an intrinsic advantage with other banks, and continued to look first to private profit. The Convention was not flexible enough at a time when the social, economic and political conditions of the country were changing rapidly.

The second objection was that the 1937 Convention endowed the BSL with a mission of public interest without giving the state effective control over its operations. The Government Commissioner's role was confined to checking the operations of the issue department, without being in any way able to determine the amount of note-issue appropriate. The third objection was that the BSL was a private foreign bank, and might have been biased towards the interests of foreign powers or establishments.[18]

To evaluate the overall commercial activities of the BSL it is useful apply three tests, regarding liquidity, solvency and profitability. For liquidity it can be argued that the BSL has on the whole kept relatively large reserves; the liquidity ratio in the period 1948–63 averaged 27.47 per cent. The ratio declined with the growth of economic activity and lending operations in the country from 48.13 per cent in 1948 to 9.7 per cent in 1957. Thereafter, a rising trend set in culminating in a 50.40 per cent ratio in 1963. These long movements paralleled an increase and then a decline in the lending activities in the country (Table 2.2).

Regarding solvency, it can be said that the BSL has attempted to improve the equity 'cushion' offered to depositors, by raising its capital resources in relation to its total activities. The equity to total assets ratio increased from 0.88 per cent in 1948 to 5.18 per cent in 1963.

Finally, with regard to profitability, book figures show that the bank's operations were quite profitable in 1948–57. Thereafter, profitability fell, largely because of increased competition from other banks.

Table 2.2. Operating indices of BSL total activities, 1948–1963

Year	Liquidity ratio %	Solvency ratio %	Profitability %
1948	48.13	0.88	8.08
1949	41.81	2.67	7.62
1950	30.01	2.39	9.09
1951	27.62	2.09	8.93
1952	17.73	1.66	9.19
1953	20.24	1.46	10.99
1954	16.18	1.44	12.63
1955	16.61	2.26	8.16
1956	17.36	2.76	7.76
1957	9.77	3.10	7.14
1958	19.44	5.73	3.52
1959	21.57	5.76	4.29
1960	19.40	4.63	4.30
1961	36.06	4.05	5.43
1962	47.63	3.94	3.56
1963	50.40	5.18	3.15

Average liquidity ratio for 1948–63: 27.47%

Source: BSL, exercises, 1948–63.

WAS THE BSL A CENTRAL BANK IN ALL BUT NAME?

The BSL peformed many of the functions of a central bank. It constituted the apex of the country's monetary and banking structure; it had the privilege of note-issue and regulation of currency; it provided banking services to the government. Though there existed no statutory provision for banks to maintain minimum reserves with it, it became traditional practice for many private banks to entrust their surplus cash to the BSL, especially for settlement of clearance differences between them.

The BSL was also the custodian of the nation's official reserves of international currency: this function was derived from its activities as a bank of issue. Moreover, the BSL acted to a limited extent as the bankers' bank, as the lender of last resort, and the bank of central clearance settlement and transfer.

However, with respect to credit control, which is accepted as the main function of a central bank, the BSL exercised little discretion in the period 1920–48. The reason is that Lebanon was on the French franc exchange standard and did not pursue an independent monetary policy. After 1948 the Lebanon severed its ties with the French franc and adopted highly liberal monetary and exchange systems. Exchange rates and the volume and composition of credit were essentially left to the free play of market forces. Only on a few occasions and at the request of the Lebanese Government did the BSL intervene in the money market to ease the tightness of credit or to prevent an undue appreciation of the Lebanese pound *vis-à-vis* convertible currencies.[19] According to Goldenweiser, 'a central bank should endeavour so to regulate the supply of money as to encourage economic activity when it shows signs of slackening and to restrain it when it appears to become too exuberant and speculative. In the simplest terms, this is still the objective and technique of monetary management.'[20] In other words, Goldenweiser adds, 'The essential principle is to ease when credit restriction seems to encourage a business recession and to tighten when there are inflationary tendencies.'[21]

It may be contended that the BSL unduly expanded its credit to the banking system in periods of boom and contracted its credit during periods of recession. The years 1953, 1956 and 1958 were recession years. The main statistical indications available are the volume of bank clearings and the volume of bank credit. Table 2.3 shows that bank clearings dropped from LL60 million in 1952 to LL48 million in 1953, and from LL121 million in 1957 to LL114 million in 1958, thus interrupting a consistently upward trend. The 1953 and 1958 recessions also witnessed a decline in the volume of bank credit.

Table 2.3. Bank clearings, bank credit, BSL discount rate and credit, 1952–1960

I	II Bank clearings (LL millions)	III Claims on private sector (LL millions)	IV Discount rate of BSL monthly average	V* BSL advances and debit accounts (French francs)
1952	60	271	6.50	28 252 676 580
1953	48	270	6.15	34 502 689 212
1954	53	345	5.48	28 363 335 425
1955	77	454	5.20	24 186 961 448
1956	102	482	5.27	23 107 899 493
1957	121	602	5.31	30 200 864 552
1958	114	585	5.58	28 158 652 369
1959	162	709	6.00	30 955 401 601
1960	185	1,002	5.85	39 625 159 330

* BSL, Exercises, 1952–1960.
Source: IFS, January 1962, Vol. 15, No. 1—Lebanon.

It is evident from Table 2.3 that the BSL did not consistently apply an anti-cyclical re-discount policy. For example, the discount rate was raised from 5.31 in 1957 to 5.58 in 1958, although the latter period was one of recession. Similarly, column (V) of the table shows that BSL loans and advances decreased in the recession years of 1956 and 1958 rather than increased. The BSL also showed little tendency to restrict credit in periods of boom.[22]

It is a fact that during the concession period of the BSL the economy witnessed an impressive prosperity. Banking activities and operations expanded in a geometric progression. It may be argued, however, that this prosperity concealed the seeds of the subsequent crisis. One should recognise that the absence of effective banking regulations was a major contributing factor to this crisis, although, of course, the BSL cannot be blamed for the absence of such regulations. Neither the BSL nor the banking system were fully up to the task of managing the business of a financial centre and entrepôt; and although the BSL laid the foundations of central banking in the Lebanon, it cannot be considered a central banking institution in the modern meaning of the term. Moreover, it might not have satisfied the concept of a central bank, which required it to perform in the national economic interest.

The BSL had been established in 1920 when the concept of a central bank was more clearly defined; it had more favourable central banking privileges than most charters of the Bank of England before, as well as after, the 1844 Act. It was established to render monetary and banking services to the governments of Syria and Lebanon, as did the charter incorporating the Bank of England in 1694. This charter proposed to lend money to the government 'towards carrying on the war against France'. It had a residual monopoly of note-issue: other banks retained their note-issues under the Act of 1844, but were restricted to the amount of notes outstanding at the time. The Bank of England, therefore, had to wait 226 years until the final abolition of these notes, in 1920, in order to have a virtually exclusive monopoly of the note-issue in England and Wales.[23] Also, not until 1826 was it authorised to open branches in other parts of England and Wales, and in 1844 its issue department was quite distinct and independent from its banking department.

The BSL, on the other hand, was granted exclusive right of note-issue as soon as it was established by the French Mandatory authorities. France had had central banking experience since 1800, when Napoleon had founded the Banque de France. Like the Bank of England, the latter became banker to the state, the bank of issue, the custodian of bank reserves, and the ultimate source of credit in an emergency. It became 'national in its operations as well as in name'.[24] It had exclusive right of note-issue in Paris and, later, in the whole of France.

In contrast, besides the exclusive privilege of note-issue granted to the BSL on its establishment, it did not have to wait very long to open branches, or to have its issue department separated from its banking department. The BSL was, to a large extent, a central bank, but it remained a foreign bank. The appreciation of this point was one of the factors which prompted the establishment of the Bank of Lebanon.

NOTES

1. Ravandal, G. B., *Turkey, A Commercial and Industrial Handbook*, Washington, Government Printing Office, 1936, pp. 220–2.
2. Himadeh, Said, *Monetary and Banking System of Syria*, Beirut, American Press. 1935, pp. 28–33.
3. There was another Lebanese banking institution, Banque Joseph Lati & Fils, established in 1925, but only by 1957 was its establishment officially effective.
4. It is to be noted that these banks were the first established in Lebanon. They were encouraged by the French Mandate because of their long experience in North Africa.

5. Foreign banks had to secure a specific authorisation to lend on mortgages (Article 3 of legislative Decree No. 196, 24 July 1942).
6. Mikdashi, 'The monetary system of Lebanon', p. 40.
7. Mikdashi, op. cit., pp. 43 and 54.
8. *The Official Gazette*, Beirut, 15 September 1956, No. 36, pp. 799–800.
9. Decree No. 304, 24 December 1942, amended in 1959, Articles 307–14.
10. Economic Research Institute, *Business Legislation in Lebanon* (mimeo), January 1956, p. 41. Also, Keesing, F. A. G., 'The Monetary and Banking System of Lebanon', Washington, DC, IMF, 1955 (typescript), p. 13.
11. Economic Research Institute, op. cit., p. 28.
12. BSL Statute, Article 3, Paris, 1949.
13. BSL Exercise, 1920, 1949, 1950, 1959.
14. The Convention of 1937, Article 4. This seems to be modelled on the United Kingdom's Bank Charter Act of 1844. See 'The Bank of England, Charters and Statutes, 1960', p. 46.
15. Such bills are classified here according to their maturity periods into different sets. Those maturing in the same week were classified together.
16. Declaration of Mr de Blettery, President of BSL, 10 December 1955, p. 1.
17. BSL, Exercise (Financial Year), 1952, pp. 7–8.
18. République Syrienne, Ministère des Finances, *Statut Organique de la Monnaie et Création de la Banque Centrale de Syrie Exposé*, March 1958, pp. 2–4.
19. Credit stringency arose in 1953 when, for political reasons, approval of the government budget was delayed for almost nine months, and again in 1960–1 when government expenditure lagged noticeably behind receipts. Also, during the Suez crisis in 1956 and the civil war in Lebanon in 1958, banks suffered a severe currency drain, which strained their liquidity positions and resulted in a tightening of general credit conditions.
20. Goldenweiser, E. A., *American Monetary Policy*, p. 69.
21. Ibid., p. 130.
22. Mikdashi, op. cit., pp. 85, 92 and 95.
23. Officially, the Bank of England had to wait 234 years, until the Currency and Bank Notes Act of 1928.
24. De Kock, M. H., *Central Banking*, p. 14.

3 The establishment of the Bank of Lebanon

REASONS FOR THE ESTABLISHMENT OF CENTRAL BANKS IN GENERAL

There are still some people who ask, says Professor Sayers, whether central banks are universally necessary. Are they not luxuries which small or poor countries can ill afford?[1] Almost every country has set up a central bank, or is in the process of doing so. Could the whole world be wrong? It is most unlikely. Central banking is a world-wide service which had its origins in the Bank of England: its apostles were either British or were influenced by British institutions. The regulation of the money supply, therefore, was thought of in terms of the British model, with the Bank of England almost always as a pattern. Britain, however, already had a highly developed banking system.

The function of a bankers' bank arose almost by accident, and the regulation of the money supply became a mechanical process linked to the gold standard by the rate of interest. Lord Keynes expounded the theory that the central banker's duty was to influence the rate of interest: the key to controlling the money supply. It was essentially a quantitative approach, and the central banker's key role was to regulate the quantity of money in the light of successful diagnosis of market conditions.[2] Could this discovery be applied to under-developed or developing countries?

It is now generally accepted that central banks are necessary to the major financial centres of the world. But it is a matter of controversy as to whether every independent political unit should establish one. This controversy is, however, of recent development. The establishment of more central banks was favoured by bankers in the 1920s as a means of protecting the value of money from the short-term fluctuations of politics. At the Brussels Conference of 1920 international banking experts persuaded their political chiefs to resolve that 'in countries where there is no central bank, one should be established'.[3] These central banks were intended to influence the national economy to pursue 'stability within as well as without', by regulating money supply.

Many bankers did not favour the universal establishment of central banks in each separate country, but politicians in countries without central banks did. They insisted that without them their countries would be at the mercy of foreign bankers.[4] In the United States, however, for nearly a century politicians feared that a central bank might sacrifice the interests of the country to those of foreign bankers, and the original central bank of the United States was liquidated in 1834 for this very reason. By contrast, during the 1950s, politicians suspected that without a central bank a country's interests might be sacrificed to those of foreign bankers, while the bankers feared the exploitation of central banks by politicians, to the detriment of monetary stability.[5]

The term 'central bank' has only come within recent years to have a standard meaning. Originally it was known as the 'bank of issue', or the 'national bank'. Even in the United States it was known as 'Reserve Bank'. To call it the bank of issue or the reserve bank covers only one of its many functions. It could, for example, be a bank of issue, but not a central bank, as in the case of the BSL.

The earlier central banks came to occupy a pivotal status by a process of trial and error. The unique status of the later central banks has arisen from their incorporation of the experience of the older banks.[6] Kent defined the central bank as 'an institution which is charged with the responsibility of managing the expansion and contraction of the volume of money in the interest of the general public welfare.'[7] Sayers states that 'the essence of central banking is discretionary control of the monetary system'. He adds, 'The purpose of central banking has been defined in various ways: To maintain stability of the price level, to keep the economy on an even keel, and so on.'[8] The history of the Bank of England is generally accepted as illustrating the evolution of central banking principles and techniques.[9] No laws defined its duties and activities. Traditions became 'guiding stars and were more potent than laws often are'. They made it 'the keeper of the financial conscience and the leader of financial activity'.[10]

The central banker is a man who exercises his discretion, he is never a mere machine that works according to rules.[11] Working to rules is in fact the antithesis of central banking. Hawtrey says 'The ostensible duty of a central bank is to maintain the monetary standard of a country'.[12] On this, Sayers comments:

> In some circumstances the purpose of central banking might be defined as the maintenance of the gold standard, the maintenance of a sterling standard, or the maintenance of a dollar standard. But these varieties are of purpose; central banking is an institutional arrangement that may be made to serve any one of a number of purposes.[13]

According to De Kock,[14] central banking has now become an entirely separate branch of banking, and has developed its own code of rules and practices, which can be described as the art, or science, of central banking.[15] It is now generally recognised, he says, as involving the following functions:[16]

1. The regulation of currency in accordance with the requirements of business and the general public, for which purpose it is granted either the sole right of note issue, or at least a partial monopoly.
2. The performance of general banking and agency services for the state.
3. The custody of cash reserves of the commercial banks.
4. The custody and management of the nation's reserves of international currency.
5. The granting of accommodation in the form of re-discounts or collateral advances, to commerical banks, bill-brokers and dealers, or other financial institutions, and the general acceptance of the responsibility of lender of last resort.
6. The settlement of clearance balances between the banks.
7. The control of credit in accordance with the needs of business, with a view to carrying out the broad monetary policy by the state.

It should not deal with the general public, unless compelled to do so in the national interest. It should not compete with commercial banks, since its success depends largely upon their co-operation.

A different view is taken by T. K. Velayudham[17] who considered the question of central-bank participation in commercial banking, and ways in which to alter its traditional role for under-developed countries. 'With no credit system, money or capital markets or even banking to control, the central banks in these countries must seek ways to help the countries develop'.

Mr Velayudham discusses the experience of the Indian Central Bank which, he says, was transformed from the traditional English style to its present form, providing development finance, promoting financial institutions and owning the largest commercial banks. Mr Velayudham disagrees with the notion that traditional central banking functions should be treated as universally appropriate even for under-developed countries. 'Central banks in these countries', he says, 'if they are to play an effective role, have to depart from traditional actions and branch out into new areas of activity including participation, directly or indirectly in commercial banking functions'. Functions and powers of 'new' central banks should be appropriate to the needs and the circumstances of these countries.

Mr Velayudham's ideas are difficult to apply in the case of the Lebanese Central Bank. If the Bank of Lebanon had been open to deposits of individuals and financial institutions other than banks, a considerable amount of commercial bank deposits would have been transferred to the Central

Bank. This is desirable only where the central bank is filling gaps left as a result of the lack of activities of commercial banks. In other words, only where commercial banks hesitate to participate because of the risk of a loss is it advantageous if the central bank steps in to foster a monetary and financial environment conducive to economic development. Thereafter, having developed a banking system, the central bank can devise methods of control; but this calls for patience. It took the Bank of England two hundred years to grow up. Although central banks mature more quickly today, substantial power and influence still come slowly.[18]

THE PARTICULAR CASE OF LEBANON

In Lebanon a central bank had become a virtual necessity, since Lebanon is an international financial centre and an entrepôt for a large region. There is a considerable need for an agency to neutralise undesirable influences of capital movements on the internal credit structure.

The legislative framework of Lebanon's monetary system rested on three main sources:

1. The Commercial Code, which regarded banking as a strictly commercial activity, and provided therefore for a few basic operations of the banking business.
2. The 1937 Convention, which allowed BSL to issue and manage the currency and to be the government's banker and financial agent.
3. The Monetary Law of 1948, implemented by a decree issued in 1949, which established the unit of the Lebanese currency linked to gold, and provided currency cover.

Rapid expansion of the banking sector and its growing prominence in the economy had induced by the mid-1950s a widespread sense of the inadequacy of the legal set-up. Some indeed had urged reform at an earlier date.[19] Among the defects were:

a. lack of government control;
b. the absence of legislation protecting depositors and safeguarding solvency and liquidity—neither the government nor the BSL supervised the development of banking conditions or controlled the credit structure;
c. the absence of a central banking institution.

The BSL performed some of the functions of a central bank according to the 1937 Convention, and these functions operated smoothly in normal times, but they did not help much in crises. The chief objections to the BSL were:

1. Its dual role. Banks cannot be expected to regard as leader a bank which is itself a competitor. BSL policy was motivated primarily by the welfare of its stockholders rather than by that of the public. Its duty as a central bank conflicted with its duty as a commercial banker.[20]
2. It confined its activities to short-term mercantile credit, without due consideration to the development of industry and agriculture.
3. It was not subject to government control in its banking operations.
4. It was a foreign bank, and this could influence policy.

The needs of the country were:

a. elasticity of currency;
b. liquidity and solvency of the banking system;
c. promotion of economic stability;
d. stabilisation of exchange rates;
e. promotion of healthy, non-inflationary, economic development.

Some argued that BSL had adapted its activities to the new conditions, and had gained much experience in managing the currency and assuring its relative stability, especially in the difficult period since 1945. It would have been willing to assume additional responsibility, provided the government gave it adequate powers of control. The argument was also advanced that the state should not be involved in banking and credit affairs; or that the Lebanese Government was inefficient, and the Ministry of Finance unfamiliar with banking conditions.[21] Thus, some reform proposals called for extension of the BSL concessions with new powers, others for an end to the concessions and the creation instead of a government-owned central bank; yet others suggested joint ownership of the BSL, with the government to participate as majority stockholder.[22]

It was true that the financial situation in Lebanon had been relatively good, and that this was partly due to the efficient management of BSL. It was also true that the Lebanese Government was inefficient, but it had not been independent for very long at that time. The BSL Convention had until 1 April 1964 to run and a breach of concessionary rights and obligations was not in the tradition of Lebanon. The government prepared, however, to take over from the BSL at the expiration of the Convention.

MONETARY LEGISLATION

The Money and Credit Board[23]

The government sought the advice of the IMF, and the Fund sent Mr Keesing, who in June 1955 recommended the collection of banking and monetary statistics and their interpretation; the enactment of the general banking legislation; the formation of the Money and Credit Board; and the establishment of a central bank.

The Planning and Development Board prepared a draft bill providing for the collection of banking statistics.[24] It recommended the establishment of a banking statistics department in the Ministry of Finance, to detail the assets and liabilities of banks, holdings in foreign exchange and other information.

Some Lebanese and other economists, however, thought that the formation of the Money and Credit Board need not await statistics and legislation. The successful working of such an institution, they held, could not in any case be assured by mere legislation. 'It is a product of years of experience and growth of sound convention. Efficient management in this field depended upon the persons more than on any legal formula'.[25] In general, it was pointed out, 'central banking was neither a science, nor an art, but a craft. Science sought facts and basic laws; art sought beauty and perfection. Central banking tried to produce a serviceable commodity —economic stability'.[26]

The Government seems to have been convinced by these views. Decree 154, of 12 June 1959, created the Money and Credit Board (CMC) as a special committee within the Ministry of Finance, with the following functions:

1. To study the monetary and banking conditions in the country, and to prepare necessary statistics.
2. To present recommendations advising the Minister of Finance on monetary and credit policy and methods of implementing it.
3. To draft the necessary legislation for organising the banking profession.

All ministries, departments and public institutions had to submit to the Money and Credit Board monetary statistics which it was to keep strictly confidential. All banks operating in Lebanon had also to submit statistics, provided that these should not conflict with the Banking Secrecy Law of 3 September 1956. Delay or misleading information would incur penalties.

The Government was silent on the final stage recommended by Mr Keesing, the establishment of a central bank. It referred only in general terms to organising the banking profession. It did not seem to have made up its mind to establish a central bank. The legislation referred to in item 3 of the decree could still organise the banking profession in such a way as to provide co-operation between the CMC and the BSL without a central bank.

After two and a half years the Money and Credit Board was formed (Decree 8211 of 15 December 1961). Its members were: Prime Minister

Rachid Karamé (President), in his capacity as Minister of Finance; Joseph Oughourlian (Vice-President), government expert on monetary affairs at the BSL; Joseph Prince, Government Commissioner at the BSL; Mohamad Atallah, representative of the Planning and Development Board; Paul Klat; and Abdul-Amir Badrud-Din.

The Board at work

The CMC held its first meeting at the Ministry of Finance. Prime Minister Karamé, who presided, outlined the aims of Decree No. 154, and stated that the ultimate aim of the Government was not only to prepare legislation but to establish a central bank. Accordingly, the BSL was to separate the issue department from the banking department, preparing to hand over the issue department to the proposed central bank. Just over ten months after the Prime Minister's statement, a licence was given under the name of 'la Société Nouvelle de la Banque de Syrie et du Liban' (decrée 10961, 26/10/1962) in which the BSL had been incorporated. Thus, the BSL disappeared *de jure*, after a life of forty-three years.

The board, discussing legislation and policy, agreed that the legislation should be based on: our geographical conditions; our human conditions; our economic conditions, particularly the nature of our national income and balance of payments.

Under the Lebanese free enterprise system:

1. The Lebanese pound had established its position as an international currency and had passed safely through the crises of 1953, 1956 and 1958.
2. Banking institutions flourished and were able to face crises safely and effectively.
3. The Lebanese economy could attain those means which would enable it to flourish.
4. The largest portion of the national income came from the trade and services sectors which could grow only in a liberal system.
5. Most external receipts on current account were supplied by invisibles which could only grow in a free economy.

The basic principles for the Money and Credit Code were, firstly, that with regard to banking legislation, the system should remain as free as possible, and Lebanon should pay the price of freedom in order to remain an international centre, with regard to capital movements. Only the central bank should have the power to supervise. Secondly, the central bank should enjoy real independence *vis-à-vis* the political authorities. In the light of these principles, the CMC proposed to establish new institutions and formulate up-to-date banking legislation.

The banking statistics

The first important work of the board was to draft forms asking for assets, liabilities, '*hors bilans*', and profit-and-loss statements. These instructions (1/62, 15 September 1962) concerned statistics which banks had to submit under Decree 154, 10523 of 10 September 1962.

These reports would enable the authorities to follow changes in the deposits of the banking system and consequently the money supply, besides shedding light on the general economic situation and the balance of payments. They would also reveal to the authorities the particular situation of each bank. This knowledge was necessary for the central bank as the controller of currency, and would indicate the credit policy of banks, and their sources and uses of funds. It would also enable the central bank to calculate liquidity ratios.[27]

Even at the outset, the working of the board was not restriced to the drafting of statistical forms. In fulfilment of its other purposes, it made recommendations on various matters influencing money and credit. On its suggestion the Minister of Finance asked the Ministry of National Economy to be cautious in licensing new banks, pending legislation. The request, however, had little impact. The increase in the number of banks in 1963 was eleven, compared with ten in 1962. Not until much later was the rush to establish banks in Beirut legislated against, on the advice of the central bank.[28] The board also set its face against inflationary policy, and resolved 'to resist any change of monetary and banking conditions which would undermine confidence in the currency and make the work of the proposed central bank more difficult'.

The Money and Credit Law

By 3 May 1962 the board was working on the draft law on money and credit, and the Vice-President went to Europe to study their central banks. Once the draft law was completed, in December 1964, the CMC consulted the Planning Board in the Ministry of Planning, and the Association of Banks in Lebanon.

The Planning Board's comments were concerned more with the form than with the spirit of the law. More searching was the study submitted by the Association of Banks in Lebanon. They were uneasy about laws and regulations, from which they had previously been free. It was hardly surprising, therefore, that they opposed the Money and Credit Law and the establishment of the central bank. This kind of feeling had occurred, indeed, in the United States over the setting-up of the Federal Reserve System, achieved in 1913 only after six years of agitation and discussion in the face of opposition by the large banks and the bankers' associations.[29]

The Lebanese Association said they would not object to the Central Bank if it were to be merely an issue department, and have nothing to do with banking regulations. 'The note issue', they argued, 'is a symbol of state sovereignty and the Central Bank is a mere government institution, while banking regulation is concerned with a liberal profession and as such is of concern to private initiative.'[30]

The Association's memorandum invoked the Banking Secrecy Law of 3 September 1956, as a weapon against central bank control, and urged the separation of the draft law into two independent parts: the first, on 'Money and the Central Bank', should be divorced from that dealing with regulations.

It also urged that the work should be achieved in stages: The 'establishment of the Central Bank to replace the BSL as a bank of issue is more urgent than the banking regulation.'[31] Control, they insisted, must be independent of the Central Bank. They hoped that the President of the CMC would invite them to discuss this with the authors of the draft law. The CMC, however, made few changes in the draft law, and replied that it did not envisage any division of the law into two parts.

On 12 March 1963 the Association issued another memorandum, insisting on separation, demanding that secrecy be respected, and that information about bank customers should go only to those responsible for the banks. They maintained that the release of such information to outsiders, such as the controllers suggested in the draft law, would endanger secrecy, and would undermine the confidence of depositors. Lebanon, they argued, was the only country in the world—except Switzerland—to have such an effective bank secrecy law. Tampering with it, even indirectly, would hurt the basis of the Lebanese economic system, the future of its wealth and the welfare of its people.[32] They renewed the suggestion of having one or two discussions before the submission of the draft to the Council of Ministers. This time the CMC did meet the wishes of the Association. Three long (four-hour) meetings were held in the Ministry of Finance between members of the CMC and those of the Association round the table, presided over by the Minister himself who was also the President of the CMC. The points made by the Association and the Planning Board will be covered in the following section.

THE MONEY AND CREDIT LAW

Major features, analysis and evaluation

The Law on Money and Credit was passed by the Lebanese Government by Decree 13513 on 1 August 1963 and took effect on 1 April 1964, when the Bank of Lebanon replaced the BSL, whose concession had ended the day before. It laid down the central banking rules, determining the policy of the Bank of Lebanon. This code of rules is regarded as the 'Bible' of the Bank of Lebanon. The discussion here follows the same scheme as the official reasoning ('*exposé de motifs*') in presenting the law.

The three basic issues—the Lebanese currency, the central bank and the regulation of the banking profession—are covered under six titles: 1. money; 2. the central bank; 3. banking regulations; 4. sanctions; 5. transitional provisions relative to (3); and 6. miscellaneous and final provisions. The next four sections discuss the points of most interest.

1. MONEY (ARTICLES 1–11; 113–116; 225–229)

The Monetary Law of 24 May 1949 determined the gold parity of the Lebanese pound as 405.512 mg. of fine gold (LL2.19448 = $1). It also stated the denominations of the Lebanese currency and regulated the note-cover. But in fact the actual value of the Lebanese pound in the free market—relative to the US dollar and to gold—had diverged a long way from the official parity declared to the IMF; the result was multiple exchange rates in contravention of IMF principles. The official rate was used for government foreign payments and for determining the value in Lebanese currency of some dues, especially customs duties and taxes, on foreign companies. In most other transactions the free market rate was used.

The disadvantages associated with the official parity were as follows.

First, the cost of some government imports was recorded at the official rate, which meant that the state budgeting did not present a fully accurate picture. On balance, this practice had increased the budgetary burden of the government. Other Treasury operations were performed at the free market rate, or at rates ranging between the free-market rate and the official rate, while operations of the private sector were at the free rate. However, the size of the operations at the official rate, or of those between the two rates, was small, compared with those at the free-market rate.

Secondly, operations at the official rate were carried out through the foreign exchange office, an institution whose very existence was unwarranted, since exchange control had been abolished.

Lastly, these were accounting complications for the institution of issue. They arose as follows: because of the divergence, between the official and free rates, the monetary authorities could not meet the provisions of the law of 24 May 1949, concerning note-cover, since they could not get dollars and gold at the official value of the Lebanese pound. Articles 2 and 3 of Decree 15105 K of 27 May 1949 sought to overcome this difficulty. Foreign exchange or its equivalent was to be entered in the cover in two accounts. In the first was to be entered the equivalent of foreign exchange and gold at the official price of the Lebanese pound. In the second, called the special account, was to be entered the difference between the official value of the bank's gold and foreign exchange and its actual purchase price (Articles 114 and 115). When the actual purchase price of gold and foreign exchange exceeded its official price, as had happened, the special account was to represent a debt claim on the Treasury. Such differences did not happen, in principle, when an appropriate parity existed.

The Government held, therefore, that the time had come for the Treasury accounts to be clarified and for the state budget to be made more accurate. A rate as near as possible to the actual value of the Lebanese pound in the free market was to be used in presenting official operations and the evaluation of gold and foreign exchange in the note-cover. This 'provisional official parity' of the Lebanese pound was also a major step towards abolishing multiple exchange rates as required by the IMF Articles of Agreement.

Thus, while Article 1 of the new law restated the Lebanese pound as the unit of the Lebanese currency, Article 2 abandoned the gold parity and provided instead for a new and more realistic parity, to be determined by law not later than December 1964. This new parity was to be a 'legal transitional rate', pending the establishment of a new gold parity for the Lebanese pound, in agreement with the IMF. However, the mere setting up of a new parity by law was no guarantee against divergence between the free market rate and the official one. Wide divergence had occurred and it was doubtful whether the government would be able to enforce the new parity.

Other Articles (3, 8, 10 and 11) regulated the divisions and fractional denominations of the Lebanese pound, and made money issue the exclusive privilege of the state, through the proposed central bank. BSL notes were to be legal tender not merely until the issue of the new notes, but also for a relatively long redemption period (seven years: Article 225). Coins in the Treasury were to be taken over (Article 226) by the central bank.

The Central Bank had to participate, as the financial agent of the government, in the negotiations for payment and clearing agreements. It had to allow time for the transfer of accounts held by private banks (Article 227). It was also to take over the holdings of the exchange office which was to be abolished. The foreign exchange acquired would be taken into account in the computation of the ratios stipulated in Article 69 with regard to note-cover.

2. THE CENTRAL BANK (ARTICLES 12–120)

The Bank of Lebanon was to be owned entirely by the state, which would subscribe all the capital, appoint the governors, and share in the profits. The Central Bank sought the public welfare and would often be concerned with long-term considerations, whereas it was reasonable for private banks to look after their own immediate interests. It was important therefore, that they should not influence the decisions of the Central Bank. This did not mean, however, that they should not be consulted or informed by the Central Bank where necessary.

Though the Bank of Lebanon was to be state-owned and supervised, it was not to be subordinate to the government. The liberal economic system was fully safeguarded by the new law. Independence, combined with co-ordination *vis-à-vis* the state, was sought by the appointment of the Central Council.

In the light of this the rules set up by the Money and Credit Law fell into seven section: (i) the legal status (Articles 12–16); (ii) organisation (Articles 17–40); (iii) supervision (Articles 41–46); (iv) functions (Articles 47–80); (v) operations (Articles 81–111); (vi) financial provisions (Articles 112–117); (vii) exemptions and privileges (Articles 118–120).

(i) Legal status

The Central Bank was a responsible authority enjoying financial autonomy, and engaged in business with third parties. Because of its special nature and functions, it was not subject to the administrative and management rules and controls applicable to other public institutions. It was to have a capital of LL15 million, mainly covering the buildings, furniture and other establishment costs. Its head office was to be in Beirut, and only the courts of Beirut had jurisdiction concerning third parties. It could only be liquidated by means of legislation.

(ii) Organisation

The Governor would be assisted by three Deputy-Governors and a Central Council (Articles 17–34). Article 17 of the Money and Credit Law, which covered this, came under criticism from the Association of Banks on the grounds that it gave the impression that the bank was to be run by one man. 'It could not be imagined', they added, 'that such management could be entrusted except to a Central Council, while not ignoring the fact that the Governor and his deputies should have special and wide powers.'[33] The Planning Board also pointed out, with regard to this article, that the Governor together with his deputies should form a committee, presided over by the Governor, empowered to determine the rules by which applications for loans, discounts and credits should be assessed, to approve private sector applications and to manage administration.

The Association agreed with the Planning Board concerning the qualifications of the Governor, both stressing that the governors should have university degrees and monetary and banking experience. 'The law should indicate', said the Planning Board,

> that the Governor and his Deputies must be highly specialised in money and banking and well known for their moral standard and patriotism, since the Governor particularly represents the monetary power of the country . . . The law provides that the Governor and his Deputies enjoy well established and independent positions. The Governor, however, is given the widest powers in the general administration and management of the Central Bank (Article 26).

The Planning Board suggested that the Central Council, not only the Governor, 'shall have the widest powers.'[34] Although I did not myself object to this criticism of the Governor's power, I thought that Articles 17 and 26 might stand as they were. The Governor was, after all, the symbol of both the Bank and the monetary power of the country, and must have adequate authority. 'Inevitably', says Chandler, 'the course of social institutions and human affairs is influenced by the vision, imagination, leadership and convincing influence of forceful men.'[35]

The governors were to be appointed for a definite but renewable period, and could not be dismissed except for reasons defined in Articles 18 and 19. They were to devote all their time to the bank and must not have any legislative mandate, public office, activities in commercial enterprise, or other professional work, paid or unpaid. Even for two years after leaving office the Governor and Deputy-Governors must not become directors, or hold any office or participate in any manner whatsoever in any bank or financial institution governed by the new law.[36]

The Central Council

The general policies and decisions of the Central Bank were to be conducted by the Central Council, consisting of the Governor, the Deputies and the Director-generals of the Ministries of Finance and National Economy. The Planning Board had proposed a different formula: the Council, it thought, should consist of the Governor and the Deputies, the Director-general of the Ministry of Finance, and five experts on money and banking, known for their integrity. The Director of Finance should represent his ministry and should have the power of holding up for ten days any decisions which he thought detrimental to monetary policy and not in conformity with the general directives, subject to the decision of the Council of Ministers.[37] The law, however, ignored this proposal and stood as it was, in that the Director-generals of the Ministries of Finance and National Economy did not necessarily represent the Government's views or policies while serving on the Central Council: 'the last two members shall not act on the Council as Government delegates. They shall exercise at the Bank only those functions belonging to their position as members of the Central Council.'[38] However, notwithstanding the restrictions on the two Government directors provided by Article 28, the Association still feared that the presence of those directors on the Central Council might conflict with the independence of the Bank *vis-à-vis* the Government. It wanted to replace them by two directors from the Central Bank itself.[39] This was also rejected, co-ordination and co-operation between the state and the Central Bank being regarded as the first essential, for discussions and decisions, albeit without encroaching on the independence of the Central Bank.

At the same time, efficiency and speed in the work of the Bank were of great importance. Here there seemed to be some confusion in the attitude of the Association with regard to the independence of the Bank. While objecting to the presence of the Government directors on the board, it suggested giving to the Minister of Finance the power to demand a board meeting. Article 29 was amended to this effect.

It will be observed that the Central Council, unlike the Bank of England, had no part-time directors. The suspected 'conflict between two separate responsibilities, or between interest and duty'[40] was thus avoided. All members of the Central Council were to participate in forming policy.

The Central Council moved with caution, restricting consultations with outsiders to an advisory committee of six, four to be selected for their experience in the fields of banking, trade, industry and agriculture. They were not, however, to act as representatives or agents of these sectors (Article 35). With regard to this the Planning Board was content with four members, and declined even to be represented on the consultative committee; it thought (with reference to Article 38) that the Central Council, not the Governor should consult the committee.[41] Against this, the Association recommended a larger committee, so as to have wider representation of the various economic sectors, as well as of more academic circles.[42] In fact, the fifth member under the new law was to be selected from the Planning Board and the sixth was to be a professor of economics. Thus, the committee would include practical experience in the various sectors of the economy, as well as theoretical knowledge.

A further amendment in the draft law was secured by the Association to shift power from the Governor to the board. This was done in Article 36, which had proposed 'to appoint the committee by decree, after consultation with the Governor'. This was changed so that the appointment would be made after consultation with the board, and not with the Governor alone.[43]

(iii) Supervision

Although the Central Council was given a high degree of autonomy, the law reserved a supervisory role to the Government over the Bank's operations through a special agency called the Government's Commissariat at the Central Bank.

This was to be part of the Ministry of Finance and was to supervise the implementation of the law as well as overseeing the Bank's accounts; but it was not to have access to accounts and files of third parties protected by the Banking Secrecy Law of 3 September 1956. The Association stressed the observation of the Secrecy Law, although Article 44 had already met this stipulation. At this stage the powers of the CMC were to be transferred to the Central Bank on the one hand, and to the Government Commissariat at the Central Bank on the other. After the establishment of the Central Bank the CMC would no longer exist.

It was entirely wrong, according to the Planning Board, that the draft law did not provide for an institution to audit the Central Bank's accounts, and they suggested that auditors should be selected by the Council of Ministers. The Government Court of Accounts, they recommended, should examine Central Bank expenditure.[44]

(iv) Functions

The ultimate objective set forth by the Money and Credit Law of the Lebanon is 'economic and social progress' (Article 70). 'The general function of the Bank', it says, 'shall be to safeguard money, to ensure the basis of a durable economic and social progress'. The word 'progress' here is more general than 'growth', covering any kind of social improvement. The aim, therefore, was economic and social progress, which is broadly similar to that of the Bank of England or the Federal Reserve.

The issue of currency. The monetary agreement of 29 May 1937 gave the BSL the right to issue currency denominations equal to or larger than the monetary unit, while the issue of smaller currency denominations was the prerogative of the state. The Money and Credit Law, however, conferred upon the Bank of Lebanon the exclusive privilege of money issue of all denominations (Articles 47, 49 and 59). It also provided for a relatively long period to withdraw from circulation all categories of notes, and their replacement by others (Articles 52, 55 and 63). The law instructed the Central Bank that the currency was to be covered in gold and convertible foreign exchange to a minimum of 50 per cent of the issued notes, and to a minimum of 30 per cent of the sum total of issued notes and the Bank's demand deposits (Article 69).[45]

The general function of the Central Bank (Article 70). This was the core of the matter: the general or ultimate objective of the Bank was economic and social progress. The particular or proximate objectives were not merely to issue currency, but to have a good currency, through control of the money supply, composition of credit, and the banking system. Moreover, it must ensure exchange stability, manage the public debt, and advise the Government on financial matters.

The Central Bank could not, however, undertake by itself the protection of the currency, since this depended ultimately upon Government policy in various fields, particularly in the budget. Inflation could not be avoided or ended by any single instrument.

Advice (Articles 71–2). Since monetary policy was only a part of the economic and financial policy, and this itself was part of the general policy of the state, the closest co-operation between the state and the Central Bank was essential. The Bank is the Governor's adviser on financial and economic policy.

Exchange stability. Article 75 gave the Central Bank the right to take over the function of the Stabilisation Fund established in the Public Exchange Control Office by Decree 8 of 6 October 1949. Here the Bank was to act as custodian of the nation's reserves of international currency, managing them to promote stability in exchange rates.

Influencing bank liquidity and the volume of credit (Articles 76–79). The instruments specified for purposes of credit control were the usual ones, namely bank rate, operations on gold and foreign exchange, open-market operations, minimum reserve requirements, regulation of consumer credit and advances against securities. It left the use of these measures singly or collectively to the discretion of the Bank authorities (Article 76). With regard to the important topic of reserve requirements, the Central Bank was authorised to establish a minimum reserve ratio for banks to deposit with it. This ratio must not be more than 25 per cent for demand deposits and 15 per cent for time deposits (Article 76 (d)).

The monthly average of actual reserves of commercial banks at the Central Bank should be at least equal to the reserve requirement ratios that have been established. If they fall short the Central Bank may charge a penalty interest rate on the deficiency. This penalty rate must not exceed by more than 3 per cent the interest rate in force on advances against securities (Article 77).

The Central Bank did not impose reserve requirements until 1969. The Bank of Lebanon thought it wise to wait until the banking system had fully recovered from the crisis of liquidity that had led to the failure of the Intra Bank, the largest Lebanese bank, in October 1966. BL circular to commercial banks No. 57, dated 6 June 1969 imposed the first 2½ per cent and circular No. 75 (7 November 1969) imposed a further 2½ per cent. In 1972 reserve requirements were increased from 5 to 7 per cent.

By 1972 the Government had issued Treasury bills for LL239 million. The issue outstanding in 1975 was LL15 million (see Chapter 6). The scope of action for the Bank here is therefore very limited, inasmuch as there is only a small volume of bills, for the market to deal in. Moreover, the Bank could conduct open-market operations only in accordance with Articles 106–108, i.e., with public or private securities maturing within 180 days. Further, the amount of public securities discounted, held under re-sale agreements or bought by the Central Bank, must not exceed the total of its capital and reserves.

Article 8 empowered the Central Bank to organise the Beirut Clearing House, and also to establish and organise clearing houses in any other city.

(v) Operations

Operations on gold and foreign exchange (Articles 81–83). These were usually entrusted to central banks. Article 83 was slightly unusual in that it aimed to facilitate the placing of gold deposits by the public against gold certificates. It enabled the Central Bank to limit speculative activities and to control the market in gold and foreign exchange.

Operations with the public sector (Articles 84–97). In addition to its advisory functions on financial and economic policies, the Bank was to be the public sector's exclusive banker (Articles 85–96) and financial agent (Article 97). Thus, it was to serve as the depository of public funds (Article 85).

Under certain conditions the Bank could also grant loans to the public sector. The law restricted such lending, in principle, to short-term advances to the Treasury, maturing in not more than four months, and to be resorted to not more than once a year. Moreover, 'those facilities to the treasury must not exceed 10% of the average receipts of the ordinary State Budget over the last three closed fiscal years' (Articles 88–89).

Article 90 states that in principle the Bank shall not extend credit to the public sector, with the exception of the above-mentioned drawing facilities. However, in cases of 'exceptional gravity', or 'absolute necessity', and after exhausting all possible means of finance, internal and external, the Bank may provide the public sector with credit facilities up to ten years (Articles 91–94). Thus, the principle embodied in Article 90, rigidly applied except in circumstances strictly defined in Articles 90 and 91, was to be the basis for confidence and protection of the currency. It was a safeguard against inflation and political intervention.

Article 93 safeguarded the currency against low rates which would make borrowing from the Central Bank more attractive. Interest was to be in accordance with the market conditions, and must not drop below a given minimum.

Article 96 set out the conditions stipulated in Article 93, under which borrowers could be asked to issue marketable and negotiable securities. Here it foresaw the possible development of open-market operations referred to in Article 76. This further aid to the establishment of a money market would be facilitated by the banking regulations, the subject of section 3.

Operations with banks (Articles 90–109). In principle, the Bank was to act as the bankers' bank. Article 96 stated that a bank might deposit funds with the Central Bank under item (d) of Article 76 or of its own free will. The conditions and formalities of the help offered to banks were defined, in Articles 100 to 106, similar to those of the BSL. It might discount commercial, industrial or agricultural papers with maturities not exceeding 180 days and bearing three accepted signatures (Article 100). It might open current-account loans to banks guaranteed by specified securities and for maturities not exceeding twelve months (Article 102).[46] Unlike the BSL, the Bank was empowered to gear its discount rate to prevailing monetary and economic conditions. It must not carry out any transactions other than those stipulated, or participate in any commercial enterprise (Article 111).

(vi) Financial provisions (Articles 112–117)

The Bank's own share in its profits was to be 50 per cent, the other 50 per cent going to the Ministry of Finance. The Bank's share was to be transferred to an account named 'general reserve', to cover any deficits incurred, so that the Bank could finance its deficits without resorting to the Treasury. When the general reserve account reached half the Bank's capital the share in the profits going to the Ministry of Finance was to be 80 per cent. The author regards the transfer of such profits to the Ministry of Finance as financially unsound. Money was invented to render a service which would promote exchange, and monetary management must aim to safeguard money. It is a medium of exchange, a store and a measure of value. In other words, in all its functions money represents goods and services or any assets in any country. Any profit accrued by the Central

Bank should not be given to the Government, but set aside as a reserve for operations strengthening or safeguarding money and the welfare of the economy. It is short-sighted and even amoral on the part of the Government to make profits out of monetary management. Besides, the use by the Government of its share in the profits is equivalent to printing money.

3. BANKING REGULATIONS (ARTICLES 121–191)

The need for regulations

There are those who regard with anxiety the increase in regulations, fearing that their steady growth 'presages the rapid "socialisation" of banking'.[47] But power and privilege of the commercial banks, says Kent, make supervision and regulation necessary in the interests of the general public. It has long been accepted that there should be supervision of gas companies, water companies and other public utilities,

> on the ground that these are 'natural monopolies', that competition is harmful, and that in lieu of competition the Government must protect the welfare of the public. While commercial banking is not a natural monopoly in the same sense, the capacity of the commercial banks to influence the economic development of the country makes them even more potent agencies for good or ill. Conservative banking policies may stifle the economic life of a community and impede sound enterprises; on the other hand, loose, reckless policies may bring about economic collapse.[48]

At the same time, regulations should not interfere with the principle of freedom which is basic to the Lebanese economy. Accordingly, the law was restricted to laying down general rules for the banks, while still allowing them wide freedom of action and of initiative. The regulations arose, indeed, out of generations of experience. They had already been practised, in the absence of any law, by any Lebanese bank concerned to honour its obligations. This third part of the Money and Credit Law was divided into seven sections, those of special interest being: (i) Bank obligations; (ii) Business related to the banking business, financial institutions; (iii) Auditors.

Bank obligations[49] *(Articles 132–151).*

a. Minimum capital. Besides the obligations to take corporate form, local and foreign banks operating in Lebanon are required to have a minimum paid-up capital of LL3 million.[50] Assets must exceed liabilities[51] by an amount equal at least to their capital. In the event of losses a bank was to reconstitute its capital within a year at most.

b. Banks' list. This laid down the principles on which an institution must act in order to be called a bank. All banks must register with the Central Bank, which was to publish periodically a list of banks.

c. Elimination (Articles 140–142). The Central Bank was also empowered to exclude from the list any bank which did not comply with the regulations, and thus effectively to close it down.

A bank could also be dropped from the list at its own request, or if it did not start operations within a year after registration, or if it suspended operations for more than a year. In neither of these three cases would the striking-off be considered a punishment under Article 208 (the ultimate administrative sanction). This Article was concerned only with violation of a bank's own statute and by-laws, or with false or incomplete statements. In the case of liquidation the Central Bank was to safeguard the interests of the depositors.

d. Accounts, statistics, control (Articles 143–151). The accounting and statistical reports required meant that balance-sheets or profit-and-loss statements would enable the Central Bank to be aware of the position of each bank, its administration, its resources and investments.

The question arises as to whether the authority given to the Central Bank to control the banks was compatible with the Banking Secrecy Law of 3 September 1956. The CMC believed that it was. The complete independence of the Control Department, the fact that its staff were sworn to secrecy, as were the Bank managers, and the fact that the Central Bank was not alien in principle to the banking system, all tended to guarantee secrecy. The Association was not satisfied, however, and after heated arguments, achieved a sort of compromise concerning control. Under Article 149 supervision was entrusted to an independent department in the Central Bank, responsible directly to the Governor. The staff of this department were to be sworn to secrecy, as prescribed by the Banking Secrecy Law, even against employees of the Central Bank's other departments, with the exception of the Governor. If additional information was deemed necessary, managers were to be asked to verify the information submitted by written confirmation, on their own responsibility. Should the Governor deem it necessary, closer examination was to be made, and managers were to give to examiners selected by the Governor access to all necessary documents.

Examiners must deal only with managers, and must not insist on customers' names, except those with debit accounts (Article 150). Banks could so organise their accounts as to not show customers names, except those with credit balances. Any Central Bank employee violating banking secrecy was to be liable to a prison sentence of from six months to two years (Article 203), instead of from three months to a year, as under the 1956 law.

In addition, three other provisions were specially stipulated, in the interests of the banks. First, the Government Commissioner supervising the Central Bank accounts was not to have access to the accounts and files of third parties protected by the Bank Secrecy Law. Secondly, Central Bank examiners must not enquire into, interfere with or give information concerning matters relating to, taxation (Article 150). And thirdly, Central Bank officials were to be bound by bank secrecy with regard to information not only about customers of the Central Bank, commercial banks and financial institutions, but also about these institutions themselves (Article 151).

(ii) Business related to the banking business (Articles 178–184)

The operations of quasi-banking institutions in the field of credit and investment had come to assume a relatively important place in the credit and financial structure. At certain times their operations were of sufficient scope to frustrate the credit policy of the Central Bank. It became necessary to bring them within its system of credit control.

The Central Bank's relations with such institutions was not, however, as close as those with commercial banks. On this basis the Law extended its regulations to non-banking financial institutions founded and operated either by individuals or by companies constituted under the commercial code, not authorised to receive deposits from the public, but performing credit and financial operations by use of their private capital and loans. The provisions were limited to registration with the Central Bank, reporting to it, and following its directions regarding credit policy. They were subject to inspection by the Central Bank and to the disciplinary sanctions relative to banks as provided for in Article 208.

(iii) Auditors (Articles 185–191)

The powers and obligations of auditors were defined in the Code of Commerce (Articles 172–178). The Law added certain provisions relating to auditors of banks and financial institutions with corporate form, both local and foreign.

4. MISCELLANEOUS AND FINAL PROVISIONS (ARTICLES 223–230)

Within two months of publication of this Law the Government would have to appoint the Central Council and remit the capital. The Central Bank would then become legal, as from 1 April 1964. The Central Bank, which was thereafter to be the bank of issue, was to determine, with the BSL, the assets and liabilities which the Department of Issue was required to transfer to the Central Bank. The Central Bank was also to arbitrate or conciliate on any questions outstanding between the state and the BSL as a result of the convention of 29 May 1937. The Central Bank was to credit or debit the Treasury by the amount resulting from these settlements.

EVALUATION

In evaluating the Money and Credit Law, the question arises as to whether the Central Bank was given adequate means of exerting influence on the foreign exchange market and on credit availabilities and money supply in a manner consistent with the responsibilities imposed upon it.

As to gold and foreign exchange, Article 75 prohibits intervention in the market by the Bank of Lebanon to buy and sell gold or foreign exchange, other than with the approval of the Minister of Finance. This may make it difficult for the Bank to conduct daily operations in the gold market. Greater flexibility would be provided by obtaining the general approval of the Ministers, leaving the Bank more or less free to operate in accordance with its own judgements.[52] However, in practice this has not been a major difficulty, since the intervention of the Bank has so far been negligible, and the Minister of Finance was always at hand. This is in any case a field where close co-operation between the Bank and the Government is especially desirable.

Article 114 states that the Bank's foreign exchange and gold assets must be recorded at the official value in Lebanese pounds, but this made operations impossible without risking losses due to differences between the official and market rates. The Bank could, of course, conduct exchange operations, but these are of much more limited scope than outright intervention. In practice, the Bank has kept out of the exchange market. This involves no major inconvenience as long as the market functions in a reasonably stable and stabilising manner. But it could prove a delicate matter in a different situation.

As regards the credit availability in the national economy, it is necessary to distinguish between direct lending to the public sector, management of the public debt, and means of influencing the volume of bank credit to the private sector.

As regards direct lending to the public sector, Article 99 stated that the Central Bank must not extend credit to the public sector. To its critics, this was unnecessarily rigorous, but it provided for three exceptions: the first was a cash facility (Article 88), limited in amount and duration, which in practice had never been used up to 1976. This was criticised as lacking flexibility, since it must not be used more than once a year (Article 89). Secondly, there could be a loan to the Government (Article 91) in circumstances of exceptional gravity. This possibility, it was argued, could be resorted to only at the cost of making the Central Bank the censor in national affairs.

The third exception was the possibility of loans to public agencies (Article 92). Although these were only to be given in exceptional cases, a considerable numbei of such loans had been outstanding at the time the Central Bank took over from the BSL.

With respect to management of the public debt, when a central bank takes up government securities—whether *en pension*, by discounting, or by accepting them as collateral for advances—it not only influences total liquidity but may also finance public expenditure. This the Bank of Lebanon may do only within narrow limits. It could perhaps extend advances to banks if state securities were considered marketable (Article 102). But this would be difficult in the absence of a developed market and would be a one-way process, since it would give supplementary liquidity, but could not check excessive liquidities. If certificates of the public debt were considered government bonds (Article 105), the possibilities of intervention by the Bank would become subordinated to the severe conditions of Articles 105 and 106, and also to those of Article 108. This latter limits the volume of public securities held by the Central Bank to the total of the Bank's capital and reserves (Article 113), and takes no account of monetary, financial or economic factors.

As regards bank lending to the private sector, Article 76 empowered the Bank to decide what reserves the banks were to place with it. Article 78 allowed a delay of thirty days for any adjustment in reserve ratios; this, it might be thought, could be exploited so as to prevent prompt action by the Central Bank. However, the banks might need time to provide liquid assets to meet increases in legal reserve requirements, especially as their freedom of recourse to the Central Banks for mobilising additional reserves was limited by the terms of Articles 100–102. The banks could get few assets accepted for re-discount *en pension*, or as collateral. There is, in fact, a disparity between the credit operations of the local banks and those which the Central Bank is authorised to re-finance, though this goes unnoticed as long as the banks have abundant liquidity. Events in 1966 forced the Bank to extend facilities beyond those ostensibly permitted, thus in effect amending the Law.

It appears to be impractical to limit the Central Bank to operations on trade bills of note more than 180 days, with three signatures: such bills represent only a small part of credit operations. It is doubtful whether even extensive reinterpretation of Articles 100–102 would meet the legitimate needs of the economy. The introduction of a system of medium-term credit would remain very difficult. In general then, the Law rigidly limited the possibilities of recourse to the Central Bank of Lebanon.

The Law has been criticised for providing brakes but no accelerator, and so preventing the Central Bank from contributing effectively to its twin objectives, monetary stability and economic growth. Some amendments, partly designed to meet this criticism, were passed by Decree No. 6102, 5 October 1973.

Thus, the general objectives of the Central Bank, in Article 70, are now stated to include the following: to safeguard the Lebanese currency; to maintain economic stability; to safeguard the banking system; and to develop the money and capital market.

This is rather more specific than before and the last item in particular is an addition to the previous text, directed to both the stability and the growth objectives. Developed money and capital markets would facilitate open market operations by the Central Bank and would also provide a means to channel domestic savings into development projects on a systematic basis.[53]

Other amendments are designed to further this new objective in detail. Article 108 would give the Bank wider scope to purchase public securities in the interests of monetary stability and not merely within the limits of its capital and reserves. To encourage the demand for public securities, Article 76 would allow the Bank to consider, if necessary, commercial banks' investments in government or government-guaranteed bonds as part of the legal reserve requirements. Furthermore, Article 109 is amended to permit Central Bank operations on public securities not only with banks and financial institutions, but also through the Beirut stock exchange.

To strengthen the Central Bank's influence on the general monetary situation, Article 76 also includes a new provision, permitting the Bank to accept special deposits from banks at interest rates determined by the Bank according to circumstances.

Another new item is added to Article 102, widening the scope of Central Bank credit to the banks and encouraging the latter to expand their medium-term loans. The Bank is permitted to grant commercial banks an advance on current account for a period of one year, renewable if necessary, against collateral in the shape of bills maturing in not more than three years, provided that such bills represent financing of agricultural or industrial operations, public works, or exports of Lebanese products.

With regard to the important weapon of legal reserve requirements, the amendments give Article 76 greater scope and flexibility. The Bank of Lebanon is to be authorised to impose:

(i) Differential reserves, i.e., different ratios on different categories of commercial bank liabilities.
(ii) Special marginal reserves on the increase in commercial banks' liabilities, or any category of liabilities, beyond a certain limit or on the increase in such liabilities after a certain date.
(iii) Special minimum reserve requirements on a given group of assets which may be defined by the Central Bank.

These amendments have been very useful in practice. Their influence on events and on the conduct of business will be observed in later chapters on the operation of the Bank.

NOTES

1. Sayers, R. S., *Central Banking after Bagehot*, 1958, pp. 108 and 113.
2. Ibid., pp. 111–12.
3. Ibid., pp. 108–11.
4. Ibid., pp. 108–9.
5. Ibid.
6. Kent, R. P., *Money and Banking*, 1957, p. 370.
7. Ibid., p. 365.
8. Sayers, op. cit., p. 1.
9. De Kock, *Central Banking*, p. 11.
10. Goldenweiser, *American Monetary Policy*, p. 68.
11. Sayers, op. cit., p. 1.
12. Hawtrey, R. G., *The Art of Central Banking*, 1962, p. 189.
13. Sayers, op. cit., p. 1.
14. De Kock, op. cit., p. 1.
15. Ibid.
16. Ibid.
17. Velayudham, T. K., 'The "New Style" Central Bank', *The Bankers' Magazine*, July 1968. A winner of the *Bankers' Magazine* first essay competition, Professor Sayers, expresses similar views, in *Central Banking after Bagehot*, 1958, pp. 115–16.
18. Sayers, op. cit. pp. 114–15.
19. Himadeh, S., *The Need for the Establishment of a Central Bank and the Organisation of Commercial Banking in Lebanon and Syria*, Al-Abhath, American University of Beirut, Vol. 4, December 1951, pp. 367–77.
20. Sayers, op. cit., p. 116.
21. Bader, Albert, lecture on 'The Economic Policy of Lebanon', in *Les Conférences du Sénacle,* 23 April 1956.
22. Yafi, T., 'A case for central banking reform in Lebanon', *Middle East Economic Papers*, 1958, pp. 111–14.

23. Conseil de la Monnaie et du Crédit (CMC).
24. Draft bill of 8 March 1956.
25. Sen, S. N., *Central Banking in Underdeveloped Money Markets*, Calcutta, Hookland, 1952, pp. 241–2.
26. Goldenweiser, E. A., op. cit., p. 1.
27. The IMF was consulted on the content of the reports, and gave a favourable opinion. IMF, Middle East Department, Memorandum on the Lebanese Call Report Forms, 13 April 1962.
28. Law No. 28/67, dated 19 May 1967 (Article 45). It was renewed for another five years.
29. Samuelson, Paul A., *Economics*, p. 32.
30. Association of Banks in Lebanon, 'Memorandum', 12 February 1963.
31. Ibid.
32. According to the Swiss National Bank authorities bank secrecy generally tends to be overestimated (see Chapter 6).
33. First Memorandum of the Bankers' Association, 12 February 1963, p. 4.
34. Memorandum of the Planning Board, 8 March 1963, p. 2 and First Memorandum of the Association of Banks, p. 4.
35. Chandler, Lester V., *Benjamin Strong, Central Banker*, 1958, p. 8.
36. For this they shall receive an indemnity equal to two years' salary (Article 24).
37. Memorandum of the Planning Board, op. cit., p. 3.
38. Article 28.
39. Association of Banks, First Memorandum, ibid., p. 5.
40. HMSO, *Committee on the Working of the Monetary System—Report*, August 1959. Comd. 827 (reprinted 1964), p. 278.
41. Memorandum of the Planning Board, op. cit., p. 4.
42. Association of Banks, Memorandum, op. cit., p. 6.
43. Ibid.
44. Memorandum of the Planning Board, op. cit., p. 4.
45. Here the Association wondered why the cover requirements should be changed, especially when they had apparently proved effective in safeguarding the currency in the past. Association of Banks in Lebanon, first Memorandum, op. cit., p. 7.
46. Article 102 was amended by Decree No. 14013, 16 March 1970, to satisfy conditions of exceptional gravity or extreme necessity. It authorised the Central Council to grant exceptional credit facilities against real guarantees other than those indicated in paragraph (d). Such guarantees are left to the discretion of the Central Council to choose.
47. Kent, Raymond F., *Money and Banking*, third edn., USA, 1956, p. 183.
48. Ibid., p. 184.
49. According to an earlier draft of the law, banks were supposed to be classified into two categories: (1) commercial and (2) specialised. Prior to this (in draft) the classification had been: (1) institutions specialised in short-term lending and (2) institutions specialised in medium- and long-term lending.
50. Originally, it had been LL5 million.
51. I.e., liabilities towards others rather than to shareholders.
52. This was achieved in practice.
53. Hoss, Salim, 'Objectives and means of monetary policy in Lebanon in the light of the draft law amending the Money and Credit Law' (in Arabic), *Businessmen*, January 1973.

4. Management and organisation of the Bank

From Lebanese central banking legislation we turn to the management and organisation of the Bank of Lebanon. The successful operations of the Bank do not depend only on the authority that it derives from the Money and Credit Law, but also upon the quality of its management. Management 'makes or breaks', not only the institution, but the whole system. 'Systems and plans are but the rules to be followed in the game in which men are the players'.[1]

The Bank of Lebanon's head office is of course in Beirut, and it has branches in Tripoli, Sidon, Tyre, Zahle, Baalbeck and, more recently (1979), Jounieh. In accordance with the Money and Credit Law, it has a governor, three deputy-governors, a central council, an advisory committee and a government commissariat. The nine directors are the heads of the departments (as shown in Fig. 4.1). The structure is simpler than, for instance, that of the Bank of England or the Swiss National Bank.[2]

THE CENTRAL COUNCIL

The Central Council, consisting (under Article 28 of the Money and Credit Law) of the Governor as Chairman, three Deputy-Governors,[3] the Director-General of the Ministry of Finance and the Director-General of the Ministry of National Economy.

The Governor is appointed for six years, and the Deputy-Governors for five years, renewable one or more times. The Governor and the Deputies are full-time (Articles 17–20).

The Council is convened by the Governor at least monthly. It can also meet at the request of the Minister of Finance (but not in the absence of the Governor or Acting Governor), or the Director-General of Finance or the Director-General of National Economy. There is a quorum of four. Decisions are by majority of members present, and the Governor has a casting vote (Articles 29–31).

It is held that, since the Central Bank deals largely with commercial banks, these latter must never be able to control its policy.[4]

> The relations of the commercial banks with trade and industry may on occasion colour their views as to what the policy of the central bank should be. Clearly a policy that should be directed by national

> considerations ought not to be subordinated to the interests of the principal customers of the central bank. Representatives elected by special bodies necessarily have to look to these bodies for re-election and may be drawn unconsciously into regarding questions of credit policy from the point of view of its effects on the special interest they represent, rather than from that of the country as a whole. Private ownership [says Regan], is an anachronism, reflecting the mistaken view of an earlier day concerning the functions of central banking ... Since the system is now primarily a public institution for the making of a national economic policy, bank ownership is inappropriate because it implies public policy-making by a private group . . . .[5]

Jacob Viner, according to Regan,[6] concedes that the private financial community 'has valuable information and experience . . . But these can be drawn upon . . . without conferring upon it any special status or authority . . . in the formulation of official monetary policy'. Regan's own comment is 'Elimination of private ownership might serve to lessen suspicion of the system as a "private interest agency" among the general public . . .'.[7] On the other hand, W. McC.Martin, the former Chairman of the Federal Reserve Board, stands with the commercial bankers in favour of the existing American mixed arrangement (publicly-controlled but privately-owned). 'Stock ownership by the banks contributes', he maintains, 'breadth of judgement and experience on the part of the reserve bank directors (two-thirds elected by owner-member banks) and has a psychological value in giving the member banks a tangible interest in, and direct connection with, their respective reserve bank.' Commercial bankers, too, support this arrangement on the grounds 'that public understanding is enhanced, regional interest promoted and Executive Branch (Treasury) dominance avoided'. Some bankers fear that full government ownership may lead to political control, making the Central Bank unable to check inflation.[8]

THE ADVISORY COMMITTEE

Since the Central Bank must always be in close contact with the business world, it has not only a department of statistics and economic studies but also an advisory committee of six, four of whom are from banking, commerce, industry and agriculture. The fifth is from the Planning Board, and the sixth is a professor of economics.[9] It can submit studies on the general economic situation or on the economic condition of any region or sector.

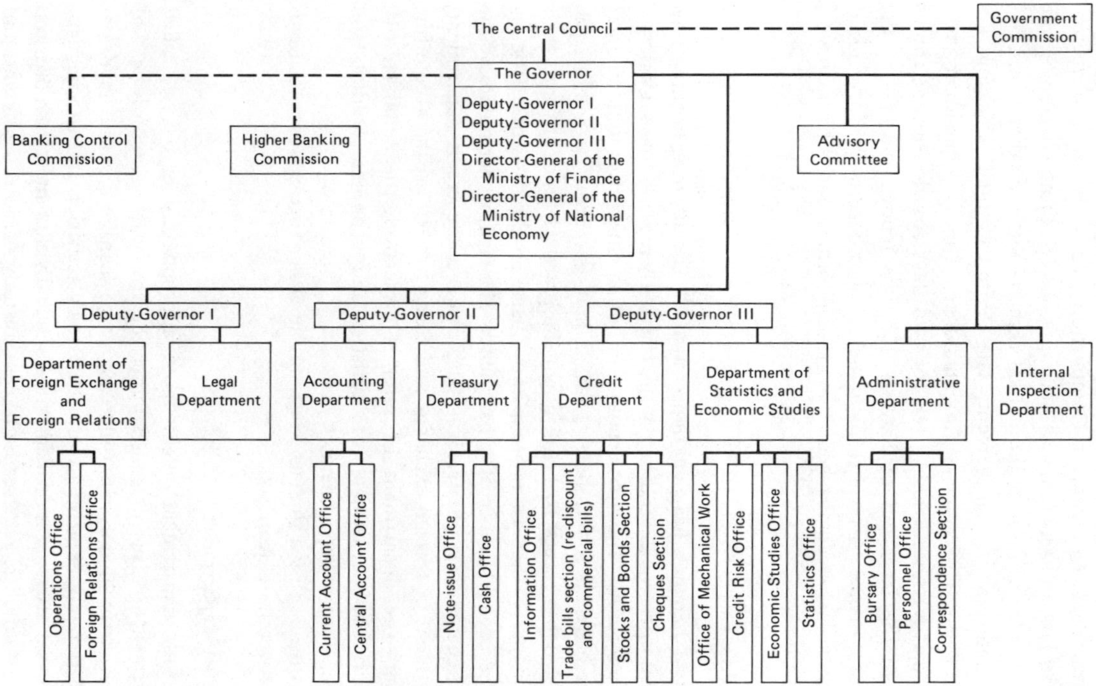

Figure 4.1.

Note: Deputy-Governor III was entrusted in October 1972 with the department of statistics and economic studies instead of the legal department, which was given to Deputy-Governor I.

THE CENTRAL BANK GOVERNMENT COMMISSION

The Central Bank Government Commission supervises the implementation of the law and examines all accounts, except those covered by the Bank Secrecy Law. It audits the Bank's cash in vault and other assets, but must not interfere in management. The Central Council's decisions are notified to the Government Commissioner. The Commissioner may request the Governor to hold back for two days any decision he thinks contrary to the laws and regulations. He then reports the case to the Minister of Finance. After five days the decision becomes enforceable if no settlement has been reached. Few, if any, other central banks have a comparable body.

THE DEPARTMENTS

The Bank of Lebanon has eight departments.[10] The differing organisations adopted by different central banks show that there is no one set pattern. What is important is the right arrangement of administrative units in order to achieve efficient functioning. Thus, it may be useful in deciding the number of departments to break down the practical functions into their component parts, then to re-group those parts on the basis of efficiency into the necessary number of departments. The eight departments of the Bank of Lebanon are: the Treasury department; the credit department; the department of foreign exchange and foreign relations; the accounting department; the department of internal inspection; the administrative department; the department of statistics and economic studies; and the banking control department.[11]

Each is headed by a director, responsible either to the Governor or to one of the Deputy-Governors.

The Treasury department

The Treasury department might more appropriately have been called the department of issue. It comes under the chief cashier, who is head of this one department only. Its functions are to manage the note-issue, and any cash transactions arising from the Bank's activities, and to safeguard gold and other assets. It is divided into an issue division and a cash division. The former supplies, receives and keeps custody of notes and coins, and holds gold and other assets. The latter conducts the cash operations of the Bank and its branches and is responsible for cash.

The credit department

This department controls the administration of credits to the public sector, to banks, and financial institutions, and when necessary administers eligible trade bills. It also examines credit applications in the light of their prospective impact on cash reserves and the sources and uses of funds both of the individual bank and of the banking system as a whole. It also supervises the execution of the law with regard to the Bank's credit operations. It includes: the information office; the trade bills section; the stocks and bonds section; the cheques section; and the credit risk office.[12]

The department of foreign exchange and foreign relations

This is concerned on the one hand with the Bank's relations with other central banks, foreign banks and international monetary institutions, and on the other with the Bank's foreign exchange operations and the administration of the Stabilisation Fund. It administers the Bank's foreign exchange assets, as well as those of the public sector. It is also responsible for the telegraphic codes and control over exchange documents. Of its two divisions, the division of foreign relations is responsible for relations with foreign monetary and financial organisations, collects information and keeps an eye on foreign legislation on exchange and trade. It may also represent the Bank in negotiations on contracting payment or clearing agreements. The operations division deals with gold and foreign exchange, either in the home market or abroad, and executes payments or clearing agreements. It also co-operates with the credit department over documentary credit. Its three sections deal with foreign exchange, documentary credit and clearing.

The legal department

The department provides advice to any division on legal precautions, as well as managing litigation. It comments on the applications submitted by banks or other financial institutions for registration, and makes recommendations. It organises the List of Banks and, with the help of the administrative department, the registration of financial institutions. It keeps an eye on the legal conditions of banks and financial institutions to ensure their compliance with the Money and Credit Law as well as the Lebanese Code of Commerce. It suggests all necessary measures when a bank or a financial institution is to be struck off the List of Banks; and it proposes sanctions which the Bank imposes under the Money and Credit Law.

The department of statistics and economic studies

This department conducts economic and monetary research and advises the Governor. It may be called upon by the Governor to prepare and distribute statistics and research studies, inside or outside the Bank. Its divisions are those of statistics, research and the credit risk office.

The statistics division receives and digests information required by the Central Bank from the other banks, and passes on all such documents to the banking control department. The economic studies division provides information on the economic, financial and monetary situation in Lebanon and abroad, through various economic, financial and monetary studies, and makes periodical reports. It also prepares the draft annual report of the Bank and is responsible for the library. The credit risk office (originally included in the credit department) receives information from the banks concerning total credits granted to each client, the kind of credit, the name of the institution granting the credit, as well as the distribution of such credits by banks to the various economic sectors. It informs the banks on request of the sum total of credits granted to any client, but without giving the names of lending institutions concerned.

All such information is distributed, with the statistical results, to the credit department, the administrative department, the banking control department and, when necessary, to the branches. This office may ask the banking control department to verify statements by banks, and informs the Governor about failures of banks in their obligations, suggesting any necessary measures.

Banking Control (Department and Commission)

As explained in Chapter 3, the struggle of the Association of Banks against banking regulations and control culminated in the arrangement stated in Articles 148–151 of the Money and Credit Law. Banking control was thereby entrusted to a department in the Central Bank completely independent of its other departments, and directly responsible to the Governor. Supervision was described as the examination of all statements, documents, information, clarification and evidence submitted by the banks or requested by the Central Bank. Bank managers may be asked to confirm the information submitted, and the Governor may order closer examination. In no circumstances may bank managers disclose customers' names, except those with debit accounts, and banks may organise their accounts in such a way as not to show their customers' names, except those with debit balances. The Banking Secrecy Law of 3 September 1956 is thus fulfilled.

An independent Banking Control Commission was established at the Central Bank by Law No. 28/67 of 9 May 1967. According to Article 8 of this new law the Commission had three members, appointed by decree of the Council of Ministers at the suggestion of the Minister of Finance. One member, and the President of the Commission, was to be a specialist in banking and financial affairs, or a professor specialising in the subject; one member suggested by the Association of Banks, and one by the Deposit Insurance Institution. A representative of the Central Bank appointed by the Central Council was to stand in until this latter institution had been established. In practice, the newly-appointed Director of the Banking Control Department was the third member of the Commission, and the whole Department was merged with it.

Article 9 of the new law defined the functions of the Commission as ensuring compliance of the banks with the Banking Law (Articles 148 and 150 of the Money and Credit Law—see Chapter 3 above). The Commission was to carry out periodical investigations of all banks and had power to exercise the control given to the Governor and the Bank by the Money and Credit Law. It could impose on any bank a plan to improve its financial position and control its expenses.

Furthermore, a Higher Banking Commission was established in the Central Bank consisting of:[13] the Governor, as President; one of the Deputy-Governors, chosen by the Central Council; the Director of the Ministry of Finance; a magistrate with at least ten years' experience, appointed by decree, with the consent of the Supreme Judicial Court; the member of the Control Commission representing the Association of Banks; and the Chairman of the National Deposit Insurance Institution.

This Commission replaced the Sanctions Commission provided for in Article 209 of the Money and Credit Law. The Governor was to be informed regularly by the Banking Control Commission about the condition of the banks, collectively and individually. The Higher Banking Commission could also demand additional information from the Banking Control Commission.

INTERNAL DISPUTES

The Bank of Lebanon is the second central bank to have three Deputy-Governors.[14] This was thought necessary to ensure representation of the major religious sections of the community.[15] To co-ordinate and strengthen the arrangement, Mr Philippe Takla, the Foreign Minister and one of the most powerful men in the country, was appointed the first Governor. The ruling in Article 20 that the Governor should devote all his time to the Bank was made effective only as from 1 April 1964, seven months after his appointment, i.e., as from the formal foundation of the Bank. The Deputy-Governors had to become full-time on appointment (in August 1963). On 18 November 1964, however, less than eight months after the Governor had become full-time, he was again needed as Foreign

Minister, and was enabled to do so by presidential decree. He delegated his powers to the first Deputy, and was away from the Bank until 1 June 1965. He stayed until 9 April 1966, and then went back to the Foreign Office. He returned to the Bank on 28 November 1966, but left finally on 18 June 1967, when Mr Elias Sarkis succeeded him. The new Governor was also unable to work full-time, since he was also Director of the presidency.[16] He was appointed for six months and this was renewed for another six months, despite protests (and threats of resignation) by the President of the Association of Banks.

Another unique feature in the Bank of Lebanon is its staff trade union. Owing to the pressure exerted by the BSL trade union, the Council of Ministers decided, in March 1963, that all the staff of the issue department of the BSL should be taken into the new Central Bank, if they so desired. This had obvious advantages in that there was no need to train new people. On the other hand, little room was left for new elements, and there were many high-ranking officials to absorb. At the head of the employees was the leader of the General Federation of Trade Unions, the late Mr Gabriel Khoury. The union grew in strength in its new position, and soon challenged the management. On Tuesday 29 December 1964 they re-elected their council, with Mr Khoury as Chairman.[17]

A critical conflict erupted between, on the one hand, the Acting Governor, and the Director of Statistics, and on the other, the staff trade union. The Council of the general union, which includes all trade unions in the country, decided on a token strike for an hour on Wednesday 3 March 1965, 'should the administration of the Central Bank continue provoking the union'.[18] They sent messages to the authorities, and met the Prime Minister, the Minister of Justice, the Minister of Labour and Social Affairs and the Foreign Minister, who was still *de jure* the Governor of the Central Bank. They demanded, among other things,[19] the abolition of the paragraph in Article 33 of the Money and Credit Law which prevented the old staff from joining the general union.

On 1 March a meeting was held, attended by the councils of the four unions comprising the general union[20] and the leaders of the petroleum workers, as well as representatives of other unions. While they were studying the results of their negotiations with the authorities over the Central Bank, the Foreign Minister (i.e., the Governor) called their leader, Mr Khoury, and discussed with him the possibility of postponing negative decisions in exchange for certain promises, but without success. A one-hour strike was in fact decided on by seventy trade unions[21] as a protest over 'the increased pressure inside the Bank on the employees who sided with Mr Khoury'.

However, the Governor met union leaders and persuaded them not to strike, in return for a change in the law which would allow the staff to join the union, and for certain increases in salaries. He made a declaration to this effect which expressed also the complete commitment of the Governors and staff to the good of the Bank and the general welfare of the country.[22]

Peace was not to last long. On the return of Mr Takla a new conflict arose. This led to the first Deputy-Governor and the Director of Statistics offering their resignations.[23] They were given leave of absence; and a settlement was reached after intervention by the President. But numerous other conflicts remained for some time between the Governors and the staff.

NOTES

1. Prochnow, Herbert V. and Foulk, Roy A., *Practical Bank Credit*, USA, 1963, pp. 283 and 291.
2. At the Bank of England only four directors are full-time. The chief committee is the Committee of Treasury, consisting of the Governor and Deputy-Governor, ex-officio, and five directors; only one of them may be an executive director. (Bank of England, Internal Administration (mimeo.), no date.)

   The Swiss National Bank is run by the following bodies:

   A. For supervision and control:
      1. The General Assembly of Stockholders.
      2. The Bank Council.
      3. The Executive Committee.
      4. Local committees.
      5. The Auditing Commission.

   B. For management:
      1. The Board of Directors.
      2. The local management committees.

   Two of the three directors are designated as President and Vice-President. All three are appointed by the Federal Council, on the recommendation of the Bank Council, for six years. The Bank Council's 40 members serve for four years. Fifteen are elected by the stockholders and 25, including the President and the Vice President, by the Federal Council.

   The Executive Committee consists of the President and Vice-President of the Bank Council and eight other members, each serving for four years. The three members of each local committee also serve for four years.

   The Auditing Commission consists of three members and three auxiliaries elected yearly by the stockholders. (Bär, Hans J., *The Banking System of Switzerland*, 1973, pp. 2-3.)
3. Although the Deputy-Governors enjoy the same status and prerogatives, for convenience they are designated First, Second, and Third.
4. Kisch, Cecil and Elkin, W. A., *Central Banks*, p. 61.
5. Regan, Michael D., *The Internal Structure of the Federal Reserve: a political analysis by the Commission on Money and Credit, Monetary Management*, Englewood Cliffs, N.J., Prentice-Hall, 1964, p. 371, quoting Bach, G. L., *Federal Reserve Policy-Making*, New York, 1950, pp. 242-3.

6. Regan, Michael, D., op. cit., p. 372. Regan quoting Sub-Committee on General Credit Control and Debt Management of the Joint Committee on the Economic Report, Hearings, Monetary Policy and the Management of the Public Debt, 82nd Congress, second session, 1952, pp. 755–6.
7. Ibid., p. 373.
8. Ibid., p. 371.
9. See above, p. 63.
10. The Memorandum concerning organisation is based on the Money and Credit Law, particularly Article 26, and on the proceedings of the Central Council in its meetings of 25 November 1963 and 10 April 1964.
11. Later, according to Law 28/67, 9 May 1967, this department was incorporated into the Banking Control Commission.
12. This office was annexed to the department of statistics and economic studies by decision of the Acting Governor on 21 December 1964.
13. Article 10 of Law No. 28/67, 9 May 1967.
14. The Reserve Bank of India is the other Bank, Aufricht, Hans, *Central Banking Legislation*, IMF, 1961, p. 345.
15. These sections are: the Maronites (Christians), the Sunnis and the Shi'is (both Muslims).
16. I.e., Director-General in the Palace of the President of the Republic.
17. Article 33 of the Money and Credit Law until 1965 prevented them from joining the general union.
18. By the 'Administration' was meant only the Acting Governor and the Director of Statistics.
19. *Al-Nahar*, 24 February 1965.
20. These are: the United Trade Union, the Trade Union League, the Independent Trade Unions and the Union of the Workers of Northern Lebanon.
21. The major trade unions were those of the banks, transportation, bakeries, mills, grocers, confectionists, commerce, fruit and vegetable workers, knitting and weaving, petroleum, workers at the American University, airlines, ships, marines, cinemas, chemists, and others joining the general union.
22. *Al-Hayat*, 3 March 1965.
23. *Al-Nahar*, 6 July 1963.

5. Operations and policies of the Bank

Having discussed the legislation and organisation of the Bank of Lebanon, it is necessary to examine its operations and policies.

RELATIONS WITH THE GOVERNMENT

To what extent is the Bank of Lebanon independent? In the nineteenth century state control or influence over central banks was taken for granted in most countries. The First World War was felt to have revealed certain threats to financial stability in this relationship and in 1920, at the Brussels Conference, there was a general feeling in favour of independence.[1]

In the United Kingdom, the Bank of England Nationalisation Act of 1946 authorised the Treasury to issue such directives 'as, after consultation with the Governor . . . , they think necessary in the public interest'.[2] In fact, this power to direct has never been employed in England.[3] Since the revival of a positive monetary policy, after 1951, it is said that the Bank of England and the British Government have been trying to evolve an allocation of respective functions. Reorganising the paramount authority of the Government under the 1946 Act, they both accept the advantages of the Bank's autonomy with a 'life of its own, capable of generating advice, views and proposals that are something more than a mere implementation of its supervisor's instructions'.[4] The Radcliffe Committee was against the proposed distinction between bank affairs and 'agency functions'.[5] It argued that if this difference were, in time, 'to harden into principles of dogma, they would be capable of producing strains in the relationship.'[6] A working and suitable relationship was more important, it maintained, than any statutory form.

On the other hand, the Committee did not approve of complete independence, on the grounds that planning and implementing national monetary policy required 'constant co-operation, strategic and tactical' between the Central Bank and the Treasury.

> The changed aspect of monetary policy which is now so inextricably connected with the government's fiscal operations and with the management of the government's debt reflects the fact that decisions about the courses which the bank is to pursue can no longer be disposed of either

according to a single set of working principles or by a single self-contained governing body.[7]

The Bank of Lebanon is a state-owned but financially autonomous legal entity.[8] It is not subject to the administrative and management rules and controls applicable to public institutions. The two government directors on the Central Council are there not to act as government delegates, but as members of the Central Council.[9] The Central Bank Government Commission, however, provides some supervision and a liaison. In practice, effective allocation of functions between government and bank is to a certain extent influenced by the people concerned, as was seen in Lebanon, where the governors were the most influential men in the country.[10] Consequently, the policies of the Bank usually had full government support.

The Bank of Lebanon provides services much like any banker to his customers, namely: receipt of money due; payments and transfers out; custody and management of securities; and, in certain cases, loans (Article 84). Besides these banking and agency obligations to the government, the Bank of Lebanon has advised on problems of the Lebanese economy and monetary system, as it is entitled and expected to do under Articles 71 and 72. On one occasion, for example, the Governor advised the Prime Minister (11 December 1965)[11] of points discussed earlier in the Bank (1946), after the default of La Banque Foncière (6 April 1964) and La Banque Commerciale (1963),[12] and after the liquidation of a third commercial bank (Sogex). The basic, underlying question (1964) was, how to ensure continuing economic development and raise the standard of living, while maintaining stability and safeguarding the value of money. More particularly, problems of the government budget were discussed by the Bank Council (11 May 1964) together with ways and means of financing public works and development projects.

As regards development activities of the private sector, the items discussed included stimulation of bank credit for the development of real estate in order to help banks solve the problem of frozen investments resulting from the general depression in real estate activity. Taxation on real estate and buildings had to be reduced and rent restrictions had to be eased. The same discussion dealt with attracting foreign capital and encouraging savings by removing tax on the interest on bank deposits, and lowering income tax on corporations. Moreover, it was advised to facilitate the establishment of institutions specialising in medium- and long-term credit, and to free these from income tax for the first five or six years.

As will be seen later, most of these points crystallised into laws and decrees.

Reaction to the Intra crisis

It is natural to have continuous co-operation between the Bank and the government on important issues of policy, and to expect even more than this in exceptional periods of stress.

> When there has been a variance of opinion between the two authorities, the government, with its exceptional responsibilities, must be able, in the last resort to enforce its will. Thus in times of crises the Bank, like many other normally independent organisations is likely to find itself to a large extent under the influence of the Government.[13]

In Lebanon the Government felt obliged to intervene over the crisis of Intra, the largest commercial bank in the country. It could be argued that the Bank of Lebanon should have accepted full responsibility. It was the body at the head of the banking system, and might have been expected to know to what extent the balance-sheet of Intra was reliable. Those who argued this way blamed the Bank of Lebanon for relinquishing its rights and surrendering to the government a matter on which it was more informed than anybody. On the other hand, it was thought that the Government should accept responsibility for any losses due to bank failures. This was based not only on the responsibility of the Government for the economy as a whole, but on the fact that the weaknesses in the banking system had been there before the Bank existed. However, at the outset of the crisis the Bank was not empowered to give exceptional help on a sufficient scale.

A new law was needed, and Law No. 62/66 (9 November 1966)[14] was enacted, authorising the necessary Central Bank assistance by:

1. the purchase of gold or convertible foreign exchange;
2. re-discounting eligible bills;
3. making advances on securities (title deeds) not exceeding 60 per cent of their value as estimated by the Bank;
4. making advances on commercial bills with maximum security of twelve months at a margin of 80 per cent for ninety days, renewable;
5. re-discounting bills with two signatures, one of them from the bank concerned;
6. granting of credit on real-estate mortgages, direct or transferred;
7. re-discounting time bills to the order of the Bank, signed by the Chairman and one member of the board of a bank, to the limit of 25 per cent of the capital of the bank. Exceptional facilities granted under this law by the BL to a bank were not to exceed 65 per cent of the bank's total deposits on 31 August 1966.

It seems that the Bank had to pay a price in this crisis. It was the surrender of the banking control function to an independent commission (see next section).

Relations between the two improved when Governor Takla returned to the Bank (29 November 1966) after the crisis. It was agreed that there must be no more bank failures. The Government accepted the view of the Governor that exceptional liquidity to banks should be provided, even beyond the above-mentioned 65 per cent limit. This, it was argued, was implicit in the law which initially sanctioned the exceptional facilities.

The attitude of both the Bank and the Government then, with regard to providing banks with exceptional liquidity, derived closely from that of Bagehot. The latter, as long ago as 1873, argued that a central bank, being the custodian of the nation's reserves, should stand ready to use these reserves in order to deal with monetary crises. 'The ultimate banking reserve of a country (by whomesoever kept)', said Bagehot, 'is not kept out of show, but for certain essential purposes, and one of those purposes is meeting a demand for cash caused by an alarm within the country'.[15]

He added:

> Whatever bank or banks keep the ultimate banking reserve of the country must lend that reserve most freely in time of apprehension, for that is one of the characteristic uses of the bank reserve, and the mode in which it attains one of the main ends for which it is kept. Whether rightly or wrongly, at present and in fact the Bank of England keeps our ultimate bank reserve, and therefore they must use it in this manner . . . In truth the Bank does not lend from the motives which should make a bank lend. The holders of the Bank reserve ought to lend it at once and most freely in an incipient panic, because they fear destruction in the panic. They ought not to do it to serve others. They ought to know that this bold policy is the only safe one, and for that reason they ought to choose it.[16]

The Government's acceptance of this view was transmitted to the Bank with the hope that the Government would seek adequate legislation from parliament. The Bank pointed out (21 April 1967) that it was bound by Articles 90 and 91 of the Money and Credit Law. Article 91 laid down that only in circumstances of exceptional gravity and in cases of absolute necessity could a loan be granted to the government and then only when there was no other solution. The Bank had acted for the Government in the Intra crisis, granting exceptional credit facilities under the Government's guarantees. It could not take any intitiative of its own in this matter unless covered by law. The Bank accordingly urged on the Government the need for a supplement to Law No. 62/66, extending the exceptional facilities; otherwise the Bank would be unable to grant any more loans. Furthermore, there was a need to speed up the whole of the draft law which included provisions to close banks found to be unable to function. The decision to close a bank must not be the responsibility of one administrative body, but must be endorsed also by the Council of Ministers. The seriousness of such a measure from the social, commercial and even political point of view means that it should be used only after all other possibilities have been explored.

RELATIONS WITH BANKS

The Central Bank's relations with the banks are founded upon the services it renders and the powers it has to regulate banking activities and operations in the country. The Bank of Lebanon, as a bankers' bank, keeps current accounts for the banks.[17] These afford to the banks some of the advantages a private customer derives from an ordinary banking account. Banks can make payments to one another through the clearing house at the Bank of Lebanon; when some banks have net claims on others, a transfer of balances takes place between the banks' current accounts at the Central Bank. Banks may also make payments to the Treasury or to the public by cheques drawn on their accounts at the Central Bank. Table 5.1 shows the banks' balances at the Bank of Lebanon, in relation to their total deposits, at the end of each year over the period 1964–74.

Further, under Article 80 of the Money and Credit Law the Bank assumes the responsibilities of a clearing house. This was transferred from the BSL immediately on the establishment of the Central Bank. Table 5.2 shows the clearing operations in the Bank of Lebanon in the same period.

Another important service rendered by the Bank of Lebanon to commercial banks is through the credit risk office mentioned earlier (Chapter 3).

The other side of the Central Bank's relations with the banks lies in its power to regulate banking activities and operations. The Money and Credit Law provides for closer relations between the BL and the banks than does the law in many other countries. Article 174 authorises the Bank 'to make recommendations and take measures designed to ensure the promotion of sound banking'. It may initiate or alter management rules to maintain liquidity and solvency, and may determine periodically the required ratios between a bank's assets and liabilities in the light of their maturity structure. It may determine the required ratios between, on the one hand, net worth and, on the other hand, acceptances, guarantees and

Table 5.1. Banks' deposits at the Central Bank in relation to their total deposits (LL Millions)

	Banks' deposits at the BL (1)	Banks' total deposits (2)	% ½ X 100
1964	65	1,901	3.42
1965	68	2,242	3.03
1966	127	2,205	5.76
1967	97	2,091	4.64
1968	211	2,464	8.56
1969	239	2,254	10.60
1970	292	2,707	10.79
1971	472	3,862	12.22
1972	537	4,765	11.27
1973	571	5,542	10.30
1974	1,705	6,770	25.18

Source: Bank of Lebanon.

Table 5.2. Cheques cleared and their value

Year	Number (thousands)	Value (LL Millions)
1964	1,179	3,683
1965	1,575	4,025
1966	1,645	4,536
1967	1,575	4,023
1968	1,775	4,608
1969	1,899	5,208
1970	2,084	5,288
1971	2,445	6,888
1972	3,011	9,297
1973	3,443	12,308
1974	4,027	15,451

Source: Bank of Lebanon.

accommodations, total credit granted to one client or concern, and total deposits (Article 175).

Non-banking financial institutions were also brought, though to a lesser extent than banks, under the authority of the Central Bank. Their relations with the Central Bank are limited to registration, reporting to it, and following its directions as to credit policy (Articles 178–184). Banks and other financial institutions are alike subject to sanctions (Articles 192–210, and 182).

New branches of Lebanese banks abroad, new branches of Lebanese or foreign banks inside the country and even the transfer of a branch from one place to another must be authorised by the Central Bank.[18] In order to have a licence to open a branch, a bank must satisfy the conditions of the Money and Credit Law.[19] There must be an economic or social advantage to its opening. The Banking Control Commission must have no serious reservations as to the soundness of the bank's operations and position. The applicant bank must show competence and demonstrate the advantages of its services. The number of branches for each bank is determined in relation to paid-up capital and reserves, which must be assigned as follows: not less than LL1,500,000 to headquarters, and not less than LL300,000 to each branch. However, the by-law regulating branches was amended in June 1978, assigning LL3,000,000 to headquarters, LL1,000,000 to each branch in Beirut, and the vicinity, Jounieh included, as well as in Tripoli, Sidon, Zahlé and Chtaura; and LL500,000 to all other branches. Even when these conditions are fulfilled, it is within the discretion of the Bank of Lebanon to withhold permission. Banks must also provide any other statistics requested by the Bank of Lebanon in addition to the regular statistical reports.

Under Article 211 (Transitional Provisions), banks and financial institutions had to apply for registration in the first banking list within three months of the bank's notification through the press and the list would be published by the Central Bank within nine months. The legal department studies the files of banks individually, under the Governor's supervision. The number of banks on the list in the years 1965–74 is shown in Table 5.3.[20]

Until 9 May 1967, as indicated in Chapter 4, supervision of banks' activities in Lebanon was a direct function of the Bank of Lebanon, and was administered by a department designated by the Money and Credit Law as the department of banking control. This department was looked upon as auxiliary to the statistics and research department. The BL management appreciated the desirability of effective control, but believed a gradualist approach to be necessary. The bankers of Lebanon, carried away by some fifteen years of prosperity and expansion at a time when

Table 5.3. Number of banks operating in Lebanon, 1965–74

Year	Lebanese banks	Non-Lebanese banks	Total
1965	74	20	94
1966	74	20	94
1967	68	19	87
1968	68	19	87
1969	56	19	75
1970	55	19	74
1971	55	19	74
1972	56	18	74
1973	59	17	76
1974	63	17	80

Source: Bank of Lebanon.

there was complete absence of control, were not at once amenable to an effective measure of control.

Mainly as a result of the Intra crisis, the Banking Control Commission was established at the Central Bank by Law No. 28/67, of 9 May 1967. The Commission officially started operations on 5 June 1967, and took over and expanded the staff of the former banking control department. Although technically the Commission is independent of the BL, the law requires it to keep the Governor informed about the position of individual banks, as well as about the condition of the whole banking system. The Governor may also ask it to conduct specific investigations.

The law did not give the Commission significantly more authority than the former department. In fact, Article 9 of Law 28/67 specifically stipulated that the Commission might exercise all the supervisory and control authorities which the Money and Credit Law assigned to the Governor. However, it had greater manœuvrability, though the secrecy rule was still a handicap. In its by-laws, the Banking Control Commission defined the task of control as having three aspects: first, the position and operation of the banks must be kept under observation, with a view to ensuring the solvency and liquidity of banks, as well as their compliance with laws and regulations. Secondly, the Governor must be informed about the position of individual banks and of the banking system as a whole. And thirdly, banks must be given encouragement and advice on improving their financial positions and reducing overheads.

With the Higher Banking Commission's approval, the Control Commission also defined the conditions which would warrant the recommendation of the take-over of a bank. These conditions included losses which would wipe out the whole or a major part of a bank's equity; deterioration of a bank's position to a point where it became unlikely that the bank would cover its overheads out of current revenues; or non-compliance with the laws and regulations in such a manner as to endanger viability of a bank.

During the first year of its existence the Commission established contacts with all banks, was able to report in preliminary fashion to the Governor on the position of practically all the banks operating in Lebanon, and experimented with alternative approaches to supervising bank activities. It did a good deal by way of training its staff and putting down detailed instructions and guidelines as to investigations. It also submitted a number of recommendations for take-over to the Higher Banking Commission, and in fact the take-over of eight banks had been effected by September 1968.

Control, ever since, has been conducted smoothly, with no serious problems. The only serious handicap to thorough and full control, as felt by the Commission, is the secrecy of deposit accounts under the Law of 3 September 1956. The Commission maintains that the secrecy of deposit accounts unduly restricts its freedom of action, and leaves certain significant aspects outside its control.

The Commission also maintains that the effectiveness of control is seriously handicapped by the fact that it has no executive powers over the banks, and by the fact that the laws do not provide for proper sanctions in the case of certain violations. For example, one article prescribes that all reports of the bank auditors shall be submitted to the Governor of the Central Bank and to the Commission by 31 March. Yet when a number of auditors did not submit their reports by the stated time the Commission could not impose sanctions. Shielded by the Bank Secrecy Law, banks are able to inflate deposits so as to give a false picture, and possibly to claim the existence of blocked deposit accounts collateralising certain debtors' obligations, without the Commission being able to ascertain this. Bank secrecy prevents the Control Commission from verifying the existence of a deposit which is assigned as a collateral for a loan. A decree was also issued by the Council of Ministers on 16 October regulating the use of funds borrowed from the Central Bank under the exceptional facilities arrangements, whereby the banks were prohibited from using such funds for payment of the deposits of members of the board of directors of a bank; but there was no way of detecting violations of this. Further, as far as monetary policy is concerned, the Central Bank may be interested in differentiating between resident and non-resident deposits. But any policy based on such differentiation would be difficult because of bank secrecy. Arguably, however, as bankers claim, the benefits that Lebanon derives from banking secrecy far outweigh its detriment to a full and thorough control of bank activities.

THE BANK'S ROLE IN THE ECONOMY: MONETARY AND CREDIT POLICY

It is the stated task of the BL, as cited earlier 'to safeguard money, to ensure the basis of a durable economic and social progress', i.e., to ensure economic stability and growth. Accordingly, the law empowers the Bank with the necessary policy instruments, as outlined in Chapter 3.

The Bank's discount policy remained almost the same as that of the BSL until 30 October 1973, when the rate was increased from 3 to 5 per cent for eligible trade bills, and from 3¼ to 5¼ per cent for trade bills *en pension*. It seems there was no urgent need to change policy as there was very little re-discounting. Also, after the Intra crisis it was felt that the banking situation did not warrant any increase in the rates. On 1 June 1974 the rate was increased from 5 to 7 per cent , and to 7¼ per cent for bills *en pension.*[21] With regard to legal reserve requirements, the Bank decided to impose a rate of 5 per cent to be paid in two instalments. The first instalment of 2½ per cent was to be paid, starting from 10 July 1969, and the second to start from 2 December in the same year. The rate was later raised from 5 to 7 per cent, starting from 1 September 1972, and to 8 per cent from 1 July 1974. Reserve requirements were initially imposed, to be paid in local currency, on total deposits, i.e., on demand as well as time deposits and deposits in foreign as well as in local currency. Foreign-currency deposits were exempted, beginning from 1 July 1974. As from 1 January 1975 the rate was increased from 8 to 10 per cent. It should also be noted that the 1973 amendment to Article 76 gave the Bank of Lebanon greater scope and flexibility with regard to the weapon of legal reserve requirement (see Chapter 3, p. 60).

Open market operations have not been used. The Bank of Lebanon could not initially buy more public securities than the total of its capital and reserves (Article 108), and it was limited to bills maturing within 180 days (Article 106). However, the amendments, according to Decree No. 6102, dated 5 October 1973 aimed to develop the money and capital market with a view to facilitating open market operations. Article 108, as amended, gave the Bank wider scope to purchase public securities in the interests of monetary stability and not merely within the limits of its capital and reserves (see Chapter 3, p. 60).

As regards the amount of Central Bank credit, bills have been considered in the same way as in the Bank of England, except that in place of the 'never refuse to lend' rule, each loan was considered on its merits. The Bank of England acts as banker to the twelve discount houses that form the London Discount Market Association; to these houses alone the Bank of England operates as lender of last resort. It can choose the method by which it provides the market with cash, and can dictate the terms on which it will lend, but it will never refuse to lend. The knowledge that the Bank of England will always lend to the discount houses as last resort helps the clearing banks to keep their cash reserves to a minimum.[22]

Once a credit ceiling was granted, the Bank of Lebanon lent at all times and virtually assumed the position of lender of first resort, not at a penalty rate, and as last resort, as in the case of the Bank of England.[23]

New applications for credit lines were studied by the credit department and passed to the Governor through the Deputy-Governor concerned. Up to the Intra crisis in October 1966, fifty-six banks had been accorded credit lines, totalling about LL184 million. Fourteen banks were using their credit lines in the form of re-discounts totalling about LL13 million. Only one commercial bank used credit *en pension* of LL1.52 million. It should be noted that the banks which used their credit lines before the Intra crash were all local banks. Other credits accorded by the Central Bank were an advance of LL67.500 million (taken over from the BSL) to BCAIF; one of LL14.400 million to the consortium which had to liquidate the Sogex Bank (see p. 74 above) and finally an advance of LL15 million to Intra Bank, given on 6 October 1966 and fully used up by 14 October 1966.

It then seems desirable to establish a more explicitly defined and uniform system of Central Bank credit, preferably after a reform of the banking system which would give the authorities closer knowledge of conditions in each bank. The rationale behind such thinking was that, first of all, an objective yardstick was needed—a formula to automatically determine credit lines and to close the door to favouritism. Secondly, Lebanese banks were like their French counterparts in that they displayed no reluctance to borrow from the Central Bank and did not regard such borrowing as a purely emergency facility. The absence of an efficient money market made it necessary for banks to resort directly to the Bank for liquidity. Consequently, the Bank should grant some credit facilities on fairly easy terms.

However, the BL's credit policy should be regarded not only as a safety valve enabling banks to get liquidity, but also as a weapon of general monetary policy, especially because other weapons, such as open-market operations and obligatory reserves, were not yet applied. It followed that there should be a first ceiling within which the BL would grant credits (all accommodation including re-discounts) in relation to the size of each bank at low and fixed rates, and a second ceiling where the terms of additional credits would be governed by the general direction of monetary policy.

To determine the first ceiling the formula suggested was (calculating in millions of Lebanese pounds):

$$0.10\,(c-b)+0.40\sqrt{\{d-(c-b)\}}$$

where c represents a bank's paid-up capital, b bad debts for which no provision exist and d deposits (annual average). The formula recognised two measures of the size and importance of a bank—capital and deposits. Moreover, by taking account of bad debts it incorporated a more realistic value of the bank's equity and also reflected to a certain extent (since bad debts indicate the quality of a bank credit portfolio) the standard of the bank's management. There were two credit coefficients: 10 per cent for net equity after deducting bad debts, and 40 per cent for deposits (more strictly, the excess of deposits over net equity). These coefficients were not final: they could be changed if there were danger of exaggerated grants or undue squeezes. It is a matter of trial and error. It will be noted that the higher the coefficient on the equity, the greater the advantage accruing to the national banks, and the higher the deposits' coefficient, the greater the advantage to non-Lebanese banks, which have larger deposits.

Use of the square root relationship ensures that, as deposits increase, credit lines rise less than proportionately. For example, if a certain bank possesses deposits of LL64 million after deducting its net equity, it will be assigned a credit line in proportion to its deposits of LL3.2 million; i.e. an equivalent of 5 per cent of its deposits. If it has LL81 million in deposits it will get LL3.6 million, or 4.4 per cent of its deposits. If its deposits were LL100 million it would be assigned LL4 million, or 4 per cent of its deposits. This arrangement was designed to avoid favouring the biggest banks, including foreign banks.

As for the second ceiling, it was suggested that this should be linked to the first ceiling, as a percentage. It might initially be equal to 5 per cent of the first ceiling, and could be raised or lowered by the Central Bank.

Alternatively, the link could be raised or lowered by the Central Bank, or the link could be made through the deposit coefficient alone. For example, instead of being limited to 40 per cent, the coefficient could be 90 or 120 per cent, as monetary policy required. In other words, the lower the figure, the tighter the policy.

Lowering the ceilings could also be a further penalty for bad judgement, in conformity with Article 104, though banks were already penalised to some extent through the deduction of bad debts in the formula.

An alternative criterion for re-discount ceilings was also proposed, considering capital, reserves, and the number of debtors of commercial banks. It was based on the amount of domestic credit instead of the amount of deposits. It envisaged a global ceiling for the banking system as a whole, divided among the different commercial banks in relation to their capital and reserves, domestic credit, and the number of their debtors. The global ceiling would be determined by the Central Bank in the light of monetary policy. For comparison, Appendix II briefly notes some similar schemes proposed and employed in other countries.

Monetary highlights, 1964–1974

Table 5.4 (a), (b) and (c), based on the usual definitions and relations[24] shows the main determinants of money supply in the Lebanon in the years 1964–74. During 1965 commercial banks' claims on the private sector increased from LL1,945 million to LL2,310 million, i.e., by about 19 per cent, whereas the GNP at current prices increased by about 10 per cent. This increase in commercial banks' credit to the private sector at a rate almost double the increase in the GNP was a reflection and a cause of inflationary pressures in the economy. Lebanon continued to experience a significant inflow of foreign funds; the banks' foreign liabilities increased by LL133 million. As a result, the banking system was able to expand credit without resorting to help from the Bank of Lebanon, which thus had little effective control. Moreover, the inflow of foreign assets to the BL was considerably greater than the LL27 million shown in Table 5.4b. A revaluation of the BL's gold holdings at \$1 = LL3.08 meant a reduction in foreign assets of LL32 million, so that the inflow from the foreign exchange market came to LL59 million. The reduction in the gold holding was balanced by an upward adjustment in claims on the public sector, because of the Government's assumption of the accounting losses involved. The introduction of minimum legal reserve requirements might have limited the capacity for expansion of the banking system. But, as in the case of the re-discount rate policy, the use of this instrument was still early in view of the circumstances of the banking system at the time.

Table 5.4a. Determinants of money supply, 1964–1974 (LL Millions) (IMF classification)

	Dec. 1964	Dec. 1965	Sept. 1966	Dec. 1966	May 1967	Dec. 1967	Dec. 1968	Dec. 1969	Dec. 1970	Dec. 1971	Dec. 1972	Dec. 1973	Dec. 1974
BANK OF LEBANON													
Assets													
Foreign assets *	747	774	830	869	839	862	1,020	1,073	1,186	1,583	1,933	2,159	3,804
Claims on public sector	62	85	81	78	77	72	70	65	63	86	127	205	308
Claims on private sector	82	83	81	81	78	76	74	69	66	57	52	51	38
Claims on commercial banks	18	24	17	166	192	219	227	311	172	103	100	173	71
Total	909	966	1,009	1,194	1,186	1,229	1,391	1,518	1,487	1,829	2,212	2,588	4,221
Liabilities													
Reserve money†	604	659	677	834	899	945	1,127	1,172	1,199	1,462	1,643	1,877	3,131
(of which circulating money outside banks)	(500)	(547)	(575)	(645)	(713)	(786)	(834)	(868)	(845)	(921)	(1034)	(1,226)	(1,353)
Public sector deposits	276	260	286	308	240	209	177	255	202	281	462	593	848
Other items (net)	29	47	46	52	47	75	87	91	86	86	107	118	242
Total	909	966	1,009	1,194	1,186	1,229	1,391	1,518	1,487	1,829	2,212	2,588	4,221

COMMERCIAL BANKS													
Assets													
Reserves	100	108	104	188	179	149	287	297	345	537	570	626	1,667
Foreign assets	1,460	1,848	1,884	1,584	1,607	1,317	1,574	1,641	2,088	2,597	3,161	3,624	3,980
Claims on private sector	1,945	2,310	2,708	2,336	2,337	2,285	2,016	2,094	2,123	2,654	3,238	4,671	5,728
Total	3,505	4,266	4,696	4,108	4,123	3,751	3,877	4,032	4,556	5,788	6,969	8,921	11,375
Liabilities													
Demand deposits	890	962	1,026	894	861	782	909	787	830	1,101	1,239	1,390	1,642
Time deposits and deposits in FX	1,271	1,705	2,175	1,891	1,862	1,784	1,721	2,062	2,590	3,322	4,106	5,112	6,578
Foreign liabilities	1,023	1,156	1,000	820	813	611	903	834	909	1,048	1,170	1,519	2,027
Other items (net)	321	443	495	503	587	574	344	349	227	317	454	900	1,128
Total	3,505	4,266	4,696	4,108	4,123	3,751	3,877	4,032	4,556	5,788	6,969	8,921	11,375

* Up to 1971 foreign assets were calculated at a 'legal transitional rate' of the Lebanese pound of $1 = LL3.08 (Article 229 of the Money and Credit Law). After 1971 foreign assets have been calculated at the market rate prevailing at the end of each year.

† Reserve money is taken to mean here, as used by the IMF, the sum total of currency in circulation outside banks + currency in commercial banks + commercial banks' deposits at the Central Bank.

Table 5.4b. Changes in the determinants of money supply, 1964–1974 (LL Millions) (IMF classification)

	Dec. 65– Dec. 64	Sept. 66– Dec. 65	Dec. 66– Sept. 66	May 67– Dec. 66	Dec. 67– May 67	Dec. 68– Dec. 67	Dec. 69– Dec. 68	Dec. 70– Dec. 69	Dec. 71– Dec. 70	Dec. 72– Dec. 71	Dec. 73– Dec. 72	Dec. 74– Dec. 73
BANK OF LEBANON												
Assets												
Foreign assets	+27	+56	+39	−30	+22	+158	+53	+113	+397	+350	+226	+1,645
Claims on public sector	+23	−4	−3	−1	−5	−2	−5	−2	+23	+41	+78	+103
Claims on private sector	+1	−2		−3	−2	−2	−5	−3	−9	−5	−1	−13
Claims on commercial banks	+6	−7	+149	+26	+27	+8	+84	−139	−69	−3	+73	−102
Total	+57	+43	+185	−8	+42	+162	+127	−31	+342	+383	+376	+1,633
Liabilities												
Reserve money	+55	+18	+157	+65	+45	+182	+45	27	+263	+181	+234	+1,254
(of which circulating money outside banks)	(47)	(28)	(70)	(68)	(73)	(48)	(34)	(23)	(76)	(113)	(192)	(127)
Public sector deposits	−16	+26	+22	−68	−31	−32	+78	−53	+79	+181	+131	+255
Other items (net)	+18	−1	+6	−5	+28	+12	+4	−5	–	+21	+11	+124
Total	+57	+43	+185	−8	+42	+162	+127	−31	+342	+383	+376	+1,633

COMMERCIAL BANKS												
Assets												
Reserves	+8	−4	+84	−9	−30	+138	+10	+48	+192	+33	+56	+1,041
Foreign assets	+388	+36	−300	+25	−290	+257	+67	+447	+509	+564	+463	+356
Claims on private sector	+365	+398	−372	+1	−52	−269	+78	+29	+531	+584	+1,433	+1,057
Total	+761	+430	−588	+17	−372	+126	+155	+524	+1,232	+1,181	+1,952	+2,454
Liabilities												
Demand deposits	+72	+64	−132	−33	−79	+127	−122	+43	+271	+114	+151	+252
Time deposits and deposits in FX	+434	+470	−284	−29	−79	−63	+341	+528	+732	+755	+1,006	+1,466
Foreign liabilities	+133	−156	−180	−7	−201	+292	−69	+75	+139	+122	+349	+508
Other items (net)	+122	+52	+8	+84	−13	−230	+5	−122	+90	+190	+446	+228
Total	+761	+430	−588	+15	−372	+126	+155	+524	+1,232	+1,181	+1,952	+2,454

Table 5.4c. Determinants of money supply, 1964–1974 (LL Millions) (IMF classification)

	Dec. 1964	Dec. 1965	Sept. 1966	Dec. 1966	May 1967	Dec. 1967	Dec. 1968	Dec. 1969	Dec. 1970	Dec. 1971	Dec. 1972	Dec. 1973	Dec. 1974
MONETARY SURVEY													
Foreign assets (net)	1,181	1,462	1,711	1,627	1,630	1,563	1,684	1,871	2,355	3,126	3,919	4,265	5,757
Domestic credit	1,808	2,213	2,581	2,184	2,249	2,259	2,158	2,258	2,172	2,523	2,817	4,127	4,840
Claims on government (net)	(−219)	(−180)	(−209)	(−234)	(−166)	(−102)	(−49)	(−84)	(−53)	(−154)	(−431)	(−595)	(−848)
Claims on private sector	(2,027)	(2,393)	(2,790)	(2,418)	(2,415)	(2,361)	(2,205)	(2,342)	(2,285)	(2,677)	(3,248)	(4,722)	(5,688)
Total	2,989	3,675	4,292	3,811	3,879	3,822	3,842	4,219	4,527	5,649	6,736	8,392	10,597
Money	1,390	1,510	1,602	1,541	1,574	1,570	1,749	1,657	1,676	2,024	2,251	2,619	2,998
Quasi-money*	1,272	1,706	2,176	1,892	1,863	1,785	1,722	2,062	2,592	3,324	4,080	5,114	6,580
Other items (net)	327	459	514	378	442	467	371	410	259	301	405	659	1,019
Total	2,989	3,675	4,292	3,811	3,879	3,822	3,842	4,129	4,527	5,649	6,736	8,392	10,597

Table 5.4d. Changes calculated from Table 5.4c above

MONETARY SURVEY												
Foreign assets (net)	+281	+249	−83	+2	−67	121	187	484	771	793	346	1,492
Domestic credit	+405	+368	+398	+66	+9	−101	100	−86	351	294	1,310	713
Claims on government (net)	(+39)	(−29)	(−26)	(+69)	(+63)	(55)	(−37)	(31)	(101)	(−277)	(−164)	(−253)
Claims on private sector	(366)	(+297)	(−372)	(−3)	(−54)	(−156)	(137)	(−117)	(452)	(571)	(1,474)	(966)
Total	+686	+617	−481	+68	−58	20	287	398	1,122	1,087	1,656	2,205
Money	+120	+92	−61	+33	−4	179	−92	19	348	227	368	379
Quasi-money	+434	+470	−284	−29	−79	−63	340	530	732	756	1,034	1,466
Other items (net)	+132	+55	−136	+64	+25	−96	39	−151	42	104	254	360
Total	+686	+617	−481	+68	−58	20	287	398	1,122	1,087	1,656	2,205

* Quasi-money includes time and foreign currency deposits.

Source: Bank of Lebanon.

From December 1965 to September 1966 the banks' claims on the private sector rose at an accelerated rate of 22 per cent per annum to reach LL398 million, while GNP increased by some 8 per cent per annum. Foreign assets increased at the beginning of 1966, owing to high interest rates in international markets; but more pressure was exerted on the Lebanese foreign exchange market by June of the same year. Bank liquidity was increasingly strained, despite continuing inflows of capital. The BL maintained its passive stance. The situation changed radically, however, in October 1966, when the Intra Bank ceased payments. From then until May 1967, the evolution of the banking system was dominated by this event.

The Intra crisis was mainly a result of the ills inherent in the banking system before the Central Bank existed. In addition, it was said that elements of local and even international politics were involved. Unsound and even illegal banking practices were rife. Among the bad banking practices rumoured was one which consisted of offering free membership on a bank board to well-known personalities. A personality was invited to join because his name lent prestige to the institution; he was lent money by the bank itself to buy the requisite shares and subsequently derived profits therefrom, without contributing any money himself. To ensure this, the interest rate paid on his loan had to be kept artificially below the rate of dividend on the shares.

Certain banks, it was also said, had fictitious capital or capital increases, and in addition their administrators 'helped' themselves to depositors' money. Fictitious companies were said to be established by some banks. The entire capital subscription in these affiliated companies was made by the bank directors with the money borrowed from the bank itself, and the funds of that company had to be deposited with the bank. Through such fictitious companies the bank granted credit and distributed profits to its directors. Other rumours claimed that individual banks bought and sold land or other assets, making use of intermediaries to artifically inflate the value of the banks' profits from these transactions. Thus, the banks' proceeds were inflated in order to derive unreal profits for distribution.

The Intra 'Empire'

In talking about the Intra Bank it is essential to mention the late Mr Beidas, who was its President and General Manager, and mainly responsible for the rise and fall of that institution. Yussuf Khalil Beidas, born in Jerusalem, passed through different banking posts in Palestine before he became one of the directors of Barclay's Bank in Jerusalem. In 1948 he left Palestine for the Lebanon and started business in Beirut, establishing at first an office in one modest room in the city centre,[25] where he dealt mainly in foreign exchange and three-way trade. After about a year and a half, with his business growing due to the co-operation of many fellow Palestinian businessmen who had moved to Beirut at the time, he transferred his business to a bigger office[26] (three rooms), with a view to establishing a bank. His efforts materialised and Intra Bank SAL was born[27] (Decree No. 6647, dated 17 November 1951). Its capital was LL12 million, divided into 25,000 shares of LL500 each. The paid-up capital was LL7,830.000.

It is clear from the name of the Bank that Mr Beidas had it in mind to play the role of an international businessman and banker. The name Intra was derived from 'International Traders', as Beidas and his friends called themselves at the very beginning. In fact, the relatively rapid and spectacular expansion reached an international level. The rise of the empire may be seen briefly from the last balance-sheet, and from the growth of capital, branches and partnerships.

As Table 5.5 shows, the authorised capital of the Intra Bank rose from LL12 million in 1951 to LL30 million in 1959 and to LL60 million in 1962. The paid-up capital as reported was LL7.830 million in 1951; LL12 million in 1959; and LL60 million in 1964. With regard to capital increases, it was said that each time Beidas felt that depositors were uneasy because of rumours about the Intra Bank, he used to declare a capital increase to allay their fears.

The same table also indicates the expansion of Intra branches, which totalled thirty-eight in 1966, spreading throughout the major cities of the world. In Lebanon there were eleven branches; three in Syria; four in Jordan; five in Nigeria; two in Sierra Leone; two in Athens, and one each in Geneva, Frankfurt, Rome, Paris, London and New York.

As to partnerships, Appendix III indicates the extent to which Beidas was involved in other banks and companies in Lebanon and abroad. Beidas, as shown, was the Chairman and General Manager of seven banks besides Intra, and of another national company. He also participated in eleven companies, most of which were key enterprises in Lebanon, and was a founding member of three other Lebanese companies. His dreams of ships, airlines, hotels and telecommunications came true when he acquired a controlling share in leading companies such as the Société du Port de Beyrouth, La Ciota (the second largest shipbuilding yard in France); Middle East Airlines; the Société des Grands Hotels du Liban, and Radio-Orient.[28] Accordingly, those who controlled Intra, with its majority holdings in key enterprises, could exercise considerable influence in Lebanese politics as well as oil politics.[29]

A glance at its last consolidated balance-sheet reveals the following:

Table 5.5. Intra Bank expansion: capital and branches, 1951–1966

Year	Authorised capital (LL)	Paid-up capital (LL)	Branches inaugurated	
			Number	Cities
1951	12,000,000	7,830,000	1	Tripoli
1954	12,000,000	7,830,000	1	Beirut
1955	12,000,000	8,425,000	1	Beirut Airport
1955	12,000,000	8,425,000	1	Damascus
1955	12,000,000	8,425,000	1	Lattaquia, Syria
1957	12,000,000	8,500,000	–	–
1958*	12,000,000	9,336,000	1	Baghdad
1958	12,000,000	9,336,000	1	Aleppo, Syria
1958	12,000,000	9,336,000	1	Amman
1958	12,000,000	9,336,000	1	Geneva
1959	30,000,000	12,000,000	1	London
1960	30,000,000	20,078,925	2	Beirut
1960	30,000,000	20,078,925	1	Jerusalem
1960	30,000,000	20,078,925	1	Doha, Qatar
1961	30,000,000	28,691,200	1	Bhamdoun, Lebanon
1962†	60,000,000	52,012,493	1	Saïda, Lebanon
1962	60,000,000	52,012,493	1	Beirut
1962	60,000,000	52,012,493	2	Jordan
1962	60,000,000	52,012,493	1	Paris
1962	60,000,000	52,012,493	5	Nigeria
1963	60,000,000	55,032,175	1	Jordan
1964	60,000,000	60,000,000	1	Beirut
1964	60,000,000	60,000,000	1	Frankfurt
1964	60,000,000	60,000,000	1	New York
1964	60,000,000	60,000,000	1	Freetown, Sierra Leone
1964	60,000,000	60,000,000	1	Bo, Sierra Leone
1964	60,000,000	60,000,000	1	Rome
1965	60,000,000	60,000,000	3	Beirut
1966	60,000,000	60,000,000	1	Quado, Sierra Leone
1966	60,000,000	60,000,000	2	Athens

* Inauguration of headquarters at Riad Solh Street, 1 May 1958.
† Syrian branches nationalised after 3 May 1963.

item 1 on the assets side shows that it had in cash and banks about LL94 million, while on the liabilities side—item 5—banks and correspondents were owed about LL97 million. (See Table 5.6.)

It appears, therefore, that the bank's liquidity was tight, since it owed other banks more than it was due. Further, items 4 and 7 on the assets side—'Portfolio-Securities' and 'Real Estate and Installations'—were about LL135 million, or twice its capital and reserves. This was unsound commercial banking, which should normally concentrate on short-term and safe assets.[30] To convey the extent of the Intra empire it is worth noting that its total deposits were then LL457 million, i.e., about 18 per cent of the aggregate deposits of the Lebanese banks (including Intra). However, its deposits at notice or with fixed maturity constituted 30 per cent of the same item of the Lebanese banks. It might perhaps have been argued that because of its 'Deposits at Notice or with Fixed Maturity', item 4, which totalled about LL100 million, Intra could reasonably carry its investments in portfolio securities. However, it may be said here that, had item 4 been genuine, the bank would have had no difficulties with its liquidity, and could have financed a portfolio of securities, assuming these were not speculative.

Moreover, it is clear that a large part of Intra's resources was invested at long term. Total resources, besides capital and banks (i.e., liability items 1 + 2 + 3 + 4 + 6) came to LL539 million, while 'Advances and Debtor Accounts', and 'Portfolio-Securities' (items 3 + 4) were LL529 million.

A considerable amount of those investments was said to be fictitious, being either of doubtful or inflated value. Also, it was said that a large number of its advances were worthless. Accordingly, extremely tight cash-liquidity and bad investments pointed to the bank's unfortunate end.

To Beidas, according to West, the Bank (Intra) was a solvent company, but in difficulty due to circumstances beyond its control, and against which it could not provide.[31] Beidas' reasoning, as described by West, was that money was pumped out of the ground in the Middle East every day: its supply seemed to have no forseeable end. But unfortunately the position had changed since there was pressure on sterling and on American gold reserves, and political pressure was exerted on Lebanon by other countries. Beidas needed to buy time in order to counter these pressures. That necessitated, according to West, a loan of $50 million.[32]

There were those who regarded Beidas as a great businessman, even a genius, ahead of most Lebanese bankers. To him, Beirut must have seemed a virgin country in the field of banking, being himself a senior executive trained at Barclays Bank in Jerusalem. There were few banks in Beirut at the time. Intra started bigger than many of them, and ended up as the largest

Table 5.6 Intra Bank balance-sheet, 30 September 1966 (LL Millions)

	Assets		Liabilities
1. Cash and Banks	93.960	1. Savings accounts	231.389
2. Portfolio-Bills	62.320	2. Checking accounts	124.835
3. Advances and debtor accounts	425.251	3. Current accounts	1.357
4. Portfolio-Securities	104.371	4. Deposits at notice or with fixed maturity	99.659
5. Shareholders	–	5. Bank and Correspondents	96.990
6. Interim dividend for the financial year	–	6. Miscellaneous Creditors	82.529
7. Real estate and installations	31.376	7. Debenture loans	–
8. Real estate and installations	26.122	8. Dividends to be paid	–
9. Results	–	9. Order and regularization accounts	35.987
		10. Profits carried forward	178
		11. Reserves	10.476
		12. Capital	60.000
		13. Results	–
Total	743.400	Total	743.400

local bank. In 1966, as shown in its balance-sheet (Table 5.6) Intra had a capital of LL60 million. Its balance-sheet totalled LL734.4 million. Even in 1975 none of the banks in Lebanon had yet reached that level, in terms either of capital or balance-sheet total. The highest figure today for the balance-sheet of a bank in Lebanon is that of 1975, LL618 million.[33]

West saw Beidas as an ambitious financier ready to do business with the devil if need be.[34] He was a banker who played games that had nothing to do with banking.[35]

According to the same author, Beidas was counting on the help of the Ministry of Finance and the Central Bank. These institutions, he thought, would help him if only to avoid civil disorder, destruction of public confidence, and of Lebanon's image as a safe haven for money and a tourist paradise.[36]

Others in Lebanon held similar views to West, considering Beidas a speculator engaged in unsound banking operations. To them, some of the credits he gave were from political motives. He spent too much on publicity, he gambled with depositors' money, participating in unprofitable enterprises with the aim of dominating strategic economic sectors. People believed that Beidas created fictitious companies; his balance-sheet was fictitious and so was his empire.

It seems that rising international interest rates and the unpopularity of Beidas were important contributory factors in Intra's difficulties. Even the Lebanese pound was affected by the considerable outflows of capital caused by such a rise in interest rates. The dollar scored a marked appreciation in rising from LP307 in January 1966 to LP324 in August of the same year. It was the first time for many years that the dollar had made such headway in relation to the Lebanese pound.

There seem to have been no Saudi or Kuwaiti withdrawals. However, Beidas could no longer draw on Gulf sources for funds for which he paid only 4 per cent while European borrowers in 1966 offered 8 per cent. It was also said that Beidas not only had competitors in banking circles, but also powerful enemies.

Apparently the liquidity problems of Intra began to be felt within the bank as early as July 1966. However, the run on the bank did not start until four months later, 8 October. Three days before (5 October) the BL Central Council met to study a credit demand from Intra whose board met the next day and authorised the acting chairman, Mr N. Salha, to sign a credit contract with the BL up to LL15 million. The BL had demanded an up-to-date balance sheet, endorsed this time by the Intra Chairman, its Director-General and its auditors. Those requirements were not fulfilled.

The BL realised the seriousness of the matter and sought to avoid the Intra liquidity crisis, with its possible dangerous consequences in the monetary and economic fields. A chance, therefore, was to be given to Intra, as requested by its representatives, especially since the loan was covered by collateral (its Portfolio-Securities).

The BL's response was, however, affected by the following factors:

1. It was impossible to rely on the figures in Intra's balance-sheet, since its representatives refused to sign it or to assume any personal responsibility. Thus, apart from the securities taken as collateral, it seems that the BL could not grant more credit. It had to warn the Government, since it was after all the Government's money, and a matter of great public interest.
2. Though the Bank of Lebanon was independent, the law limited its power to give credit not only to banks but to the Government also.
3. The Bank could not go beyond Article 102 of the Money and Credit Law: the only alternative was an amendement, whose proposal in parliament would have made the collapse inevitable even if Intra's name had not been mentioned, since rumours were in the air.

The Central Council, therefore, decided on 8 October to inform the Minister of Finance immediately about the Intra liquidity crisis, and report to him the decisions of the Central Council. The Government Commissioner was also to be consulted as soon as possible, and to be presented with the minutes of that meeting.

On the evening of 12 October the Central Council met Intra representatives[37] who explained the situation at Intra, declaring that all resources available, including the credits accorded by the BL, had been used but that immediate liquidity was still needed. They also reported that the Intra Chairman was abroad on Intra business. They said that Beidas was providing them with a million pounds sterling and another million dollars, due on Friday 14 October.

After the representatives had left, the Central Council decided to continue to grant credit, up to the whole amount of LL15 million. As mentioned above, an Intra balance-sheet was demanded by 15 October, to be endorsed by the Intra officials and auditors.

Continuing rumours increased Intra's difficulties. Nothing was received from the Intra Chairman as promised, and the entire BL credit of LL15 million had been used up by 14 October.

The Central Council had hoped that the LL15 million would have enabled Intra to surmount the crisis and allay the fears of depositors. Even the Intra representatives thought at first that about LL6 million (and a little later, LL11 million), would be enough. Unfortunately it was not, and consequently more credit was sought from the BL, allowing a higher margin on the collateral already presented.

In the end the credit had gone by noon on Friday 14 October, and the Acting Governor met the Council of Ministers and the Intra representatives at the Presidential Palace at 5 p.m.

It was natural to take the matter to the Council of Ministers, since it was a matter of national concern. The Acting Governor felt that he could not accept the responsibility on his own. The meeting lasted until about 1.30 a.m., but without reaching any decision. Their inability to come to a decision sealed the fate of Intra. At 3 a.m. on Saturday 15 October, Mr Salha, for Intra, announced the decision to close down.

Later that morning the Central Council met to determine ways of stemming general alarm and providing any necessary liquidity to other banks. In view of the exceptional circumstances, the Council authorised the BL to override Article 102.

The Council of Ministers met on the Saturday evening, and again on the Sunday morning, when the Chairman of the Association of Banks made suggestions. After hearing the Acting Governor, the Director of Finance and the Chairman of the Association of Banks, the Council decided:

— to ask the BL to help all banks operating in Lebanon, providing them with the necessary liquidity to ensure the demands of depositors, according to specified conditions;[38]
— to adopt a generally lenient attitude to banks in these circumstances;
— to declare a three-day bank holiday;
— to authorise the Ministry of Finance and the BL to draft amendments to the Money and Credit Law so as to increase the powers of the BL with regard to banks and the financial and money market;
— it was also agreed that the Treasury would assume full responsibility for all the burdens of the BL and for losses resulting from the crisis.

Further steps were taken by the Council of Ministers on the Wednesday afternoon (19 October), to strengthen confidence in the banking system. It was decided to present two draft laws to parliament: the first authorised the Government, as from 16 October, to give the BL power to provide liquidity to banks; the second authorised the Government to grant up to LL50 million to small depositors in Intra, provided that the Government took over the claims of the depositors upon Intra. Following this decision, which became Law 62/66 (9 November 1966), the Bank of Lebanon made available extra credit facilities. Total Central Bank credit available to fifty-six banks up to 14 October 1966, i.e., immediately before the crisis, was

LL183.950 million, of which LL12.826 million were drawn (by way of re-discounts). Credit lines were then increased to LL663.400 million,[39] of which by 20 October 1966 LL142.320 million had been drawn as follows:

— re-discounts (three months and three signatures), LL28.634 million;
— advances on securities (title deeds—60 per cent of their value being lent), LL9.659 million;
— advances on commercial bills (maximum twelve months—margin 80 per cent for ninety days), LL89.934 million;
— advances on real estate mortgages, LL2.050 million;
— re-discounting bills to the order of the BL, signed by the Chairman and one member of the board of a bank and limited to 25 per cent of the bank's capital, LL5.750 million.

To strengthen its own external position the Bank of Lebanon also concluded, on 20 October, swap operations in US dollars for amounts equivalent to LL132.594 million with foreign banks, and equivalent to LL48.083 million with Lebanese banks; and in sterling for amounts equivalent to LL9.956 million.

Lebanon's experience over the Intra Bank was similar to some of the nineteenth-century banking panics in Britain, when the Bank of England felt obliged to extend special credit to the banking system. For example, the crisis of 1825 was recounted by Bagehot as follows:

> The way in which the panic of 1825 was stopped by advancing money has been described in so broad and graphic a way that the passage has become classical. 'We lent it,' said Mr. Harman, on behalf of the Bank of England, 'by every possible means and in modes we had never adopted before; we took in stock on security, we purchased Exchequer bills, we made advances on Exchequer bills, we not only discounted outright, but we made advances on the deposit of bills of exchange to an immense amount, in short by every possible means consistent with the safety of the Bank, and we were not on some occasions over nice. Seeing the dreadful state in which the public were, we rendered every assistance in our power. After a day or two of this treatment, the entire panic subsided, and the "city" was quite calm'.[40]

The disappearance of Intra brought about a massive change in the monetary situation. The run on banks forced a halt in the expansion of credit, as well as major recourse to the BL in order to meet withdrawals of deposits and to constitute more reserves as a precautionary measure. This appears in Table 5.4b above in the increase of LL149 million in BL claims on the commercial banks.

The precarious banking situation resulting from the Intra crisis was studied at many meetings of the Central Council. As a result, certain solutions were proposed for application by the BL and the Government in co-operation. The Council pointed out that the exceptional credit facilities were to expire on 15 April 1967 (i.e., six months after the crisis). Thereafter, the BL would be unable to help except within the ordinary limits of the Money and Credit Law. Moreover, some banks were already violating the law under which the extraordinary facilities were granted, and were using them for more than the repayment of deposits. It was difficult, however, to apply the sanctions provided by law—appointing a controller or ending credit facilities—since this would probably lead to suspension of payment by those violating the rules.

In view of these considerations, and the provisions of Articles 70, 71 and 72[41] the Central Council suggested the formation of a ministerial committee,[42] advised by experts, with the following objectives:

1. To establish permanent machinery for supervising publicity and the management side of banking.
2. To avoid the suspension of payment by any bank in the existing circumstances. For this it was proposed:
   (i) to renew the exceptional credit facilities if necessary when they matured;
   (ii) to extend the effect of Law 62/66 (9 November 1966) beyond 15 April 1967; and
   (iii) to formulate legislation providing for the take-over before suspension of payments of any bank clearly unable to continue functioning according to the Law, and then to simply liquidate it, while ensuring, as far as possible, the rights of depositors.
3. To set up an institution for deposit insurance.
4. To encourage bank mergers.
5. To pass a law encouraging the establishment of institutions specialising in medium- and long-term credit.
6. To set up the development bank.
7. To remove the tax on the interest on bank deposits.
8. To arrange for the issue of Treasury bills.

To achieve these aims the Central Council advised the Government to seek special legislative powers for six months in the banking field, and after that, to issue decrees rather than resorting to parliament, where arguments and disagreements would be subject to much publicity and would aggravate the problem, weakening confidence and defeating the desired aim. As a result, a special law was passed (22/67),[43] on 16 January 1967. Its main provisions were as follows.

If a bank suspended payment the Government would ask the Court of Commerce to invoke the new law. The court would appoint, within forty-eight hours, a new provisional manager, who would place the bank's affairs in the hands of a committee of administration, composed of six to ten members. The committee would assume, when necessary, the powers of the board of directors and of the ordinary general meeting. It could conclude agreements conducive to the resumption of the bank's activities by way of financing or any other arrangement. If it considered that the resumption of the bank's activities might be achieved through an increase in capital, it would convene an extraordinary general meeting of shareholders, to authorise the increase.

If, within six months, the committee thought the bank could resume activities, it would consult the court which, after referring to the BL, could convene a general meeting of shareholders and elect a new board of directors. If the bank seemed unable to resume activities the court would wind it up. This gave the bank the chance to resume activities or postpone liquidation, thereby preventing considerable losses; the word bankruptcy disappeared from the banking vocabulary in Lebanon.

The next period, until May 1967, was the logical result of the events of October 1966. Table 5.4b shows the considerable change in the policy of the public sector in this post-crisis period. Its deposits increased by LL68 million between December 1966 and May 1967. In May laws were formulated by the Government to restore confidence and strengthen the economic situation; but immediately following this, the Middle East war increased the difficulties again.

When the Central Council met on 30 May 1967, Egyptian and Israeli forces stood face to face and the powder barrel only needed a match. Banks increased their demands for exceptional facilities from the Bank of Lebanon, either to pay deposits, or as a precautionary measure to provide for larger withdrawals. The Bank advised the Government either to resort to Article 21 of Law 28/67, which empowered it to adopt any measures necessary to reinforce the banking situation, or to assume special powers to issue emergency decrees in the banking, financial and economic fields.

Immediately the Governor heard of the clash of the Arab–Israeli forces he called an emergency meeting, and members undertook to be available as long as the war continued. The Central Council kept a close watch on that morning's withdrawals by banks, and in the afternoon it met the Association of Banks. With the Government's assent, a three-day bank holiday was declared.[44] It so happened that the Bank was expecting three orders of notes due from London. One of these was due by ship before 20 June, and special arrangements were made for its arrival, since the dockers were boycotting American and British ships. The second and third deliveries, it was decided, must be brought by plane. At the same time the Government, on the recommendation of the Bank, limited the use of notes.[45] On the advice of the Bank it also secured special powers for two months (Law 45/67) to rule by decree in the economic and monetary fields, as well as in matters of public security.[46] The first decree issued under this law defined the relations of banks with clients until 29 June. Regrettably, and for the first time, it was considered necessary to impose a moratorium. Depositors could not withdraw more than LL1,000 in cash during this period. Any creditor could use his balance for the day-to-day needs of his business, but not in banknotes and coins. On 19 June this decree was replaced by Decree No. 5, stipulating that up to 24 June creditors could withdraw in cash from one bank up to LL5,000.[47]

The war did not last long and on 15 June Decrees 1 and 5 were cancelled, on the recommendation of the Central Council. At this stage Law No. 28/67 was put into effect, which allowed the Bank to extend exceptional credit facilities until 10 May 1968, provided that all were repaid before the end of that year. The Law established the Banking Control Commission inside the Bank of Lebanon, but independent of its authority. This Commission was to exercise the powers of control previously vested in the Governor.[48] The Control Department, under Article 148, was merged with it.[49] The Bank thus surrendered the control vested in it by the Money and Credit Law. The new law also established the Banking Higher Commission to replace the Sanctions Committee previously formed under Article 209; and a Deposit Insurance Institution was set up, consisting of representatives from the Ministry of Finance, the Bank, the Association of Banks, and an expert in insurance. Four of its seven directors were to be elected by the banks, and three appointed by the Government. Article 23 empowered the Banking Higher Commission to take over any bank unable to meet its obligations. This power was for a year, but could be extended to the end of 1968; it would require a decree from the Council of Ministers. Article 44 permitted the Government to issue Treasury bills up to LL75 million within a year. Article 45 imposed a five-year ban on the issue of new licences to established banks, except for institutions specialising in medium- and long-term credit. Article 46 authorised the Government to grant facilities, tax exemptions and other measures to encourage mergers or self-liquidation.

In accordance with the preceding law two banks were taken over and the exceptional facilities to commercial banks were extended at a lower interest rate. By the end of August 1967, the period given by the Money and Credit Law[50] for banks to complete the minimum of capital required, had expired for all banks. In accordance with this same law the Higher Banking Commission granted to these banks an additional period of grace.

More significant at that stage, was the rescue of the Intra Bank, under Law 2/67, under the following conditions:

1. Fifty per cent of all deposit balances, totalling less than LL250,000, were to be repaid in three instalments over a period of three years, including initial payment of 15 per cent. The Central Bank was to provide the necessary funds in the form of an advance.
2. Remaining deposits were to be converted into equity in the new company (specified in paragraph 3).
3. A holding investment company was to be set up, to own and administer the assets of Intra. The banking business of Intra was to be organised into a small bank of LL3 million capital, which would be a subsidiary of the holding company.
4. The various parties involved were to be represented on the board of directors of this company. These would include the Lebanese Government, the CCC (Commodity Credit Corporation of the US Government), and the Qatar and Kuwait Governments.

On the foreign exchange market the war with Israel had, contrary to all expectations, a favourable influence on the dollar rate. For a few days it hovered around LP325.50 = $1, but later it reverted to about LP322 (the level before the Arab–Israeli crisis), in spite of important purchases of dollars by the BL for the Government account. This decline was due mainly to the banking institutions' need for liquidity in Lebanese pounds, after the massive withdrawals by depositors in view of a possible bank holiday. This need was met by many banks by repatriating foreign exchange funds on a large scale and selling them back against Lebanese pounds in the local market.

The situation on 31 December 1967, as seen in Table 5.4, reflects the influence of all these factors. The contraction of resources since May, and particularly that of the foreign exchange assets of the commercial banking system by LL290 million, resulted mainly from the great outflow of savings deposits and other assets into gold, following the sterling crisis. Both residents and non-residents were involved. Commercial banks' liquid reserves decreased by LL30 million. The drop of LL52 million in claims on the private sector was partially the result of the rush on gold, but was mainly due to stagnation of the economy which induced businessmen to liquidate stocks and led to a fall in imports. The BL's claims on the banks increased between May and December by LL27 million, while its foreign assets rose by LL22 million, as a result of dollar support operations in the Beirut market. The dollar exchange rate fluctuated between a high of LP326 in May and a low of LP312 in November/December. Additional liquidity was also created by the anti-deflationary expenditure of the public sector, whose deposits decreased by LL31 million (Table 5.4b).

Thereafter, money increased by 6–7 per cent per annum between the end of 1967 and the end of 1970, and by 34.3 per cent per annum from the end of 1972. Quasi-money increased by 45.2 per cent per annum and by 57.4 per cent per annum in the same two periods. The relative shift towards time deposits helped to stabilise the resources of the commercial banks. The combined total of money and quasi-money went up by 8.5 per cent per annum in the years 1968–70 and by 23 per cent per annum in the years 1971–2. Allowance must be made for an accounting change which swelled the statistical total of quasi-money. In 1972 the deposits of the social security funds, totalling LL172.2 million, previously included in money and quasi-money, were transferred into the deposits of the public sector. Even allowing for this, however, the expansion of money and credit was massive and inflationary, especially after 1970. It reflected the international monetary situation as well as certain internal causes.

On the assets side, foreign claims on the banking system, including the Central Bank, increased by 50.6 per cent per annum in 1968–70 and by 66.4 per cent per annum in 1971–2, reflecting the massive inflow of funds from abroad, much of which was reinvested overseas. Domestic credit decreased in the first period by only 3.9 per cent per annum and increased in the second period by 29.6 per cent per annum. The public sector's demand for credit was negative because the Treasury situation was good. In fact, after the decrease in Government deposits from LL102 million at the end of 1967 to LL53 million at the end of 1970, they increased to LL431 million by the end of 1972. The major part of the increase resulted from two factors: readjustment in the value of the Central Bank foreign exchange reserves, and the aforementioned transfer of social security funds to the public sector.

The rapid growth in the money supply in 1973 and 1974 was in particular a result of credit expansion, and the massive inflow of foreign capital to Lebanon. These trends induced the BL to take several contractionary measures. The effect of this is clear in Table 5.4c from the slowdown of the expansion of domestic credit (from LL1,310 million in 1973 to LL713 million in 1974).

Monetary aggregates, 1975–1977

In the years 1975–77 the Lebanese banking system stood its hardest test, due to the civil war and the attendant economic dislocation. The worst period of the war was from August/September 1975 to the end of 1976. The behaviour of the money supply is summarised in Table 5.7a below.

The increase in the narrow money supply by LL838 million (or 28 per cent), from the end of 1974 to the end of 1975, does not give the full picture. In effect, the first seven months of 1975 witnessed a normal development unaffected by the political events of April. During those seven months M1 rose by LL20 million (3.3 per cent), of which demand deposits accounted for only LL43 million, while currency in circulation increased by LL177 million (see Table 5.8), due to insecurity. Thus, by the end of July 1975 currency in circulation represented about 47.5 per cent of M1, compared with 45 per cent at the end of 1974. M3 increased during this same period, by LL1,178 million (12.3 per cent), because quasi-money rose from LL6,580 million at the end of 1974 to LL7,538 million at the end of July 1975, i.e., by LL958 million (14.6 per cent). The counterpart on the side of bank assets was an increase in the net foreign position by LL840 million and a growth in domestic credit of LL579 million (10.2 per cent). The net claims on government hardly changed. The drastic change occurred from August/September 1975 onwards and continued all through 1976.

This seventeen-month period was characterised by a rapid expansion of M1, particularly in currency in circulation combined with a noticeable contraction in quasi-money. There were massive withdrawals of deposits and capital outflows.

M1 rose by LL1,070 million (or 28 per cent) during 1976, and its currency component by LL843 millions. This meant that currency in circulation accounted for 63 per cent of M1 at the end of 1976, as against 47.5 per cent in July 1975. M3 rose by only LL556 million (5 per cent) in 1976 (see Table 4.8), because quasi-money decreased from LL6,816 million at the end of 1975 to LL6,302 million at the end of 1976, or by LL514 million (7.5 per cent).

In 1977, by contrast, the development of the monetary aggregates reflected the state of relative security in Lebanon. M1 increased by only LL157 million, and there was a decrease in currency in circulation from 63 per cent to about 54 per cent at the end of the year. M3 increased by LL3,166, or 22 per cent, as a result of capital inflow. Net foreign assets rose by LL2,404 million over the end of the previous year.

Table 5.7a. Monetary survey, 1974–1977 (LL Millions)

	December 1974	July 1975	December 1975	December 1976	December 1977
Foreign assets (net)	5,750	6,590	6,101	6,609	9,013
Domestic credit	4,715	5,291	5,673	6,116	6,996
Claims on Government (net)	−980	−981	−1,142	−1,089	−959
Claims on private sector	5,695	6,272	6,815	7,205	7,955
Total	10,465	11,881	11,774	12,725	16,099
Money	2,998	3,218	3,835	4,905	5,062
Quasi-money	6,580	7,538	6,816	6,302	9,311
Other items (net)	887	1,125	1,123	1,518	1,636
Total	10,465	11,881	11,774	12,725	16,009

Table 5.7b.* Monetary aggregates, 1974–1977

	1975	Change %	1976	Change %	1977	Change %
M1†	+838	28	+1,069	28	+157	3
M3+	+1,074	11	+555	5	+3,166	22

* Calculated from Table 5.7a above.

† M1 = Money in circulation outside banks (and naturally, outside the Central Bank) + demand deposits of commercial banks.

+ M3 = Money (M1) + quasi-money (monetary aggregates).

Table 5.8. The development of money supply, April 1974–January 1977 (LL Millions)

Date	Currency in circulation (net) 1	Demand deposits 2	Money supply (M1) 3	Percentage: Currency in circulation 3/1	Percentage: Demand deposits 3/2
30 Apr. 9164	498	861	1,359	36.64	63.36
1 Dec. 1964	500	890	1,390	35.97	64.03
31 Dec. 1965	547	963	1,510	36.22	63.78
31 Dec. 1966	645	896	1,541	42.60	57.40
31 Dec. 1967	786	784	1,570	50.06	49.94
31 Dec. 1968	834	925	1,759	47.41	52.59
31 Dec. 1969	868	789	1,657	52.38	47.62
31 Dec. 1970	845	831	1,676	50.42	49.58
31 Dec. 1971	919	1,115	2,034	45.19	54.81
31 Dec. 1972	1,033	1,242	2,275	45.40	54.60
31 Dec. 1973	1,226	1,393	2,619	46.81	53.19
31 Dec. 1974	1,353	1,645	2,998	45.13	54.87
31 July 1975	1,530	1,688	3,218	47.55	52.45
31 Dec. 1975	2,241	1,595	3,836	58.42	41.58
31 Dec. 1976	3,084	1,821	4,905	62.87	37.13
31 Mar. 1977	2,761	1,960	4,721	58.48	41.52
30 June 1977	2,653	2,030	4,683	56.65	43.35
30 Sept. 1977	2,722	2,154	4,876	55.82	44.18
31 Dec. 1977	2,729	2,333	5,062	53.91	46.09

Source: BL.

Foreign exchange and currency reserve policies

In the years 1964–71 the BL was not generally very active in the foreign exchange market: in fact it pursued the same policy as that of the BSL before it.[51] It absorbed most of the Government's foreign exchange revenues from such sources as oil company royalties. On occasion it had to buy foreign exchange from the market in order to mop up an undesirable excess supply and check upward pressures on the foreign exchange rate. Speculation was also a stabilising factor. In 1971–74, however, the weakness of the dollar (see Table 5.9), reflecting the effect of the United States' domestic and international financial policies at that time and in previous periods, led to a major increase in exchange market intervention.

Thus, the BL confirmed the free foreign exchange system and the flexible exchange rate already practised in Lebanon since 1952. Arguably, however, such a system was not ideal for Lebanon as a financial centre. The main argument against the flexible rate system are:

1. It is a 'rubber yardstick' which contributes to 'walls of uncertainty' around countries and to 'economic isolationism'.[52]
2. It is liable to become a continuous invitation to economic warfare as countries manœuver their rates against each other.
3. It deprives the authorities of a potent weapon, such as the bank rate, for causing a helpful movement of funds to cover passing deficits due to seasonal, random or business cycle causes.[53]
4. Contrary to those who believe that flexible rates would provide an alternative to the need for larger reserves, Sir Roy Harrod suggests that larger reserves are needed to support a flexible rate.[54]

Table 5.9. Dollar rates in the Beirut market, 1964–1974, in Lebanese piastres

Date	Average rate	Maximum rate	Minimum rate
1964	307.48	312.25	303.75
1965	307.23	209.15	305.30
1966	313.12	324.00	307.15
1967	321.75	326.00	312.00
1968	315.80	318.40	312.00
1969	325.61	336.75	317.95
1970	326.75	330.90	324.00
1971	323.10	328.05	310.00
1972	305.07	315.50	296.00
1973	261.04	301.83	237.01
1974	232.70	251.50	221.00

Source: BL.

A comparison, however, between the relative merits of fixed and flexible exchange rates in this particular respect can only be made on a hypothetical basis. The general economic conditions during the 1960s, when relative stability reigned, were vastly different from the more turbulent conditions of the 1970s. In fact, it is highly unlikely that a system of fixed exchange rates would have survived this turbulence.

As regards the case of Lebanon in particular, a similar point can be made. It is highly improbable that a fixed exchange rate system would have survived the wartime shock to the economy during 1975–6, and even in the post-war period. In contrast, flexibility in the exchange rate served the economy well during that time and in the present state of uncertainty. Thus, the best policy for Lebanon seems to be to let the exchange rate move freely and to intervene only to smooth out erratic short-term fluctuations.

In view of these arguments, and of Lebanon's long experience with flexible rates, it is of interest to glance at the way in which the Lebanese foreign exchange market has fared, since 1971 in particular.[55] The suspension of dollar convertibility by the United States reflected fear of the consequences of Bretton Woods and lack of confidence in the dollar. This contributed to the dollar weakness which began at the beginning of the year and accelerated in the last four months. The average dollar rate retreated for the first time in many years in the Beirut market. There were substantial conversions to purchase the D-Mark, the Japanese yen and the French franc. In such a situation the intervention of the Stabilisation Fund had to be much more frequent than in the previous year.

In the first quarter of 1972 the dollar was in better condition in Beirut than in the wider international markets, being demanded as a vehicle for conversion into other currencies. Hence, the Stabilisation Fund saw no need to intervene.

In April, however, the Fund started to buy dollars and the movement quickened in May. In June increased lack of confidence in the dollar caused a rush of purchases of the D-Mark and the Swiss franc. Consequently, strict measures were taken by Germany and Switzerland to stop capital inflow. The floating of sterling also had a bearing on the dollar weakness which intensified in spite of the intervention of central banks. Thus, in July and August the Beirut market was irregular. Some world-wide improvement in the dollar started in August and continued until November, due to an increase in interest rates in the United States as well as a relative improvement in the United States' balance of payments and GNP. In Beirut, however, the dollar remained weak and the Fund had to intervene heavily. The raising of the banks' legal reserve requirements by the Bank of Lebanon from 5 to 7 per cent also helped to weaken the dollar as banks had to liquidate part of their foreign assets in order to constitute legal reserve requirements.

The year 1973 witnessed a spectacular fall in the dollar rate, with a further (10 per cent) devaluation in February and then a floating dollar from mid-March onwards. The uncertainty which reigned in international markets pressed the dollar rate in the Lebanese market to the lowest level ever since the institution of the country's free foreign exchange system. Another unfavourable factor was the shortage of liquidity in local currency in the Beirut market where inter-bank interest rates were abnormally high. The retreat of the dollar persisted through 1974 and the Stabilisation Fund had to intervene heavily, purchasing five times more dollars than in the previous year.

The currency reserve policy of the Bank of Lebanon until the collapse of Bretton Woods in 1971 was to hold the major part of its reserves in gold. The law required that reserves in gold and foreign exchange be not less than 50 per cent of the note-issue; the Bank of Lebanon consistently held 86–90 per cent in gold and foreign exchange, of which gold was (then) by far the largest proportion. The BL was cautious with regard to these reserve elements, in order to avoid, as far as possible, losses that might arise out of currency devaluations.

The sterling crisis which erupted in 1964, and the dollar crisis which followed, further strengthened the Bank's preference for gold. On this matter, the author brought the views of Sir Roy Harrod to the attention of the Central Council in January 1968, in a written memorandum.[56] The memorandum recalled Sir Roy's warning that world reserves of gold relative to world trade had been falling (Table 5.10).

World gold reserves as a percentage of annual imports fell from 99.6 per cent in 1937/8 to 56.8 per cent in 1948, and to 26.4 per cent in 1963.

Table 5.10. World reserves as percentage of annual imports, c.i.f.

	1937/8 average	1948	Reserves proper: 1963 (4th quarter imports at annual rate)
Gold only	99.6	56.8	26.4
Gold plus foreign exchange	107.1	88.6	42.8
Gold plus foreign exchange plus gold tranche, at IMF			45.3
			Reserves plus credit facilities
Gold plus foreign exchange plus total tranche, at IMF			54.2
As above, plus special US bonds and swap credits			56.8

Source: Harrod, Roy, *Reforming the World's Money*, London, 1965, p. 12.

Even including foreign currencies, IMF facilities and other elements such as swap facilities, total world reserves were far lower relative to trade than gold alone had been.

> In the present set-up [Harrod wrote in 1965] the quantum of reserve currencies available is not likely to grow very much in the coming years. Unless the price of gold is raised, gold and reserve currencies together will constitute a dwindling part of the sum total of reserve assets in one form or another. Thus there will be a gradual shifting over, an ever smaller fraction of a country's so-called reserve being usable at its own discretion. This is perhaps the most important point of all in favour of a rise in the price of gold.[57]

Harrod believed that a rise in the price of gold was essential to any increase in international liquidity, and that it was essential to ensure its natural increase along with the need of world trade. There is more than one way to reform the international payments system, but a rise in the price of gold is crucial, whatever the method chosen. The United States, Sir Roy believed, needed to take the initiative, as soon as possible, to reconsider the official dollar value in gold, or it would be obliged one day to allow the dollar price of gold to rise *de facto*, if not *de jure*. The existence of short-term and demand liabilities on the United States equal to twice its reserves would no doubt force it one day to abandon its commitment to exchange dollars for gold at a fixed price. Subsequently, the free market price of gold would soar, and thus the dollar would be devalued *de facto*, if not *de jure*.

'I have been in favour of a once-over increase in the price of gold, as expressed in terms of the dollar, sterling, and the other principal currencies',[58] wrote Harrod.

> It is not the contention of this book that raising the price of gold would be a panacea, or that it would dispense with the need for the many improvements in our existing system and in the working of the IMF . . . rather, it should be regarded as a helpful first step which could make the problems that remained more manageable.
>
> It is not indispensable. But, if it is not done the changes required to get a smoothly functioning international system will be much greater than they would otherwise need to be, and it is going to be difficult enough, in all conscience, to get any substantial changes at all.[59]
>
> I do not regard raising the price of gold as an alternative to the various other methods of adjusting reserves, but hold that, if nothing is done about gold we shall place too great a strain on those other methods. The change in the price of gold should help, not hinder, the gradual

perfection of the world's monetary system as desired by the 'enlightened' school.[60]

The revaluation should be represented as a delayed tidying-up operation, remedying the great disturbance caused by the war, and bringing the price of gold back to its traditional relation, more or less, with all other prices.[61]

The author has concluded, on the basis of Harrod's analysis, that the dollar price of gold would inevitably rise, in one of two ways: either by official reconsideration by the United States authorities of the exchange rate, as a necessary step to adjusting international payments—which would be highly desirable; or, by the emergence of a free gold market as a result of the United States abandoning its obligation to exchange dollars for gold at a fixed price—this being inevitable if the first solution were not adopted—especially when the United States reserves dwindled to a minimum level.

The prevailing view at that time (1968) was that American measures taken to limit the US balance of payments deficit would be effective to a large extent. Such measures, however, whether they succeeded in decreasing the American deficit or in eliminating it, would in fact only postpone the problem of international liquidity, not solve it. This was because the United States deficit had been the most important source of international liquidity for the rest of the world. If this source were lessened the shortage of international liquidity would affect other countries, and consequently would start the problem all over again (the so-called Triffin dilemma). Thus, the problem would not be solved by limiting the United States balance of payments deficit. Some other solution would have to be sought implying, as Harrod recommended, reconsideration of the gold exchange rate of currencies, including that of the dollar, either *de jure* or *de facto*.

Harrod's prognosis in fact came true.[62] The first step came when the United States could no longer support the London gold pool. A communiqué issued by the Central Bank governors (those who were members of the gold pool) in Washington on 16 and 17 March 1968, declared that officially-held gold would henceforth be used only to effect transfers among monetary authorities, not to supply gold to the London or any other gold market. The governors also stated that:

> as the existing stock of monetary gold is sufficient in view of the prospective establishment of the facility for special drawing rights, they no longer feel it necessary to buy gold from the market. Finally, they agree that henceforth they will not sell gold to monetary authorities to replace gold sold in private markets.

At the same time the governors agreed to co-operate fully to maintain existing exchange parities, and the United States maintained its commitment to buy and sell gold at the official price of $35 an ounce in transactions with monetary authorities. A little over three years later, however, on 15 August 1971, the United States suspended convertibility.

Gold thus became a commodity with a free market price. Because the price is variable in the market from day to day, any central bank that holds gold in its reserves faces a difficult decision as to whether to dispose of the gold it has at a certain price or to hold fast to it in the hope of a further rise in price.

The BL's gold assets have still been valued at the sometime official price of $42 an ounce. However, it has been natural for BL to diversify its new foreign exchange reserves in several currencies besides the dollar.

The significance of the gold element in the reserves of the BL seems in part to reflect a French influence, inherited from the BSL. At the same time, the fear of over-indulgence in creating paper money induced the authorities in Lebanon to stipulate gold as a necessity for the note-cover (Article 69).

The gold reserves seem to the authorities to be more important than ever. This is a concrete source of wealth for a country, in particular in the present post-war period of uncertainty.

RELATIONS WITH THE IMF

Lebanon has been a member of the IMF since 1947. Article 81 of the Money and Credit Law states that the Governor and the Deputy-Governors may be appointed governors or members of the board of directors of the International Monetary Fund, the International Bank for Reconstruction and Development, or any other international institution of which Lebanon is a member. According to Article 72, the BL shall insure the liaison between the Government and international financial institutions. The official parity of the Lebanese pound initially declared to the IMF was LL2.19148 to the US dollar, based on the sterling–dollar cross rate at the time of $4.03 = £1.

However, Lebanon has never been an active member of the Fund, despite its role as a financial centre. It never needed to use Fund facilities because of its strong balance of payments position. Its initial quota was one of the smallest in the world. Following a general increase of 50 per cent in Fund quotas in 1959, Lebanon's quota in the Fund was $6.75 million and that in IBRD $9 million. In February 1963 the IMF board of directors passed a resolution permitting voluntary increases in the quotas of countries whose participation was considered small relative to their national income and foreign trade. A further general increase in IMF quotas of 25 per cent was agreed in 1964–5.

Besides advising Lebanon to re-establish a fixed exchange parity, the Fund suggested that Lebanon would gain by increasing its quotas in the Fund and the Bank to $35 million and $37 million respectively. It was pointed out that there were virtually no costs involved in Lebanon in increasing quotas. Drawing rights in the gold tranche were, then, automatic in the event of any payments problem. Furthermore, the creation of a more adequate quota for Lebanon in the Fund would have opened up the possibility that the Fund would wish to include the Lebanese pound among the currencies which it makes available to other members in their transactions with the Fund. Given the importance of Lebanon as an international financial centre, the case for a larger quota was particularly strong. The fact that the Lebanese pound is not legally convertible should not suggest that it is not in the same category as other currencies for which legal convertibility has been established. In fact, it has generally been stronger than some of these currencies.

Against the Fund's advice it might be argued that 25 per cent of any quota increase would have to be paid in foreign exchange, and Lebanon would have earned more by investing its reserves on a commercial basis. Lebanon opted, therefore, to increase its quota to the minimum required by the Fund, i.e., to the equivalent of 9 million SDRs. Under the sixth general review of quotas adopted, on 22 March 1976, Lebanon had to increase its quota to 12 million SDRs, which still represents only 0.03 per cent of the total IMF quotas. Of this increase 25 per cent was paid (10 June 1978) in foreign exchange. It should be noted that in accordance with the second amendment to the Articles of Agreement, which entered into force on 1 April 1978, Lebanese currency can now be utilised in the Fund's lending operations, in common with all other currencies of Fund members. Mainly for these reasons, Lebanon has participated late in the SDR allocation scheme.

Further, there were those who thought that it was pointless to 'waste' the foreign exchange reserves held in the Stabilisation Fund of the Bank of Lebanon in order to borrow more heavily from the IMF. 'When the time comes for Lebanon to use all its reserves and to remain still in need of help from the Fund, it will be the end of the world . . . It might look easy to pay money now, but to get it back afterwards there would be so many restrictions'. To this self-centred view one might reply that to have ample reserves is an additional reason for contributing to the welfare of the international community and its institutions.

NOTES

1. Kisch, Cecil H. and Elkin, W. A., *Central Banks*, London, 1937, p. 17.
2. HMSO (Cmnd 827), op. cit., p. 271.
3. Ibid., p. 273.
4. Ibid., pp. 271–2.
5. Bank affairs would be those relating more specifically to the bank, such as bank-rate, management of the money market and management of the issue department portfolio. Agency functions include the exchange equilisation account and exchange control.
6. HMSO (Cmnd 827), p. 273.
7. Ibid., pp. 275–6.
8. Article 13 of the Money and Credit Law.
9. Article 28.
10. Mr Philippe Takla, the first Governor, was the man closest to both President Chehab and President Helou; the Acting Governor was the brother-in-law of the former President (1966) while Governor Sarkis was the Director-General in the Presidential Palace and was also a candidate for the presidency in 1970. On 8 May 1976, Governor Sarkis was elected President of the Lebanese Republic.

    The present Governor, Cheikh Michel El-Khoury (1978–), is a former minister and a statesman besides being the son of the first Lebanese President of the Republic.
11. In his capacity as the Minister of Finance.
12. Though La Banque Commerciale ceased payment in 1963, it was declared bankrupt in 1967.
13. Kisch, C. H. and Elkin W. A., op. cit., p. 18–19.
14. Exceptional credit facilities had been granted earlier (from 18 October 1966) by decree of the Council of Ministers, and this law confirmed them.
15. Bagehot, Walter, *Lombard Street*, 14th edn., reprinted, London 1873, p. 53.
16. Ibid., pp. 63–4.
17. Apart from the obligatory reserves in Article 76, Article 98 stipulates 'The bank shall open deposit accounts for banks and financial institutions. These accounts shall not yield interest'.
18. Law No. 28/67, 9 May 1967, Article 1, put into effect by the Governor's Decree No. 233, 10 October 1967; amended on 20 June 1978.
19. See Chapter 7, and Chapter 3, sections 3 and 5.
20. Out of those registered as Lebanese banks, there were in 1974 twenty-one whose capital was shared by non-Lebanese.
21. '*En pension*' means a sale and re-purchase agreement. According to Article 101 of the Money and Credit Law the maximum period for such transactions is thirty days, renewable once only. The time limit is the only difference from the procedure of the BSL.
22. HMSO, Cmnd 827, op. cit., pp. 120–1.
23. Ascheim, Joseph, *Techniques of Monetary Control*, 1961, pp. 84–8.
24. Banking sector's foreign assets (net) = A; banking sector's domestic credit = B; money = M; quasi-money (includes time and foreign currency deposits) = N; other items (net) = O. Domestic credit (B) can be divided further into: claims on private sector = $B1$; and claims on government (net) = $B2$. Money is composed of: circulating currency outside banks = $M1$; and demand deposits = $M2$. The fundamental equality between these elements can be presented in the following formula: $A + B = M + N + O$.

$$A + B1 + B2 = M1 + M2 + N + O.$$

Money supply is then derived as follows:

$$M = M1 + M2 = A + B1 + B2 - (N + O).$$

Variations in the money supply M, are related to the variations of the other factors, as follows:

$$\Delta M = \Delta(M1 + M2) = \Delta M1 + \Delta M2 = \Delta A + \Delta B1 + \Delta B2 - \Delta N - \Delta O.$$

25. Isabelle Fakhoury Building.
26. At Khan El-Shuna, off Allenby Street.
27. Place de l'Etoile, Beydoun Building.
28. See Appendix III.
29. West, Morris, *The Tower of Babel*, London, Heinemann, 1968, p. 224.
30. It was also considerably in excess of the limit set in Article 153 of the Money and Credit Law, i.e., 75 per cent of net worth may be placed in such fixed investments as real estate and equities.
31. West, op. cit., p. 99.
32. Ibid., pp. 51–2.
33. Banque Libano–Française SAL, 31 January 1975.
34. West, op. cit., pp. 23–4.
35. Ibid., p. 227.
36. Ibid., p. 525.
37. Mr Salha and Mr Ayoub.
38. As indicated by the list on p. 00 above, Law No. 62/66 (9 November 1966).
39. This figure was based on Law 62/66, which stated that the exceptional facilities were not to exceed 65 per cent of the banks' deposits on 31 October 1966.
40. Bagehot, op. cit., p. 52.
41. pp. 74 above.
42. The committee was to include the Ministers of Finance, National Economy, Planning and Information.
43. Referred to as the Intra Law.
44. This bank holiday was subsequently extended for the whole week of 6 June 1967.
45. 10 June 1967.
46. *Official Gazette*, Annexe to No. 45n 5 June 1967.
47. *Official Gazette*, No. 50, 22 June 1967.
48. See Chapter 4 and also this chapter.
49. Article 9 of Law 28/67, 9 May 1967.
50. See Chapter 3, p. 55 above.
51. See Chapter 1, pp. 14–19.
52. Friedman, Milton and Roosa, Robert V., *The Balance of Payments: Free Versus Fixed Exchange Rates*, p. 85.
53. Ibid.
54. Harrod, *Reforming the World's Money*, p. 45.
55. For earlier years, see Chapter 1, pp. 14–19.
56. The memorandum was entitled 'Gold and Dollars as the Two Competing Elements of International Reserves', 22 January 1968. It was based on the theme of Sir Roy Harrod's book *Reforming the World's Money*, London, 1965.
57. Harrod, *Reforming the World's Money*, p. 80.
58. Ibid., p. 58.
59. Ibid., p. 59.
60. Ibid., p. 71.
61. Ibid., p. 70.
62. Also in Harrod, R. F., *Money*, p. 310.

6. Central banking in Switzerland and Lebanon

DEFINITIONS AND DISTINCTIONS

An *international financial centre* is defined by W. M. Clarke as: 'a place where both domestic and international money can flow fairly freely both in and out, where money can be found for trade, and capital can be found for industry and where foreign merchants, traders and industrialists can find wider commercial facilities. All the leading financial centres are providing, in different degrees, both domestic and international markets in money, in capital, in securities, and occasionally in other commodities. Above all they provide markets with depth and markets open to foreign traders on a significant scale.'[1]

Clarke further indicates that these centres exist where wealth exists, and a dominant economy produces a dominant centre. According to him, what makes them live and flourish is economic prosperity, political stability and the ability to make ready use of a safe currency.[2]

The related term of 'financial entrepôt' is defined by Paul Einzig as 'The role of lending to foreign borrowers capital owned by non-resident investors.'[3] The interesting point here is the similarity of the financial entrepôt to the entrepôt in goods. Just as the goods in the latter are outside the control of the authorities, the money in the former is outside the control of the central bank as it is outside the economic circuit. The essence of this is that the financial centre is strictly an intermediary in capital transactions without any contribution in capital from its own residents. The financial centre does not need to run an export surplus. It should be able to lend borrowed money, or re-borrow money lent in excess of its export surplus, without straining its balance of payments. To perform such functions it must possess efficient banks with good international connections inspiring confidence abroad. Einzig suggested the role of an entrepôt for London as a way of resuming its international banking function in the field of long-term lending without aggravating pressure on sterling. In making this proposal, Einzig was following the Governor of the Bank of England, Lord Cromer, who told bankers and merchants of the City of London on 3 October 1962,

> I want to see more foreign business attracted to our markets so that we can earn more foreign money. The time has now come when the City

> once again might well provide an international capital market where the foreigner can not only borrow long-term capital, but where, equally important, he will once again wish to place his long-term investment capital. This entrepôt business in capital, if I may so describe it, would not only serve this country well but would fill a vital and vacant role in Europe in mobilising foreign capital for world economic development.[4]

Lord Cromer envisaged the issue of foreign loans in London without the participation of British capital even in the form of re-lending borrowed foreign capital. The role of London bankers was to be restricted to that of placing foreign bonds with foreign investors. This is entrepôt trade in its purest form.

Einzig goes on to spell out how the requirements of a financial entrepôt differ from those of an international capital market where local capital is lent. He concludes that an entrepôt market need not possess plentiful supplies of local savings or a balance of payment surplus. However, he pointed out that these do inspire confidence in a country's financial institutions, and conversely persistent deficits are detrimental to prestige and confidence.

For the entrepôt, local investors and the local currency are not important. Even exchange restrictions affecting the local currency do not prevent foreign issuing activity unless they affect transactions between non-residents. Further, a good market in Euro-dollars and other Euro-currencies is an advantage, though not of decisive importance. Foreign bonds issued must be listed on stock exchanges both in the issuing centres and abroad. Above all, Einzig insists that the issuing banks should have good connections with banks and investors abroad.

FINANCIAL CENTRES OF THE WORLD

Clarke's list of major financial centres includes New York, London, Zurich, Frankfurt, Paris, Hong Kong, Amsterdam, Milan and Brussels. In Europe, Zurich, according to Clarke, is well known for security, Frankfurt for the volume of money and London stands out clearly for its unrivalled facilities.[5] The latter continues to dispute first place with New York in spite of many sterling crises, while Paris still has the structure, but hardly the flexibility or the convenience to compete with London and New York. Frankfurt has been progressing steadily, helped by Germany's exceptionally strong current account, but still lacks the financial and commercial institutions to make it a hub of European business. Amsterdam is the nearest copy of London on the continent, but its volume of business is comparatively limited.

Financial centres, Clarke says, are liable to move with wealth. From the Italian city states in the fifteenth and sixteenth centuries, business shifted towards northern Europe through Holland to Britain in the nineteenth century, and to the United States in the twentieth.

It is necessary here to have a very quick glance at the first three of the centres listed by Clarke. New York and London are the largest and most important examples and Zurich, besides being a major centre, is the best to be taken as a model for Beirut.

New York

The United States became the greatest creditor nation during the First World War; this helped New York to emerge from the struggle as the financial centre of the world. It has maintained its position since 1918 as the most fully-developed money market ever known, due to its importance as a centre of domestic and international trade. An ever-increasing number of financial institutions have established their offices in that city. New York is the headquarters of 3,500 companies, worth over $1,000,000 each. It is the home of the nation's two largest security exchanges, accounting for 93 per cent of shares treated in the United States. More than two out of every three dollars deposited in the United States are deposited in New York.[6]

The Federal Reserve Bank of New York has a great influence on its money market operations: it is a correspondent of all leading central banks of the world, a fiscal agent for the United States as well as for many foreign governments, the depository of legal reserve balances of commercial banks and foreign central banks and governments. Further, it holds deposits of the IBRD and the IMF. It acts as a custodian of gold and securities of foreign banks and international institutions. It deals in foreign currencies and bills arising out of foreign trade.

The large commercial banks of Wall Street are not only the hub of the domestic money market, but they also perform the operations required to make New York an international financial centre. They have well-developed foreign departments dealing with instruments of foreign trade and investment. They extend credit to foreign banks acting as United States' correspondents. They also hold deposits of foreign governments and corporations. They act as transfer agents and registrars for foreign corporations whose securities are bought and sold in American markets. They are the custodians of American corporations' bonds and stocks owned by foreigners.

Beside the Federal Reserve Bank and the large commercial banks, New York has numerous foreign-exchange brokers and acceptance and discount houses. New York is also the greatest capital market in the world, due to its investment bankers dealing in long-term credit and the brokers and dealers in corporate and government securities. It is further the largest security exchange in the world and the home of many savings banks, insurance agencies, and trust companies.[7]

The financial power of the United States fascinates Swiss bankers themselves. There is no comparison between New York's financial power and that of Switzerland.[8]

London

Within this international finance city are to be found the largest gold market, the largest international insurance market, the world's main shipping and air chartering exchange, several of the world's leading commodity exchanges, the biggest concentration of foreign banks, and the centre of the largest network of overseas bank branches in the world.

Nearly a hundred foreign branches can be found in this small area, far more than in New York or Paris—the only comparable centres. And if London has more foreign banks in its midst than any other centre, it is also operating far more branches abroad than any other. While New York can boast nearly two hundred overseas, London-based banks now have over four thousand. These are the outward signs of London's links with the world.[9]

London has emerged and continued as an international centre for many complex reasons, such as the pattern of world trade, the role of the United Kingdom, its history and traditions, and so on. Twenty years of war had concentrated the world's trade in the British Empire and had made Britain the one country in the world where capital might be invested with the maximum of contemporary safety.[10]

Russia, for example, normally keeps a fair-sized portion of her foreign currency in the form of sterling in London. The ruler of Kuwait reputedly keeps over £100 million of his investments there. Communist China at one stage had some £100 million in the City and other foreign countries continue to do the same.[11]

Zurich

Zurich is today one of the leading world financial centres, thanks to its industrial development, the great capacity of capital formation possessed by its people, its favourable location with respect to international transport facilities, and the close economic ties of Switzerland with foreign countries. During the first half of the century Zurich rose to be the leading financial and banking centre not only of Switzerland itself, but of continental Europe—thanks to Swiss economic liberty, freedom of capital movement and private initiative, all assisted by political stability, neutrality, sound finance and currency. Such a formula for success resulted in Zurich becoming a traditional source of capital exports, an import reservoir and turn-table of foreign capital and a principal centre for foreign exchange dealings, trade in banknotes and gold.

The dominance of Zurich in the Swiss banking system is manifested in the number and size of its banks, and by the fact that the Swiss National Bank has established its international headquarters in the city, recognising its importance as a financial metropolis.[12] Further, Zurich's insurance institutions are intimately interrelated with the Swiss banking system and capital market. Zurich also holds a prominent position in the Swiss money market; the city plays a predominant role with respect to foreign balances in domestic and foreign currencies and investments abroad. Zurich's foreign exchange market is also of marked prominence.[13]

The most important development in international finance since the Second World War has been the growth of truly international money and capital markets centred on Europe and dominated by the dollar. Savings are channelled through these 'Euro-currency' and 'Euro-bond' markets from all over the non-communist world to finance trade and investment.[14] Moreover, these international markets have contributed to the finance of surpluses and deficits in countries' balance of payments. Central bank reserves receded to a second line of defence.[15]

The Euro-dollar market is an important institutional change in the international monetary system. It has introduced a new element in the international credit structure with strong influence on money markets, discount markets, foreign exchanges, foreign trade financing, domestic interest structures, speculation, arbitrage, and the banking system.[16]

SWITZERLAND

The Swiss money market

The remarkable feature of the Swiss money market is its relatively high degree of liquidity. In view of the strong influx of foreign funds into Swiss banks, which made the market extremely liquid, the National Bank had to absorb the incoming dollars, giving Swiss francs in exchange. Then, this liquidity had to be absorbed also by the National Bank. In actual fact in 1960 'sterilization bonds', amounting to Sw.fr.400 million were placed on the market. Again, in the spring of 1961, the Swiss National Bank (SNB) had to block Sw.fr.1 billion held by the banks as balance on drawing accounts, in a special account with it.[17]

In effect, the Swiss banking system became interwoven with the international market.[18] An interesting phenomenon showing the close ties between the Swiss money market and the international market is revealed in the dynamics of the position of the banks and the relative stability of the reserves of the Central Bank. The position of banks increased in importance whereas the changes in currency reserve of the SNB declined in importance. The positive side of the 'Euro-money market' here is its great contribution to an international levelling of liquidity. The Swiss National Bank (1968) had to do less and less with hectic inflows such as had been the case in 1960 and 1961, because the Swiss banks ceased to sell to the Bank inflowing foreign exchange. Instead they invested their funds in the Euro-market.[19]

At present dollars are offered to the SNB only rarely, i.e. when the banking system lacks the desirable degree of liquidity, as may be the case on balance-sheet dates. Thus, the currency reserves of the SNB rise less sharply now than before. The evidence is that in the period 1956–62 they increased from Sw.fr.7.4 to Sw.fr.11.4 billion, or more than 50 per cent. But in the six years that followed the rate of increase slowed down to 15 per cent.[20]

The contrast between the dynamics of the position of the banks and the relative stability of the reserves of the Central Bank is quite striking. Between September 1966 and September 1968 foreign assets of Swiss banks increased from Sw.fr.17,662 million to SW.fr.32,500 million, i.e. 80 per cent. In the same period foreign liabilities increased from Sw.fr.16,710 million to Sw.fr.27,462 million (60 per cent). Thus, the banks' net foreign assets increased in this period from Sw.fr.952 million to Sw.fr.5,038 million (435 per cent). In contrast to the huge increase in foreign balances of the banks, the total currency reserves of the SNB in the same period rose from Sw.fr.13,611 million to Sw.fr.14,461 million (i.e. only 6.2 per cent).[21] In the above period therefore (1966–68) the country's balance sheet relative to the rest of the world closed with a huge surplus.

In this situation the need for liquidity on balance-sheet dates at the end of every quarter necessitated the liquidation of foreign investments. The SNB, for example, at the end of March 1969, had to take dollars equivalent to about Sw.fr.1 billion and open credits on securities or on bills of exchange for about the same amount. Thus, the close relationship between the Swiss money market and the international markets results in a steady influx and outflow of funds with corresponding fluctuations in currency reserves. The higher the interest rates on the Euro-market, the more the banks are inclined to invest there. As a result, the Swiss money market is tightened at the end of a quarter. At the end of March 1969 the interest rate on the Euro-market went up to 9 per cent for Swiss francs, but at the close of the quarter it fell back to 3½ per cent. This shows how the small money market of Switzerland is very tightly interwoven with the Euro-market.[22]

In comparison to the foreign markets, figures for the domestic money market are small: short-term treasury bills are missing; the shortest maturity term for Government bonds is one year; the banks can deposit about Sw.fr.80 million of these bonds with the National Bank at any time for a shorter or longer period. They are therefore suitable for investing cash in hand. At the end of 1968 Government bonds amounted to Sw.fr.889 million in the market, and the Cantons issued bonds of Sw.fr.70 to 80 million.[23] At the same date, the Bank's total holdings of money market instruments was Sw.fr.6,859 million.[24]

Central Bank credit facilities are normally used by the banks only in small measure and mostly temporarily on balance sheet dates. At the end of October 1968 the porfolio bills of exchange rose to over Sw.fr.300 million. At the end of December it was Sw.fr.290 million, and at the end of June 1969 it rose to Sw.fr.1,137 million. At the latter date the total volume of Central Bank credit used was Sw.fr.1,433 million.[25]

Apart from balance sheet dates the Bank's portfolio of bills of exchange in 1968 was under Sw.fr.100 million, of which about Sw.fr.80 million were 'inventory bills'.[26] Thus, the level of commercial bills in the proper sense was kept at Sw.fr.20 million. The average credit securities used in the year was about Sw.fr.27 million.[27]

The capital market

The degree of liquidity in the Swiss capital market is not as high or as permanent as that in the money market. The basic tendency of availability of capital in the capital market resides principally in the high formation of savings in the country, which commonly exceeds investments and necessitates capital exports.[28] In 1970 the estimated Swiss investment rate was 28 per cent (ratio between gross Swiss investments and gross national product). In absolute figures, however, the gross investments of Sw.fr.25,000 million or Sw.fr.15,000 million net investments are small compared to those of other, larger countries. The same applies to Swiss savings and to Swiss capital export potential, which are substantial relative to the size of the country but modest in comparison with the large capital markets of the world. Among the more constant types of Swiss savings is household savings, in the form of savings and deposit accounts with banks, and medium-term bonds and shares. Next comes saving through private insurance companies. With regard to foreign issues, savings in the form of subscriptions to foreign bonds and securities are estimated at 35 to 40 per cent of total private savings.[29]

Holdings of securities administered by the big banks for their clients may be estimated to average 200 per cent of their balance-sheet total. Those administered by the cantonal banks vary between 10 and 80 per cent of their balance-sheet totals.

The big banks do not handle long-term industrial financing in Switzerland, since they were originally established as commercial banks. Investment companies, also called trust banks, finance the majority of domestic industrial investments, mainly from their own resources. The two components of capital exports—Swiss savings employed for long-term investments abroad and other bank credit to foreign countries—are subject to government supervision and control. However, direct acquisition by the public of foreign securities is free and substantially a function of the stock exchange and of economic and political developments abroad. Part of the purchase of foreign securities is indirectly handled by Swiss investment trusts.[30]

Thus, the Swiss capital market not only provides capital for the needs of the domestic economy, but also for foreign economies. Rates of interest paid on capital market paper are mostly lower than those prevailing abroad. The yield of federal bonds at the end of 1968 was 4.35 per cent and that of cantonal bonds was 4.66 per cent. Prior to this it had been even lower. In the period 1949–55 the Federal Government could borrow in the market at 2.75 per cent. Only in 1966 did the Government have to offer 4.5 per cent and in 1967, 5 per cent. Such low rates were due to the fact that investment demand in the economy was still relatively low. The level of interest rate in the capital market peaked in September 1969 when it reached the level of 5.37 per cent.

The efficiency of the Swiss capital market can be inferred from aggregate investment which amounted to Sw.fr.18.7 billion in 1966, of which Sw.fr.7.1 billion (38 per cent) were financed from external sources and Sw.fr.11.6 billion (62 per cent) from internal ones, representing largely undistributed profits and depreciation allowances. Although it was relatively high, it did not exert any undue pressure on the capital market because of the high degree of self-financing displayed by both the private and the public sectors. In the former sector internal financing, as a percentage of total financing, is higher in Switzerland than in most other European countries. Free funds are therefore normally available in the capital market for capital export.

Capital export

Capital export on a large scale was resumed after the Second World War. Foreign bonds floated on the Swiss market, which represented the major vehicle for foreign financial investment, reached Sw.fr.9.1 billion by the spring of 1969. The geographical distribution of total capital exports was as follows:

— the EFTA countries participated, with about 25 per cent;
— the EEC countries participated, with about 10 per cent;
— North and South American countries participated, with about 20 per cent;
— other countries participated, with about 7.5 per cent;
— international institutions participated, with about 17.5 per cent.

The most important debtors are shown in Table 6.1.

Table 6.1. Major Swiss debtors

	Sw.fr.million
The United States	1,486.6
Great Britain	1,157.0
The Federal German Republic	836.1
France	668.1
Italy	429.0
Belgium	352.0

Despite the rise in interest rates from 5.46 per cent in 1968 to 6.25 per cent in 1969 they were still below those on other markets. The average of all loans was 4.88 per cent, making the annual proceeds Sw.fr.419 million.

At first the loans were subscribed generally by Swiss investors; later the share of foreign subscribers rose to 40 per cent. Foreign participation therefore in the Sw.fr.7.6 billion loans raised on behalf of foreigners would be Sw.fr.3 billion.[31]

Capital export is in the form of bank credits and security purchases, and direct investment also developed rapidly from a level of Sw.fr.100 million in 1952 to Sw.fr.1,243 million by 1968, constituting roughly 12.6 per cent of total capital exports in that year.

Thus, in 1968 total capital exports amounted to Sw.fr.9.825 billion and were as shown in Table 6.2.

As a rule, 20 to 25 per cent of the Swiss banks' assets are deposited

Table 6.2. Switzerland: total capital exports

	Sw.fr.billion
Foreign bonds	7.64 (77.7%)
Loans via Swiss financial companies	0.942 (9.5%)
Bank credits, security purchases and direct investments	1.243 (12.6%)
Total	9.825

with American and English banks in London—the centre of the Euro-money market—about 33 per cent in EEC countries and about 20 per cent in the United States and Canada. The remainder is scattered through the other European countries and overseas.

As to private capital export by security purchases, United States statistical records on purchases of American securities for foreign accounts show that Swiss net purchases developed from Sw.fr.259 million in 1951 to Sw.fr.5,671 million in 1968. On the Eurobond market the figure was $3.2 billion. As for the volume of Swiss portfolio holdings of foreign securities, the estimate was $13 billion in 1960, $15.7 billion in 1965, and about $35 billion in 1968.[32]

The issues market and the stock exchange

The importance of Zurich as a financial centre in the mortgage market is only local, but its influence on new issues and stock exchange business is incomparably more extensive. Zurich's average share in the national potential for absorbing new issues was estimated at about one-quarter. The big banks often assume leadership in the preparation and execution of public issues, and possess a comprehensive placing mechanism. The Cartel of Swiss Banks and the Association of Swiss Cantonal Banks assume a virtual monopoly. These two cartels combine into one when making issues for the public authorites.[33]

Apart from domestic issues, the capacity of the Swiss market during the post-war period enabled numerous foreign loans to be placed. Compared with other capital export centres, such a share of foreign issues in the total issues is probably close to the top.

As regards turnover, the Zurich stock exchange is among the foremost markets of the European continent. Its business volume in 1956 was at least as large as that of the Paris Bourse and twice as large as that of the Frankfurt Stock Exchange.[34]

In 1971 1,566 securities, 1,328 bonds and 228 shares were quoted at the Zurich stock exchange. The ratio of stocks to bonds has shifted markedly in favour of the latter. Cantonal and communal issues account for the highest share among the bonds quoted. One of the peculiarities of the Zurich stock exchange resides in the large share of foreign securities in the transactions.[35]

What characterises this stock exchange is first, the securities clearing organisation for cash transactions, controlled by the Swiss National Bank; second, the *criée* system on which it operates at one level for bonds and another for stock transactions; third, registered stockbrokers in Zurich comprise twenty-six banks and brokerage firms, including the big banks and various private bankers (these constitute the members of the Zurich Stock Exchange Association); fourth, the consulting service in securities is probably nowhere so well developed, so strongly internationally orientated and so specialised as it is in Zurich.[36]

Switzerland is also a centre for business transactions in foreign exchange, banknotes and gold. The dollar has played a major role on the Swiss foreign exchange market,[37] serving as the key intervention currency. Foreign exchange arbitrage is still active in a fairly wide field; it has, however, lost some of the importance it had at the time of restricted international payments. Today Switzerland may be regarded as the world's biggest centre of trade in banknotes. It has not only developed into a fully-fledged gold trade centre since the Second World War but also the most important gold market in existence.[38]

To sum up Zurich's significance as an international centre mention must be made of Switzerland's investments abroad and foreign balances held in Switzerland. Switzerland is a typical creditor country: in 1970, income from capital invested abroad totalled Sw.fr.3,440 million, while the yield of foreign capital in Switzerland amounted to Sw.fr.400 million. The balance of payments surplus therefore was about Sw.fr.3,040 million.[39]

In 1970 total Swiss investments and holdings abroad were estimated at Sw.fr.166,000 million. Against this the total of Swiss francs balances and investments of foreigners in Switzerland, plus direct investments, may have been assessed at Sw.fr.86,000 million. This shows that the balance in favour of Switzerland was Sw.fr.80,000 million.[40]

From mid-1956 to 1958 it was necessary to protect the tight capital market by restricting capital exports. But more recently it has been necessary to promote capital exports in re-admitting foreign issues because the market has become highly liquid. The danger of an excessive influx of undesired foreign funds has been more permanent than the temporary threat of excessive capital exports. The policy of the National Bank was that the volume of money must maintain a reasonable relationship to the economic potential of the country. The influx of foreign funds, which is not connected with Swiss foreign trade, leads to an inflation of the money supply. Further, there is the inherent danger that foreign funds may be withdrawn at an inopportune moment. Moreover, the Swiss economy is so small that major inflows and outflows of capital may cause heavy domestic disturbances. The Swiss franc is never likely to become a world currency, due to the small size of the Swiss economy.

The National Bank, against these dangers, concluded gentlemen's agreements with the banks during 1937–9, and from 1950 to 1951 and from 1955 to the beginning of 1958. These were designed to discourage foreigners from making sight deposits in Swiss francs by not allowing interest on foreign short-term deposits, and it subjected them to a minimum of sixty days notice. Also, the National Bank has always discouraged the establishment of foreign banks whose existence was not connected with Swiss foreign trade. These precautions reveal the limitations on Switzerland as an international financial centre.[41]

CENTRAL BANKING IN A FINANCIAL CENTRE: OPPORTUNITIES AND RESTRAINTS

Switzerland and Lebanon: similarities and differences

There are special opportunities for and also special restraints on the central bank of a country which is a financial centre for a region larger than the country itself. There is some analogy here, although not a complete one, between Lebanon and Switzerland. Up to the middle of the last century Switzerland was rather a poor country: at the foot of the Alps, without access to the sea and with no natural wealth. It lacked all the natural endowments that were possessed by London, Paris, Amsterdam, and, later, New York. 'It could certainly never have been foretold that Switzerland would one day become an international financial centre.'[42]

Lebanon has been called 'the Switzerland of the Middle East'. Its geographical position has natural advantages comparable to and in some ways greater than those of Switzerland. Apart from its beautiful setting, and important land communications, it has direct access to the sea. Like Switzerland, Lebanon has neither oil nor raw materials. The people in both are multilingual and of many races and religions. As to economic similarities, the Lebanese trade balance, like the Swiss, is normally in deficit. Lebanon, like Switzerland, has kept to the principle of permanent economic liberty and to freedom of capital movement, as shown by the absence of exchange control.

'It could be said that it is the difficulty of existing that has made Switzerland what it is', says the Vice-President of the Board of Management of the Swiss National Bank. Having no raw materials of its own, it processed raw materials bought elsewhere. Swiss success is due to the inventive spirit which has put the country in the forefront of technical progress. Economic progress has been furthered by the country's political stability and the absence of labour conflicts. The Swiss political institutions are of an almost legendary stability, and the Swiss came through the two world wars unscathed.

With only 6.3 million inhabitants, and only enough land to scrape a bare living, it has become a prosperous country in which industry, particularly export industry, is a vital function, and only 8 per cent of the population live by agriculture, as against 18.9 per cent in Lebanon. In Switzerland 48 per cent are in industry and construction and 44 per cent in services, whereas in Lebanon 25.7 per cent are in industry and construction, and 55.7 per cent in services. The importance of exports for Switzerland is shown by the high ratio of exports to the national income. The strength, stability and convertibility of the Swiss franc make it increasingly sought-after, an ideal refuge and one which some would like to make an international reserve currency.

Yet, it was not until the middle of the nineteenth century that the Swiss Credit Bank, the first of any size in Switzerland was established. It was followed a few years later by the Swiss Bank Corporation. Both were founded with the help of foreign capital. Before and after the turn of the century the thriving Swiss textile industry brought in money, part of which was invested outside. Thus, exports were under way before the turn of the century. Besides industry the banks also began to extend their business beyond national frontiers. According to Dr Jöhr, of the Swiss Credit Bank, the international expansion of banking business assumed great proportions at the end of the nineteenth century, when declining interest rates led Swiss capitalists to look for more profitable investments abroad and at the same time alarmed foreign capital which had sought refuge in Switzerland.

After the Second World War Switzerland found itself in a world in which its trading partners were restricting foreign payments by means of exchange control and other measures. In order to pave the way for Swiss exports, the Swiss confederation found it necessary to grant substantial credits to the major countries of Western Europe, and suffered considerable losses through 1949 devaluations. However, with its productive capacity intact, Switzerland moved rapidly into a creditor position, carrying out substantial capital exports. After the war the confederation offered to reinvest about Sw.fr.250 million in Germany, and extended long-term loans to France and Italy and, later, to Austria.

This was not the end of Switzerland's role as an international banker. Up to 1964 appreciable balance of payments surpluses were recorded in the federal accounts which for reasons of economic policy had to be sterilised; the confederation placed some of these funds with the Bank for International Settlements, some on the American money market and some in US Treasury bills, denominated in Swiss francs. The World Bank was also granted a medium-term loan. The Swiss short-term money-market investments reached a total of Sw.fr.1.2 billion in 1960, and at the end of 1965 they stood at Sw.fr.1.08 billion. Since the war Switzerland has moved steadily to its present position as an international financial centre.

The contributing factors to the Swiss 'miracle' are claimed to exist to a large extent in Lebanon and have certainly contributed to its economy's evolution. One of those factors has been *political stability*. Switzerland had again been spared war in the 1939–45 period, and was able to keep its currency relatively stable. This had a favourable influence on the Swiss capital market, in contrast to most continential European markets, in which war and inflation had weakened capital resources, while post-war reconstruction called for large-scale investments. Although the Lebanese political scene was intermittently plagued by the violent eruptions of civil disorders, rooted mainly in the division of the population along religious lines and by income disparities, yet, until 1975, compared to the neighbouring Arab countries it was a haven of stability and peace.

Another factor that contributed to Switzerland's progress as an international financial centre was its *highly developed banking system*; the foreign business of the big banks is probably just as important as their domestic business, if not more so. Although Lebanon's banking system may still be regarded as undeveloped as yet in some respects, such as medium- and long-term lending, it has certainly long been the most developed in the Middle East.

Also, the importance of the part played by *bank secrecy* and so-called 'numbered accounts' in the expansion of the Swiss banks' foreign business, generally tends to be overestimated. Bank secrecy, it is said, is not a peculiarly Swiss phenomenon. Any banker worth the name exercises discretion. Swiss banking secrecy only goes beyond that observed by banks in other countries in that it also applies *vis-à-vis* the tax authorities. On the other hand, it affords no protection in demonstrably criminal cases. Bank secrecy was introduced in Lebanon in 1956, and apparently proved to be an attractive feature for the wealthy classes of the neighbouring countries. Thus, bank secrecy may well have been a more effective contributing factor to Lebanon's financial development than to Switzerland's.

Then the international character of the Swiss banking system has also been supported by the *small size* of the country, and the limited scale of its short-term public debt. Without a very broad internal money market, excess Swiss money and funds entrusted to it from abroad have to be placed in London, Paris, the United States and Canada. This has resulted in very close links between the Swiss banking system and other countries. The same has been true of Lebanon. The narrow investment possibilities of Lebanon compelled the banks to enhance their ties with the Western markets in order to find outlets for the enormous volume of funds that flowed in from neighbouring countries, particularly the oil-producing Arab countries.

Further, according to Jöhr, Swiss *neutrality* is one of the main factors in Switzerland's unique position.

> The banking system of a country that has written on its banner the principles of non-intervention in the quarrels of the great powers of Europe, and whose neutrality is acknowledged by all and is in the interest of all, is bound, if it is prudently managed in other respects, to have a head-start over others in the confidence inspired in citizens of less fortunate lands that are more exposed to the accidents of diplomacy and of international policies—a head-start that rebounds to its benefit.

Swiss neutrality has evolved slowly over four hundred years. Protestants and Catholics held a balance of power that became self-neutralising. If one religious group in the confederation had sought to give military support to a particular camp in Europe, the other would have been immediately aroused. The result would have been the spread of European war to Swiss territory, and the outcome would have been terrible. In the case of Lebanon, it has maintained a nominally neutral position as between East and West, although it tended to lean to the West. However, the highly valued position of neutrality which it maintained until 1975 was that between its quarrelling Arab neighbours.

Switzerland: special opportunities

If a central banker were given the choice between the management of a central bank in a country which was a financial centre and a country which was not, naturally his preference would be for the former, if he is hard-working, committed and adventurous. His task would be more difficult, but also more fruitful. He would accept the challenge to exploit the special opportunities provided by that type of economy. Those opportunities are to strengthen the central bank reserves, to promote growth as a result of capital inflows, which benefit the economy, and capital exports, which help international monetary co-operation.

Switzerland has a very high rate of savings and surpluses in the current balance of payments; easy conditions on the money and capital market are normally insured and the rates of interest are among the lowest in the world. In addition, the current surpluses help to strengthen the monetary reserves of the central bank and make it possible for a considerable amount of capital to be exported in different forms, such as foreign loan issues, bank credits, purchases of foreign securities or direct investments. Switzerland acquired a strong position as a creditor country.

Administering foreign funds is part of the traditional business of Swiss banks. Almost assimilated, it has presented no danger for the Swiss economy, unlike 'hot money' which may at any time enter or leave the country without warning. Since Switzerland usually has a surplus on its current balance of payments and the tendency to save is high, the economy has funds to secure its growth, which is the concern of both the central bank and the whole economy. As a general rule, in fact, it tends to have an over-abundance of funds.

Capital exports perform for Switzerland the important function of a valve through which surplus funds can escape. It also helps the Swiss initiative in the field of international monetary co-operation. Given the liquidity of the market and the strains due to the boom, it was only natural that Switzerland should promote the flow of funds to foreign countries, by taking care not to cause a rise in domestic interest rates and by authorising, as far as possible, capital export transactions submitted for the National Bank's approval. That huge gross outflow of capital enabled the National Bank to relieve, by natural means, the domestic market of surplus funds and thus to reduce substantially the effects of liquidity pressure on the economy. In 1961 alone gross capital exports reached a figure of about Sw.fr.2 billion.

In March 1961, owing to the simultaneous speculation on a revaluation of the Swiss franc and a fall in the value of the pound, an inflow of about $300 million was recorded in less than a week. An advance of $200 million was made to the Bank of England, putting back at its disposal a large part of the funds that had moved from the United Kingdom into Switzerland. The Swiss National Bank granted the Bank of England assistance on a swap basis equivalent to $120 million. The sum of about Sw.fr.520 million was entered on the central bank's balance sheet as item: 'forward-covered balances with foreign central banks'. Added together, the foreign exchange credits that had been granted from 1961 to 1968 in the form of swaps and the taking up of Treasury bills in Swiss francs, amounted to Sw.fr.9.5 billion.

This foreign policy of the National Bank had a dual purpose: first to rid the Swiss market of surplus funds, and second to help, as far as Swiss resources allowed, to restore or preserve international monetary equilibrium—an equilibrium in which Switzerland has a very direct interest, since 'any disturbance of international monetary stability generally means that Switzerland receives an undesirable inflow of funds'.

The Swiss National Bank concluded in 1966 a swap arrangement on a stand-by basis with the Federal Reserve Bank of New York which had been gradually raised to $1,000 million. In addition, it made it possible by means of a gold/Swiss franc swap, for the BIS to make available to the United States, on a swap basis, Swiss francs to the equivalent of $600 million. The swap arrangements have been drawn up on a number of occasions by the United States at times when there were substantial dollar flows to the Swiss National Bank.

Subsequently, the confederation took up Roosa bonds to a total of Sw.fr.680 million. Later the Swiss National Bank also purchased US Treasury bills of this kind, and issued in their place sterilisation rescripts,[43] in order to skim off surplus liquidity from the Swiss banking system. A similar skimming-off operation was carried out through the BIS, which took up Roosa bonds to a total of Sw.fr.400 million and placed promissory notes in the Swiss banks. The Swiss francs acquired by the US Treasury were used to meet swap commitments *vis-à-vis* the Swiss National Bank.

With regard to direct investment, Swiss industry embarked at a relatively early stage upon the establishment of subsidiary companies abroad. First there were investments by the textile industry in Italy and other neighbouring countries, and in the United States. Next came the engineering industry, and investments abroad in building materials. At the end of 1970 direct investments by the Swiss economy, excluding the insurance companies, were estimated at about Sw.fr.34 billion, compared with Sw.fr.10 billion at the end of 1960.

Another category of capital transactions is capital export, in the narrower sense of the term. Here there are three categories to be distinguished: public issues on behalf of foreign borrowers, which reached Sw.fr.13.6 billion in 1972. Then comes the category of private acquisition of securities, which was estimated at about Sw.fr.38 billion in 1972. The third category of capital export is the acquisition of foreign securities by investment trusts. In 1963 these organisations held securities worth Sw.fr.2.7 billion, at which point their rapid growth came to a stop.

Switzerland: special restraints

Although central banking in a financial centre offers great opportunities to the central banker it also contains risks which require special restraints. Constant vigilance and tact are required to manage the domestic economy and the bank's affairs. Much depends on the central banker himself. Opportunities would become, in the absence of tact and constant supervision, disadvantageous to the central bank as well as to the economy. The international financial centre's links with foreign countries call for much hard work and a high degree of liquidity, to be maintained by the banks and the central bank. 'The house should be kept in order, to maintain the confidence of foreign countries in the country and its currency. This means that public authorities must balance their revenue and expenditure, to ward off inflation.' Being an international financial centre therefore not only brings advantages for the country in question; it also entails additional responsibilities and obligations. 'Behind the high asset and liability figures lurk risks and dangers.'

Thus, while the central bank is following a credit restraint policy, it could be faced with a sudden inflow of funds which would defeat that aim. On the other hand, when the country is attempting to relax credit restrictions, there might be an outflow of funds over which it has almost no control.

Also, there is the danger of inflation. The problem of keeping the volume of money and credit in line with the real needs of the economy is made more delicate and complicated in a financial centre by the sensitivity of international capital movements to the general monetary conditions. In Switzerland, for example, money stability attracted an inflow of funds with every major political or monetary event in other countries. The economy of a small country runs the risk of being thrown out of balance by huge inflows of funds. One can imagine the effects of the wave of about $300 million, or approximately Sw.fr.1.2 billion, that swept Switzerland in the space of a few days in 1961, if one remembers that the fiduciary note-issue stood, as it then did, at Sw.fr.6 billion. The twofold danger for the economy is, first, that such inflow of funds may spark off a process of inflation and over-expansion, and second, if they have been allowed injudiciously to enter the economic circuit, they may give rise to fresh disequilibria if later they suddenly leave the country again.

The danger involved in the inflow of foreign funds is so serious and so ever-present that the Swiss National Bank has been compelled to make repelling the inflow of hot money one of the principles of its policy. If the Swiss refuse to let their franc become a refuge currency or an international currency, they do not do so, according to Motta, out of xenophobia or false modesty. 'This course is dictated by prudence and the overriding consideration of preserving the balance of their economy.'

The Swiss National Bank seeks to protect the purchasing power of the Swiss franc and to counter the invasion of foreign funds seeking refuge. In 1961 the expansion of business activity had been promoted to a large extent by the development of bank credit, as shown in the yearly rise in advances. The increase in advances of the sixty-two banks covered by the statistics in 1959 was 15 per cent. It rose by 24 per cent and 25 per cent in the years 1960 and 1961 respectively.

The instruments with which the Swiss National Bank is provided by the law are very limited, due mainly to the liberal economic policy of Switzerland. Liberal economies, it is said, are the most defenceless against the forces of the market. 'To some extent', says Motta, 'this lack of means of action is a result of the fact that the National Bank law still reflects the classical Gold Standard system.' Some of the weapons at the disposal of the National Bank seem to have been designed to combat a shortage rather than an excess of funds. The instruments available to the Swiss National Bank under its charter for influencing the liquidity of the economy were: the discount rate, open market operations, and the right of veto in respect of certain kinds of capital exports.

The discount rate was left unchanged in Switzerland for more than twenty years.[44] The authorities were persuaded against raising it, although at first sight it would have seemed appropriate, in order to check the powerful economic upswing. The reasons were the easy market conditions and the negligible extent of the banks' recourse to the assistance of the central bank. Also, a rise in the price of money, instead of inducing a contraction of credit, might tend to have the opposite effect of increasing the banks' liquid funds and thus their lending powers. In fact, a rise in the Swiss money rate would constitute an added attraction for capital seeking refuge or investment openings.

The instruments of monetary policy are those means which enable the central bank to regulate the money supply in accordance with its stability and growth objectives. Additionally, in a financial centre the central bank should try to insulate the internal credit structure from temporary movements in the balance of payments on current account or on capital account. At various times, however, when large foreign balances made it difficult for the Swiss National Bank to make its rate effective, some method was needed to reduce the liquidity of the market: it would then resort to open-market operations.[45]

The Swiss National Bank's scope with regard to open-market operations is very narrow. The term to maturity of the securities that the National Bank may include in its cover for the fiduciary note-issue is at present limited by law to two years; this impeded the creation of a bond portfolio. Further, the Swiss National Bank has only had this freedom (to hold securities at two years) since 1953. Since that time, however, market liquidity and the level of economic activity have for the most part been such that the National Bank has had hardly any opportunity to make security purchases, so that it still lacks a sufficiently large *mass de manœuvre* to sell securities for the purpose of reducing liquidity. As regards short-term paper, because of the country's easy cash position there is not enough of it to allow open-market operations on any substantial scale.

While discount-rate action depends only on its indirect influence on money and credit through primary changes in short-term interest rates or yields, open-market operations are designed to have a direct and immediate effect on the volume of money and credit, as well as on money and interest rates generally. It is therefore a more direct as well as a more comprehensive instrument of credit control, provided that there are broad and active markets in the types of short-term and long-term securities in which the central bank can legitimately deal, and that such securities constitute a sufficiently sensitive and decisive part of the whole capital or credit structure.[46]

It may be argued that if full use is made of open-market operations, the technique of varying cash-reserve requirements for contra-cyclical purposes, the techniques of non-penal discretionary re-discounting, and the techniques of moral suasion can be dispensed with.[47]

The Swiss National Bank has the power to control certain types of capital exports by refusing to authorise the issue of foreign loans in Switzerland, purchases or issues of foreign shares and credits to and investments in foreign countries for more than twelve months, when these operations are being carried out by banks and amount to Sw.fr.10 million or more. This is an instrument that works in only one direction, as it enables the National Bank to slow down or regulate the flow of funds to foreign countries when the situation—such as a shortage of funds on the domestic market—demands this. In the reverse direction, on the other hand, it does not provide the National Bank with the means of opposing too powerful an inflow of funds from abroad. The only facility open to the National Bank in times of high liquidity and large inflow of foreign funds is 'to open wide the gates to capital exports'.

What the Swiss National Bank has done

To conclude, the instruments available to the Swiss National Bank gave it hardly any direct bearing either on the money supply or on the volume of bank credit. To cope with the situation it had taken measures to counteract excess liquidity and limit the expansion of credit, taking care not to bring about a rise in interest rates that might attract fresh funds from abroad, or slow down exports of capital, or contribute to the price rise. The National Bank, therefore, concentrated on having a direct bearing on the sources of liquidity and credit, refraining from acting on interest rates.

Since the excess of liquidity was due to the inflow of funds from abroad, it was natural that the Bank should think first of checking this inflow and, if possible, of inducing an outflow. It concluded, in August 1960, immediately following the first wave of foreign funds, a gentleman's agreement with the banks designed to stem the flow of foreign funds, or at all events to reduce their volume. Under this agreement, the banks undertook to accept no further sight-funds from abroad, but only deposits repayable at three months' notice, and not to pay any interest on such balances; these provisions applied to all foreign deposits placed after 1 July 1960. Deposits received after 18 August 1960—the date on which the agreement came into force—and repayable at less than six months' notice became subject to a commission of 1 per cent per annum. Ultimately, it is for the owners of the funds to decide whether they prefer a remunerative investment elsewhere or the security which they consider they have in Switzerland.

The persistence of the inflow led the National Bank to take steps to sterilise part of the surplus funds, in order to prevent them from entering the economic circuit and giving further impetus to the boom. Thus, at the beginning of October 1960, the National Bank placed with the banks Treasury bills to the value of Sw.fr.400 million issued by the confederation specifically for this purpose, the interest on which is paid by the National Bank. This was basically an open-market operation carried out by means of *ad hoc* paper. Later, at the end of March 1961, in order to neutralise the inflow of funds provoked by the German and Dutch revaluations and the speculation against the pound, the Swiss National Bank persuaded the large banks to deposit with the central bank, on 'temporarily tied current accounts', an amount of just over Sw.fr.1 billion. This measure bears some resemblance to the creation of minimum reserves, with the difference, however, that it affects only the few institutions which receive the bulk of inflow of foreign funds.

Together with the export of capital, the measures adopted to stem the inflow of foreign funds and sterilise part of the money supply seem to have avoided the worst; these measures were not sufficient, however, to check the pace of expansion and avert all signs of inflation, as was shown by the sharp rise in prices in the few months prior to June 1962. Having influenced the level of bank liquidity, the Swiss National Bank had to take further action to limit the level of credit; not by manipulating the discount rate but by directly restricting growth. To this end, it concluded an agreement with the banks under which they limited new credits to a specific percentage of the increase recorded in 1960 or 1961. Along with this, the Swiss National Bank increased its contacts with the public authorities and the economy, in order that those sectors might also, in their specific fields, help to put a brake on the excessive expansion.

However, about 1960 the Swiss National Bank's sense of powerlessness in the handling of monetary policy started to grow. This powerlessness was felt in the Bank's ability to fight inflation; neither the instrument of open-market operations, nor that of minimum reserves, was provided by law; and it was felt that gentlemen's agreements were not enough. Thus, in 1967, when Mr Alexander Hay, Vice-President of the Swiss National Bank, found himself defending the extension of powers of the central bank to fight inflation, he said:

> Les propositions d'extension des moyens d'action de la banque d'émission visent exclusivement à limiter un accroissement exagéré des liquidités bancaires et du crédit et sont assorties de clauses qui interdisent d'utiliser le nouvel instrumentation à des fins déflationnistes . . . La Banque Nationale s'abstienne de créer de la monnaie pour empêcher une expansion malsaine de crédit.[48]

The evidence is that in Switzerland the instruments of monetary policy—rediscount, open-market operations, and a well-defined exchange policy—had all been restrained.

As the instruments of rediscount and open-market operations became largely ineffective, the Swiss National Bank had to count on the collaboration of the banking system. But immediate measures were necessary, and although the banks never refused to collaborate, the gentleman's agreements were not always scrupulously respected.

The new instruments Hay advocated were: minimum reserves, limitation of credits, and open-market operations. A fourth instrument proposed was the supervision of the capital market. It was also proposed to provide the National Bank with the power to issue its own interest-bearing bonds.

The minimum reserve instrument envisaged was the first and most important. It was meant to touch only the increase in deposits, after a determined date, and not their total. The heavier rate affected only sight obligations. Its maximum was to be 40 per cent on the increase in the bank deposits of Swiss residents, and 80 per cent on those of foreign non-residents.[49] But if the minimum reserves and the other instruments were not sufficient, the National Bank must limit its credit granting directly. These extensions of power for the central bank, as Hay rightly recognised, would help the international financial centre in Switzerland. Investors of capital, as he argued, would refuse to invest in a country which refused to give its monetary authorities the power to fight inflation. Finally, he called for sacrifices to defend the stability of the Swiss franc and added that it was in the interests of the Swiss liberal economy to fight inflation, since monetary disorder would eventually open the door to *dirigisme*, possibly even to dictatorship.

The extension of the powers of the central bank, defended by Hay, was proposed by the Government in a draft law for amending the National Bank Law of 1953. This draft law granting the National Bank powers to issue its own interest-bearing bonds and to fix minimum reserves, credit ceilings, and control over new issues, met with determined opposition.[50] Credit restrictions were considered a form of control alien to liberal Swiss traditions. The dilemma was finally resolved by a proposal which advocated a private agreement between the banks and the National Bank. That was accepted as an ideal solution.

The agreement—effective on 1 September 1969—was concerned with imposing minimum reserves on the increase of liabilities from a date periodically specified, as shown in Table 6.3.

It can be seen in Table 6.3 that a maximum of 80 per cent of the global increase of foreign deposits, which includes funds retransferred abroad, was set for the calculation of the minimum reserves. The rates applicable were to be revised twice annually and the monthly minimum reserves determined were to be deposited with the National Bank in interest-free accounts.[51]

The agreement, further, imposed ceilings, restricting internal credit expansion to 9 per cent of the total in force in July 1969. Credits to foreign borrowers were excluded from those ceilings, as the aim was to slow down economic growth in the country, and capital exports naturally were officially welcomed. Those restrictions were valid for a period of two years and the rates were to be revised every six months.[52]

Moreover, after the floating of the pound (23 June 1972) the Swiss franc—becoming much more attractive 'hard' currency—was seriously in danger as a target for speculation. Excess liquidity was considered

Table 6.3. Maximum rates to determine the fixing of minimum reserves

Nature of the funds	Swiss funds	Foreign funds
	Percentage increase	
Bankers' deposits	40	80
Demand deposits	40	80
Time deposits		
(a) to 3 months	30	60
(b) 3 months to 1 year	20	40
(c) to 3 years	10	20
Savings deposits	5	10
Cash bonds (certificates of deposit with a duration of up to 5 years)	5	5

detrimental to the Swiss economy, the annual rate of inflation being over 6 per cent. Thus it was that emergency countermeasures were resorted to. The Federal Government implemented six ordinances (26 June and 5 July 1972) in order to discourage the influx of foreign funds (the federal decree on the protection of the currency would expire on 8 October 1974). It is to be noted that the National Bank reserved its right to modify such directives at any time in the light of subsequent experience.

Accordingly, all new deposits made after 30 June 1972 were subject to a 2 per cent quarterly commission, i.e. 8 per cent per annum, to be levied by the banks concerned and paid to the National Bank.[53]

LEBANON

The remaining part of this chapter is concerned with the extent of the financial centre and entrepôt in Lebanon, the Beirut money market, and the scope of activity of the Central Bank of Lebanon. Lebanon acts as a financial centre chiefly with respect to short-term capital. Long-term capital movements constitute a fairly modest portion of its total capital flow. At the short end, business has been substantial and the country has been a net exporter of funds. At the end of 1971, short-term foreign assets (total net foreign assets) of the Central Bank and commercial banks combined totalled LL3.126 billion and reached LL5.757 billion in 1974, while foreign liabilities of banks amounted to LL1.048 billion in 1971 and LL2.027 billion in 1974.

In the period 1975–8 foreign assets (net) of the Central Bank and commercial banks combined increased considerably from LL6.101 billion to LL9.567 billion, and LL14.474 billion in September 1980. However, foreign liabilities of the commercial banks increased from LL2.863 billion in 1975 to LL3.096 billion in 1978, and to LL5.1 billion in September 1980. Hence Lebanon can be considered a financial centre that has imported a substantial amount of short-term capital which has been more than offset by capital exports.

It is important to stress the role of the entrepôt for international capital in Lebanon, as in Switzerland, for the financial centre's survival as international or inter-regional bankers. It is a matter of necessity. Both countries are geographically small and have limited natural resources, particularly Lebanon, and cannot compete with other centres if they rely solely on the exploitation of their natural resources. So, by its nature, Lebanon is left with this role of banker to play as the most advantageous one for its viability and prosperity.

The United States can afford to ignore the entrepôt role, being the richest country in the world, with foreign trade contributing only about 5 per cent to its economy (GNP), while according to Einzig, Britain is not in a position to relinquish that role because London cannot repay the huge foreign balances out of its dwindling gold reserve.[54] The large amount of foreign holdings of sterling, therefore, compels London to continue to play the part of a world banker. Here it is the efficiency of London's international banking mechanism that counts. The same may be said of Lebanon: an efficient international banking mechanism would more than compensate for the shortage of domestic sources of funds. The advantages of this role as enumerated by Einzig are: keeping the lending mechanism in practice, earning invisible exports, strengthening valuable international connections, gaining prestige, stimulating exports and supporting friendly countries.

Naturally, on the other side of the balance sheet, this practice entails risks and disadvantages. It is, however, very profitable not only for large economies, but also, and to a great extent, for smaller ones.

Promoting Lebanon's role as an international financial market was the subject of a seminar organised in November 1974 by the Association of Banks in Lebanon, and official concern for the entrepôt appeared in Decree No. 9976, 1 April 1975, which created a 'banking free zone in Lebanon'. It exempted non-resident deposits as well as other banking liabilities in foreign currencies from income tax on interest, from legal reserve requirements, and from deposit insurance fees.

For the sake of clarity the term entrepôt will be used here in the restricted sense to mean the part or parts of the financial centre concerned with importing and exporting foreign capital, as defined by Einzig. Certain modifications are needed, however: it should not be restricted to long-term capital, but extended to short-term funds as well. Thus, it would be applicable to a country like Lebanon that lacks a developed capital market.

The Beirut money market

A money market, as defined by one authority, is a market that facilitates the borrowing and lending of short-term funds (i.e., up to two or three years to maturity), and one that is usually concentrated in a particular centre or closely related centres.

It is generally accepted that for a money market to exist there must be a supply of temporarily idle funds seeking short-term investment in an earning asset. There must also exist a demand for temporarily available cash, either by the banks, etc., for the purpose of adjusting their liquidity positions, or by the government when it decides to finance itself by adding to the floating debt or by issuing short-dated bonds. The supply of funds must be regular; this is sometimes called a 'revolving fund of cash'.[55]

Another definition of the market concept states that:

> The term 'money market' does not refer to a 'place' in the sense that the market is housed in a single building, as is a stock exchange or commodity market. It is, rather, a group of institutions and arrangements that bring lenders and borrowers together. It brings into focus all the forces of supply and demand for funds. Commercial banks are the chief source of short-term funds in the money market.[56]

Hence, to refer to a money market is to refer to institutions, instruments and transactions.

It is worth mentioning here that the most important achievement towards the development of the Beirut money market was the establishment of the Lebanese Financial Institution which was approved by the Bank of Lebanon on 12 January 1981. Its purpose was to develop a secondary market, to introduce the concept of secured lending; to activate the money and capital markets and further enhance professionalism in this sector; to create fixed-term, unbreakable (but negotiable) certificates of deposit (CDs); and to mobilise savings by creating new investment alternatives, thereby discouraging speculative activities.

In Beirut, as in other markets, commercial banks are the most important institutions since they are the main dealers in short-term funds. Next are the discount houses, money-lenders and exchange dealers. The Lebanese Government has played the role, since 1968, of seller of bonds, mainly to commercial banks. Other instruments included trade bills—bills of exchange and promissory notes—mortgage contracts and letters of credit. The major segment of transactions in the market is inter-bank deposits.

Commercial banks

Table 6.4 below shows the geographical set-up of the Lebanese banking system (December 1974–May 1977). A considerable change appeared in the structure of the system as a result of the war and the consequent dislocation of economic activity. Thus, at the end of May 1977 the number

Table 6.4. The structure of the banking system, 1974–1977

	December 1974		August 1975		May 1977	
	Head-quarters	Branches	Head-quarters	Branches	Head-quarters	Branches
Beirut	75	84	75	132	74	185
Mount Lebanon	1	77*	2	29	2	51
Bekaa	2	8	2	9	2	12
South Lebanon	–	29†	–	27	–	31
North Lebanon	2	35‡	1	37	1	46
Total	80	233	80	234	79	325

* 4 branches were seasonal.
† 5 are offices.
‡ 1 was an office.

of banks was seventy-nine, and twenty-eight of them had to move their headquarters. The number of branches was 325. At the end of 1978 the number of operating banks on the banks' list was eighty-one. At the end of 1980 the number of banks increased to eighty-seven, and that of branches became 382.

It is to be noted that the change in the banking structure occurred on the initiative of the banks themselves, without the prior authorisation of the Bank of Lebanon (BL). The latter, on 20 June 1978, issued new regulations concerning branches (the Governor's Decree No. 1283).[57]

Thus, the official banks' list at the end of 1974 included eighty banks, seventy-four of which were commercial banks and six were specialised in medium-term and long-term credit. The identity of the former banks may be classified as in Table 6.5.[58]

Foreign banks have always played a dominant role in the Lebanese banking system. Those foreign and jointly-held banks accounted for 63 per cent of the total deposits in September 1966 although they constituted only a third of the total number of banks. By the end of 1970 those foreign and jointly-held banks constituted about 53 per cent of the total number, accounting for about 81 per cent of the total deposits. The largest —twenty—include eleven foreign and seven jointly-held banks. The foreign banks are: six Arab, three American, two French, two British, and one of each from Italy, Holland, the Soviet Union, Pakistan, Iran and Canada. These accounted for 51 per cent of the total deposits at the end of 1970, and 32.6 per cent in 1974.

Table 6.5. Banks by origin

	1972	1974	1978
Lebanese banks	34	31	35
Lebanese–Arab banks	6	4	6
Lebanese–foreign banks	14	22	22
Arab banks	6	5	5
Foreign-bank branches	13	12	12
Total	73	74	80

In 1974 there were seventeen foreign banks, five of which were Arab. The foreign and jointly-held banks constituted 58 per cent of the total number and accounted for 74.9 per cent of the total deposits. The twenty commercial banks in 1974 included seven foreign, seven jointly-held and six Lebanese.

In 1978 foreign banks numbered seventeen, the same number as in 1974, five of which were Arab, but the jointly-held banks increased by two, and the Lebanese increased by four. The foreign and jointly-held banks constituted 56.25 per cent of the total number (in 1978) and accounted for approximately 61 per cent of deposits.[59]

The foreign share in the Lebanese banking system looks considerable. While it is preferable to keep the banking sector in local hands, foreign influence seems to have been important in the development of banking in Lebanon. Indeed, foreign banks may be considered as the backbone of the Lebanese banking system. Moreover, foreign business is vital to Lebanon as an international financial centre and an entrepôt.

It is clear that most of the banking institutions have been commercial banks. When the Central Bank was established there were over a hundred commercial bank licences, but only one medium and long-term lending institution (BCAIF). Commercial banks looked so numerous that the authorities had to discourage new institutions. On the advice of the Central Bank, therefore, a ban was imposed on the establishment of commercial banks for five years and extended for another five years (Law No. 28/67, 9 May 1967) i.e., until May 1977. As a result, and due to the demand for bank licences, the premium paid for a licence reached about LL8 million in 1977. On 27 June 1977, however, the ban on the establishment of commercial banks was removed by Decree No. 77, dated 27 June 1977. The new decree raised the minimum capital required to LL15 million, half of which to be deposited with the Treasury until liquidation of the bank. In 1980 the BL, by discretion, demanded not less than LL30 million, even LL50 million as the minimum capital required for the establishment of a commercial bank.

On the other hand, Law No. 22/67 of 21 April 1967 stipulated tax incentives for the establishment of medium-term and long-term banks. Not until 1972 was the first private bank of this category established; in 1973 the National Bank for Industrial and Touristic Development was established; and in 1974 three such institutions were added to the banks' list.

Out of the six medium-term and long-term credit banks, two are semi-government: BCAIF and NBITD (the National Bank for Industrial and Touristic Development). Total resources of those banks by the end of 1974 were LL175 million, compared to LL94 million at the end of 1973, i.e., it increased by LL81 million. On the other hand, their total credit given to the private sector was LL146 million in 1974, while in the same year total commercial bank credit was LL5,649 million.

It seems that the above-mentioned tax incentives were not sufficient. The Central Bank, in June 1975, had to reduce the rate of legal reserve requirements on time deposits (for not less than two years) from 10 to 5 per cent. In December 1975 there were five such banks, as one of them (the Union Bank SAL) went into voluntary liquidation. Their total capital in 1977 was LL162 million; and their total resources were LL196 million, out of which savings and time deposits were only LL33 million. Their advances, on the other hand, in 1977, were LL251 million—almost twice what they were in 1973. It seems that those institutions had not been active in attracting deposits, not only because of the high liquidity preference of the depositors, but also because interest rates paid on time deposits were not an important incentive.

Financial institutions in Lebanon, such as discount houses or *comptoirs*, have increased from 200 in 1972 to 337 in 1974. In 1978 financial institutions with a minimum capital of LL2 million (Article 180 of the Money and Credit Law) were only five, while the *comptoirs* were 359. They are supposed to register with the Central Bank, report to it, and follow its directions. The law gave them the privilege of rediscounting with the Central Bank.[60] This has not been put into practice because the Central Bank has not yet developed the necessary control over them that it had over the banks. Further, in October 1973, an amendment to the same law (published as Decree No. 6102, dated 5 October 1973) distinguished between those institutions with regard to their capital, form, subject and intention.

A trend developed at this time for foreign banks to establish in Beirut representative offices whose sole function was, virtually, to arrange placement of large foreign deposits in their European branches. Their activities covered many Middle East countries and their presence in Beirut placed them in close touch with the sources of funds in the whole area and made it possible for them to keep abreast of economic and business developments in the area. This explains the presence of representative offices for foreign banks already established in Beirut. They supplemented Lebanon's banking system and contributed to the Lebanese banking and financial preponderance in the Middle East region. The banks with registered offices in Beirut increased from forty-three at the end of 1972 to sixty-two by the end of 1974, and in 1978 they were seventy-four, though five had closed.

Liquidity

The liquidity of the Lebanese banking system in local currency increased in 1971 by LL206.1 million, reaching LL535 million.[61] In 1974 it reached LL1,661.4 million, increasing by LL1,053.2 million on the previous year. In 1975 it dropped to LL772 million, i.e., by LL889.4 million, to resume a rise in 1976 of only LL288.8 million. Liquidity in 1977 increased by LL836.9 million, but in 1978 the increase was only LL133.4 million. In 1979 liquidity decreased by LL639.1 million to rise again in September 1980 by LL704 million.

Other evidence of the relatively high liquidity in the Beirut money market could be detected from the development of both inter-bank deposits and banks' deposits with the Central Bank. Table 6.6 shows that banks' deposits at the Bank of Lebanon increased from LL474.2 million

Table 6.6. Inter-bank deposits and loans—1971–September 1980 (LL Millions)

End of year	1971	1972	1973	1974	1975	1976	1977	1978	1979	1980*
1. Deposits at the BL	474.2	505.9	548.5	1,541.1	637.8	870.9	1,703.3	1,648.5	1,178.0	1,870.0
2. Sight deposits and day-to-day loans	468.7	586.6	445.8	424.9	397.6	437.6	485.5	658.0	782.0	715.0
3. Other loans	154.4	343.2	427.4	414.3	410.0	359.9	451.3	259.7	296.0	361.0
Total of 2 + 3	623.1	929.2	873.2	839.2	807.6	797.5	936.8	917.2	1,078.0	1,076.0
Total	1,097.3	1,435.1	1,421.7	2,380.3	1,445.4	1,668.4	2,640.1	2,566.2	2,256.0	2,946.0

* September.

at the end of 1971 to LL548.5 million at the end of 1973. The increase by 180 per cent in 1974 in banks' deposits at the BL which created excessive banking liquidity was a result, on the one hand, of the Central Bank intervention in foreign exchange market as mentioned previously, and on the other hand, the Central Bank restrictive measures imposed on commercial bank domestic credit. It then decreased to LL637.8 million in 1975, then resumed its increase to LL1,870 million in September 1980.

The liquidity crisis of 1974 caused interest rates on inter-bank deposits to rise to 33.3 per cent. In February and March of the same year it was decreased, to increase again to about 19 per cent. However, at the year end it fell to 1 per cent or even 0 per cent, due to the Central Bank creation of excess liquidity by its intervention in the foreign exchange market, and also to the Central Bank restrictions on domestic credit.

In 1975 banks' deposits at the BL decreased by LL903.3 million. Banks, then, had to pay back depositors. This figure was also clear in the increase of currency outside banks which was LL887.9 million. The remaining LL15.4 million could have been used by the banks themselves. Inter-bank deposits and loans have decreased by LL31.2 million as each bank had to collect its loans and deposits as a precautionary measure. The banking losses of LL46.6 million (15.4 + 31.2) could have been due to the banks' expenses in setting up new branches.

From the same table it appears that the total increase in inter-bank deposits and loans was also high in 1974, decreasing only in 1975, and resuming its increase to LL2,946 million in September 1980.

Further evidence of excess liquidity in the Beirut market could be noticed from the decrease in Central Bank credit to commercial banks, as discussed in the next section.

Central Bank credit to commercial banks

Re-discounts

Table 6.7 shows the amount of rediscounted eligible bills with the Central Bank held by the commercial banks. Those bills as mentioned earlier, have to carry three signatures, and a maximum maturity of 180 days.

It appears from Table 6.7 that since 1971 commercial banks were sufficiently liquid to resort very seldom to the Central Bank credit facilities. The amount of re-discounting which was about LL37 million in 1969 dropped to about LL22 million at the end of 1970, and stood at LL3 million in 1971, and LL4.6 million at the end of June 1972.

During the last quarter of 1973 re-discounting rose due to the liquidity crises when the inter-bank interest rates were ranging between 20 and

Table 6.7. Re-discounting with the BL at the end of each year—1968–1979 and in September 1980

	(LL millions)
1968	12.192
1969	36.801
1970	31.835
1971	3.867
1972	4.615
1973	17.290
1974	5.492
1975	36.2
1976	13.1
1977	0
1978	0
1979	2
1980 (Sept.)	0

36 per cent in November and December. The increase in re-discounting continued to reach LL70 million in April 1974 due to the same crises. Thus, the figure of LL5.492 million, which appears in Table 6.7 as re-discounting for the year 1974, is only the outstanding balance of bills re-discounted in June of the same year. After that date there were no re-discounting operations in 1974.

It appears that re-discounting increased at the end of 1975 to reach LL36.2 million, to decrease in 1976 to LL13.1 million. However, in 1977 and 1978 there was no re-discounting, and only LL2 million in 1979. But in March 1980 re-discounting was LL19 million, to disappear entirely in June and September of the same year.

Central Bank credit on other trade bills: (‘*avance sur effets*’)

These bills are different from bills eligible for re-discounting in that they carry two signatures only, and a margin of 80 per cent of their value is given. Their maximum maturity is one year and the rate is 5 or 5½ per cent. Such bills existed in normal operations only in 1969 as a Central Bank credit given to banks taken over under Decree No. 10956, dated 2 October 1968. Their amount increased from LL14.5 million at the end of 1968 to LL24 million at the end of 1969.

As to Central Bank credit against shares of stocks, they were also exceptional facilities for banks taken over. Their amount increased from about LL39 million at the end of 1968 to about LL67.5 million at the end of 1971, and they stood at about LL60.9 million by the end of 1972, at LL63.5 million at the end of 1973, and at about LL45 million at the end of 1974.

Treasury bills

As we have seen, the instruments of the money market have been almost non-existent at the Central Bank due to the high liquidity of the operating banks who did not resort to Central Bank credit. It was not possible therefore to resort to open market policy because of the scarcity of Treasury bills. However, since the end of 1967 the Government has started to enter the market as a seller of Treasury bills: this would encourage their use in the future open market policy. Their balance on 4 August 1972 was LL40 million, resulting from the total of all issues of Treasury bills until August 1972 which was LL239 million. It was at an end by 4 August 1975.

Treasury bill issues were resumed on 30 June 1977, mainly because the Government needed that internal loan. Their balance until 28 July 1979 was LL1,121.55 million. The purpose was sometimes, and especially in the earlier issues, to absorb liquidity from the market, saving to a certain extent the conversion of Lebanese pounds into dollars to be invested outside. Liquidity created by the inflow of foreign funds had also to be absorbed. Later, the war necessitated this. At the end of 1980 the issues outstanding amounted to LL742.2 million in medium-term bills, and LL1,733.85 million in short-term bills. Rates on the former were 5 per cent for two years and 5.75 per cent for three years for issues of 10 April 1979. Those rates were raised on June and August issues to 7.5 per cent for two years and 8 per cent for three years. On short-term bills (three months) the rates started at 6.5 per cent and reached 9 per cent on 19 November 1980 and 11 per cent by the end of 1980. On 15 January 1981 interest rates on Treasury bills (3 months) were 11.5 per cent and the issue was LL339.35 million.

THE RELATIONSHIP BETWEEN THE BEIRUT MONEY MARKET AND THE EURO-DOLLAR MARKET

Two roles have been played by the banking system of Lebanon with respect to Western money and capital markets:

1. By accepting foreign currency deposits from residents and placing them abroad, and by taking long foreign exchange positions, it has directed a substantial volume of domestic savings to the Western markets.

Table 6.8a. Foreign assets and foreign liabilities of the commercial banks and foreign assets of the BL at the end of each year 1968–79 and September 1980 (LL Millions)

	1968	1969	1970	1971	1972	1973	1974	1975	1976	1977	1978	1979	Sept. 1980
Foreign assets of banks	1,574.4	1,640.7	2,087.7	2,596.7	3,178.4	3,624.3	3,980.2	5,112.2	4,524.5	5,770.4	6,063.0	9,379.0	12,119.0
Foreign liabilities of banks	902.9	834.3	908.9	1,048.0	1,174.2	1,520.8	2,027.1	2,862.8	2,806.8	2,557.6	3,096.0	3,909.0	5,101.0
Foreign assets (net) of banks	671.5	806.4	1,178.8	1,548.7	2,004.2	2,104.1	1,953.1	2,249.4	1,717.7	3,212.8	2,967.0	5,470.0	7.018.0
Foreign assets (net) in BL	1,012.2	1,064.2	1,175.6	1,725.0	2,041.0	2,161.1	3,805.4	3,858.7	4,949.5	5,864.6	6,674.6	6,242.0	7,456.0
Foreign assets (net) in BL (excluding gold)	847.8	954.6	1,038.5	620.0	987.0	1,182.0	2,916.3	2,913.2	3,809.6	4,696.9	5,504.9	4,973.9	6,115.9
In percentages	%	%	%	%	%	%	%	%	%	%	%	%	%
Foreign assets (net) in banks	39.9	41.1	50.1	49.5	49.5	49.3	33.9	36.83	25.76	35.39	30.77	46.70	48.52
Foreign assets (net) in BL	60.1	56.9	49.9	50.5	50.5	50.7	66.1	63.17	74.24	64.61	69.23	53.30	51.48
Total	100.0	100.0	100.0	100.0	100.0	100.0	100.0	100.0	100.0	100.0	100.0	100.0	100.0

Table 6.8b. Net changes calculated from Table 6.8a

	1969 minus 1968	1970 minus 1969	1971 minus 1970	1972 minus 1971	1973 minus 1972	1974 minus 1973	1975 minus 1974	1976 minus 1975	1977 minus 1976	1978 minus 1977	1979 minus 1978	Sept. 1980 minus 1979
Foreign assets of banks	66.3	447.0	509.0	581.7	445.9	355.9	1,132.0	−587.7	1,245.9	292.6	3,316.0	2,740.0
Foreign liabilities of banks	−68.6	74.6	139.1	126.2	346.0	506.9	835.7	−56.0	−249.2	538.4	813.0	1,192.0
Foreign assets (net) of banks	134.9	372.4	369.9	455.5	99.9	−151.0	296.3	−531.7	1,495.1	−245.8	2,503.0	1,548.0
Foreign assets (net) in BL	52.0	111.5	401.9	468.7	114.8	1,644.3	53.3	1,090.8	915.1	810.0	432.6	1,214.0
Total	186.9	483.9	771.8	924.2	214.7	1,493.3	349.6	559.1	2,410.2	564.2	2,074.4	2,762.0
In percentages	%	%	%	%	%	%	%	%	%	%	%	%
Foreign assets (net) in banks	20.1	46.2	31.4	29.4	5.0	−7.2	15.2	−23.6	87.0	−7.7	84.4	28.3
Foreign assets (net) in BL (excluding gold)	12.6	8.8	−40.3	59.2	19.8	146.7	− 0.1	30.8	23.3	17.2	−9.6	23.0

2. By acting as intermediary between neighbouring Arab (mainly Gulf) sources of funds and Western markets, it has channelled a much larger volume of Arab savings to Western markets.

Table 6.8 illustrates that the claims of the Lebanese commercial banks on the outside were over one billion dollars, i.e., LL3,178 million at the end of 1972. To this the foreign assets of the BL could be added which were, at the same date LL800 million excluding gold. Thus, the sum total of the Lebanese banking and monetary system placements abroad was about LL4 billion.[62] In 1974 claims of the Lebanese commercial banks from outside were LL3,980.2 million, and the foreign assets of the BL excluding gold (gold was LL888 million) were LL2,916 million. Therefore, the sum total of the Lebanese banking and monetary system placements abroad was about LL6,896 million in 1974, increasing by 5.4 per cent on 1974. Those placements increased in 1975 by 16.3 per cent and in 1976 by only 3.8 per cent. However, in 1977 they resumed their increase to LL10,467.3 million, i.e., by 25 per cent. It is to be noted that 1977 was a year of recovery after the two previous war years. In 1978 the increase was 10.5 per cent, to proceed to 24 per cent in 1979, and to 27 per cent in September 1980. Considering that most of those assets were invested in the Euro-currency markets (in practice the Euro-dollar market), the importance of the role of the Lebanese banking system in the Euro-dollar market is clear.

A further point to indicate this relationship could be inferred from the influence of the fluctuations of interest rates in the Euro-dollar market on the Beirut money market. The increase in the interest rate in the former market causes an increase in the foreign investments of the Lebanese banks, making domestic credit investments less attractive.

Further, the susceptibility of the Lebanese market to the international market is quite clear. As in other centres, Lebanese investments abroad are greatly influenced by the stability of the major currencies as well as by fluctuations in interest rates. Any instability in the reserve currencies or rumours of depreciation make the Lebanese withdraw their funds from abroad to reinvest them locally, increasing liquidity in the local market as was mentioned previously, and vice versa.

Exploring Table 6.8, it can be seen that from the end of 1968 to 1972 foreign assets of the commercial banks were more than doubled, increasing from LL1,575 million to LL3,178.4 million. On the other hand, in the same period, the foreign assets of the BL (excluding gold) increased by 16.4 per cent from LL847.8 million to LL987 million. In 1973 BL foreign assets increased to LL1,182 million (excluding gold), i.e., by 19.7 per cent, while in 1974, the increase jumped to LL2,916.3 million, i.e., by 146.7 per cent, as a result of the heavy increase of the BL intervention in the foreign exchange market. It is evident here that the BL was active in its intervention in the local market due to the balance of payments surplus, which was caused primarily by a great capital inflow into Lebanon. Internal liquidity has considerably increased, prompting the BL to raise the 7 per cent legal reserve requirements to 8 per cent and 10 per cent in 1974.

During the period of the 1975–8 war, banks were involved in investments outside Lebanon since the local situation rendered business impossible. Short-term interest rates on the Euro-dollar market were rising. Foreign assets of banks increased in 1975 by LL1,132 million (part of this increase was due to the decrease in the exchange rate of the Lebanese pound). In 1976, however, those foreign assets declined by LL587.7 million due to the total paralysis of the Lebanese economy in the war period of February to October 1976. But in 1977, as the situation improved, foreign assets increased by LL1,245 million and by LL292.6 million in 1978. In 1979 the increase was LL3,316 million, and in September 1980 it was LL2,740 million.

Though commercial banks in Lebanon had been investing funds on the Euro-market the Bank of Lebanon continued to deal with inflows of foreign currencies. Table 6.8 shows how net foreign assets of the commercial banks increased from LL671.5 million in 1968 to LL7,018 million in September 1980, i.e., by 945 per cent or by 72 per cent annually. On the other hand, the foreign exchange reserves of the BL, excluding gold, have risen in the same period from LL847.8 million to LL6,115.9 million, i.e., by 621 per cent or by 47 per cent annually. The BL could have stood aside, keeping its reserves as a second line of defence, as the Swiss National Bank had done.[63] It could have left Lebanese commercial banks to invest the inflows of foreign exchange on the international market, but it intervened in order to stop the Lebanese pound from appreciating, which the authorities thought would be detrimental to the services sector. Comparison with Switzerland in this case is not exact since the BL has witnessed difficult times all along.

In order to determine precisely the effect of outside developments on the Beirut market we shall compare the percentage change in foreign assets of the banks and the percentage change in their domestic credit. The former stood at LL1,574 million at the end of 1968 while the latter was LL2,097 million. Thus, foreign assets were 43 per cent of the total claims of the commercial banks. This percentage increased in 1972 to about 48.6 per cent because the banks' foreign assets reached LL3,161 million and the domestic credit was LL3,332 million. In 1974 foreign assets were LL3,980 million and domestic credit was LL5,764 million, i.e., about 41 per cent.

As is clear in Table 6.9, foreign assets dipped in 1976 to resume rising, reaching LL6,063 million in 1978. Domestic credit, on the other hand, kept increasing from LL6,835 million in 1975 to reach LL10,991 million in 1978. The ratio of foreign assets to total claims was 42.7 per cent, in 1975, and decreased to 35.5 per cent in 1978, to increase to 41.02 per cent in 1979 and to 42.54 per cent in September 1980. Outside developments, therefore, had great bearing on the Beirut market.

The relatively large volume of monetary reserves in the Lebanon confirms the hopes of the Lebanese that their country can act as a financial centre and an entrepôt. Additional favourable factors are the liberal economic and monetary policy, the free foreign exchange system, the means of communications, the many languages spoken in the country, its strategic position contributing to its role as an intermediary for inter-regional trade and transit as well as financial operations, the presence of the giant international banks, the mixed ownership of many local banks, and (most important) the secrecy law and the joint account system. All of these are contributing factors to the character of the centre and the entrepôt.

The proportion of the entrepôt in the centre

In discussing a financial entrepôt Paul Einzig makes the following points. In any active international financial centre there are constant flows of foreign capital in both directions, inward as well as outward. To the extent to which the amounts lent abroad and borrowed abroad are balanced the financial centre does fulfil the role of entrepôt for foreign capital.[64]

Further, a financial centre may be a net importer or a net exporter of capital, but it may be labelled as an entrepôt only to the extent that capital imports are matched by capital exports. In other words, a country which re-exports none of its capital imports may qualify as a financial centre, but would not qualify as an entrepôt. And a financial centre which is a net importer of capital is labelled as an entrepôt only to the extent that its capital imports are offset by capital exports.[65]

The financial entrepôt, therefore, is the extent of the non-resident foreign assets matched by non-resident foreign liabilities in a financial centre. In other words, it is the extent of non-resident capital (long-term, or short-term), lent to foreign borrowers matched by the same amount of capital or part of the capital owned by non-resident investors.

Here the entrepôt character of Lebanon is an established fact since the non-resident foreign liabilities of the commercial banking system have

Table 6.9. Foreign assets and domestic credit of commercial banks, at the end of each year 1971–1979 and in September 1980 (LL Millions)

	1971	1972	1973	1974	1975	1976	1977	1978	1979	Sept. 1980
Foreign assets	2,597	3,161	3,624	3,980	5,112	4,524	5,770	6,063	9,379	12,119
Domestic credit*	2,729	3,332	4,714	5,764	6,835	7,244	8,506	10,991	13,488	16,368
Ratio of foreign assets to total claims	48.7%	48.6%	43.4%	40.8%	42.7%	38.4%	40.4%	35.5%	41.02%	42.54%

* Domestic credit = claims on Government (net) + claims on the private sector (portfolio-securities are included).

been more than offset by the foreign assets of the Lebanese banks. Moreover, since in Lebanon foreign assets have always exceeded foreign liabilities and as the part of the non-resident foreign assets that exceeds the non-resident foreign liabilities is to be ignored—since there is no match for it in non-resident foreign liabilities—the volume of non-resident foreign liabilities, therefore, could be considered as representing the extent of the entrepôt in the Lebanese financial centre. For example, in September 1980, foreign assets, or the outflow, of the commercial banks in Lebanon, amounted to LL12,119 million, and the non-resident foreign liabilities were LL5,101 million. The latter figure is the extent of the entrepôt. It represents the amount of the inflow of foreign funds which is then lent to foreign borrowers and is included in the foreign assets. The remaining LL7,802 million included in the foreign assets came from foreign exchange deposits of the private sector. The component parts of such foreign liabilities are the deposits of foreign banks in Lebanese banks; loans of foreign banks to the Lebanese banks; as well as the foreign deposits of the non-banking sector in the Lebanese banks.

The following list shows that the size of the entrepôt or non-resident foreign liabilities has increased steadily:

end of 1969	LL834 million
end of 1970	LL909 million
end of 1971	LL1,048 million
end of 1972	LL1,174.2 million
end of 1973	LL1,520.2 million
end of 1974	LL2,027.1 million
end of 1975	LL2,862.8 million
end of 1976	LL2,806.8 million
end of 1977	LL2,557.6 million
end of 1978	LL3,096.0 million
end of 1979	LL3,909.0 million
Sept. 1980	LL5,101.0 million

The counterpart of the Lebanese liabilities to the outside is shown in the foreign assets of the Lebanese commercial banks invested abroad. These may be divided into the following four basic items: the deposits of the Lebanese commercial banks abroad; their claims on banks abroad; their claims on the non-banking sector abroad; and their shares and other investments abroad.

The foreign assets of the Lebanese commercial banks stood as follows:

end of 1969	LL1,641 million
end of 1970	LL2,087 million
end of 1971	LL2,597 million

end of 1972	LL3,178 million
end of 1973	LL3,624 million
end of 1974	LL3,980 million
end of 1975	LL5,112.2 million
end of 1976	LL4,524.5 million
end of 1977	LL5,770.4 million
end of 1978	LL6,063.0 million
end of 1979	LL9,379.0 million
Sept. 1980	LL12,119.0 million

It is clear, therefore, from the above lists that the ratio of foreign assets to foreign liabilities has developed from the end of 1969 to 1972 from 197 per cent to 270 per cent. In 1974 this ratio was 196 per cent. Also, the ratio of foreign assets invested in banks abroad to total foreign liabilities has developed during the same period from 160 per cent to 214 per cent in 1972 and to 199 per cent in 1974. This is evidence of the entrepôt character in the Lebanese centre. Besides, this excludes the reserves of the Bank of Lebanon which were more than LL1,933 million at the end of 1972 and LL3,804 million at the end of 1974. If these BL foreign assets are added to those of the commercial banks, foreign liabilities being the same, the ratio would then be about 435 per cent at the end of 1972 and 384 in 1974. Thus, the total of the Lebanese foreign assets covers the total of foreign liabilities by about 435 per cent, and 384 per cent in the years 1972 and 1974 consecutively.

Only in the first year of the war period did this ratio drop, and then it rose again. Thus, in 1975 it dropped to 313.9 per cent; to rise in 1976 to 337.5 per cent and to 454.8 per cent in 1977. In 1978 it was 411 per cent, 400 per cent in 1979 and 384 per cent in September 1980.

It appears in Table 6.10 below that the ratio of foreign assets of the commercial banks to their total assets would be about 41 per cent at the end of 1971, 32.3 per cent in 1974, 37.9 per cent in 1975, and 29.6 per cent in 1978; 34.7 per cent in 1979 and 35.5 per cent at the end of September 1980.

The ratio of foreign liabilities to the total resources of the system at the end of 1971 would be 19 per cent, 24.5 per cent in 1975, 17.7 per cent in 1978, 17.1 per cent in 1979 and 17.9 per cent in September 1980.

It can also be observed in Table 6.10 that the share of the entrepôt has decreased slightly in the later years. The role of the entrepôt, however, except for the years 1976 and 1977 has improved, considering the absolute figures of the foreign liabilities which increased from LL834 million to LL1,170 million, and LL2,027 million in the years 1969, 1972 and

Table 6.10. The relative share of the entrepôt factor in the centre in Lebanon, end of years 1971–1979 and September 1980

	1971	1972	1973	1974	1975	1976	1977	1978	1979	Sept. 1980
I Foreign liabilities as a percentage of total resources*	19	17.5	18.4	19	24.5	24.8	17.5	17.7	17.1	17.9
II Foreign assets as percentage of total assets	41	41.8	37.36	32.3	37.9	32.7	33.4	29.6	34.7	35.5

* Total resources = demand and time deposits plus deposits of the public sector in banks plus foreign liabilities, or total liabilities minus other items net (capital plus regularisation accounts).

1974 respectively. In 1978 it increased to LL3,096 million, and LL3,909 million in 1979 and LL5,101 million in September 1980.

The ratio of foreign assets of the commercial banks to their total assets was 41 per cent in 1971 and 29.6 per cent in 1978. The decrease in this ratio does not mean a reduction in the foreign assets of banks, but seem to be the result of a higher increase in claims on the private sector. On the other hand, commercial banks had to restrain their foreign assets because of the amount of legal reserves imposed on them by the BL.

The ratio of foreign liabilities to total resources of the system started at 19 per cent in 1971 and ended at 17.7 per cent in 1978. In 1979 it was 17.8 per cent, and in September 1980, 17.9 per cent. In 1975, however, it was 24.5 per cent and in 1976 it was 24.8 per cent. This does not necessarily indicate higher foreign liabilities in both years but a stagnant amount of time and demand deposits which are included in total resources.

In spite of the dark picture of the war the extent of non-resident foreign liabilities of the Lebanese banking system has dropped by only LL56 million in 1976 and by LL249 million in 1977, to rise again by LL538 million in 1978, reaching LL3,096 million when security conditions improved relatively. In other words, the relatively small drop in 1966 and 1977 of foreign liabilities was characteristic of the war conditions. Its effects, however, were not detrimental to the entrepôt as foreign liabilities resumed rising in 1978 by 21 per cent.

The same could be said for foreign assets which dropped in 1976 only by LL588 million, to rise again in 1977 by LL1,246 million, and by LL293 million in 1978, to rise sharply in 1979 by LL3,316 billion and in September 1980, by LL2,740 billion or by 54.6 per cent and 29.2 per cent respectively. And the entrepôt survived.

The outlook seems promising with regard to the growth of the centre and the entrepôt, provided the right conditions are maintained. Developments in the area, especially with regard to oil revenues, would be a great contributing factor.

With regard to the capital market in Lebanon, the obstacles retarding its development are the predominance of the individual proprietorship over the corporate form and the preference of the Lebanese public for saving and investing in tangibles rather than in intangibles like stocks and bonds. Thus, capital investment was carried out by individuals rather than by corporations. The shortage of investment outlets and large-scale industry left one or more families in control of investment instruments. This is often the case in small countries with small populations. Besides, outside competition is high against local industries. Nevertheless, industrialisation in Lebanon has improved, though not to a very great extent. The projects which needed collective savings such as electricity, telephone, water supplies and to a certain extent, transport, etc., have been nationalised and therefore financed from the Government budget or by foreign loans. In some cases industry is financed by medium-term bank credit. Lebanese seeking investment opportunities resort to foreign stock exchanges such as New York, Paris, London or Frankfurt, because the Beirut stock exchange has operated only on a limited scale.

The development of the Beirut capital market would benefit if Lebanon adopted greater industrialisation in new outlets such as, perhaps, petrochemicals, chemical or electronic industries. Oil passes through the country, and salaries and taxes are relatively lower than in other countries.

The pre-condition for the establishment of capital markets—a minimum financial infrastructure—exists in Beirut. Medium-term and long-term banks have been established alongside a reasonably well-developed commercial banking system. The latter has been the first to provide long-term investments, sometimes disguised behind short-term credit indefinitely renewed. At present the amendments of the Money and Credit Law, Article 102 have encouraged longer-term investments by commercial banks. The Central Bank accordingly could grant current-account loans to the commercial banks up to one year, renewable only once, against bills of three years maturity originating from industrial, agriculture, public works and export operations.

The Beirut stock exchange has existed since 1920 and many efforts have been made to develop it. Its progress reflects the developing Lebanese economy. There are also plenty of insurance companies in Lebanon, including branches of leading world companies.

In the early 1970s Lebanon was providing medium-term loans to the outside world to absorb ample liquidity. In December 1972 the Lebanese banks lent a sum of LL20 million to the State Bank of India for five years, and the sum of LL75 million to the IBRD in January 1973. In February 1973 a loan of LL50 million to Regie Renault was announced. In December 1974 the Arab Finance Corporation arranged a loan of $25 million to the Federal Republic of Brazil for ten years. The same corporation arranged in April 1975 another loan of $25 million to Honda for five years, and $30 million loan in July 1975 to Toshiba for fifteen years.

Consequently the BL, being in an international banking centre, had to become more concerned in the international sphere. With a free foreign exchange system the Central Bank in an international financial centre is not completely sovereign or independent in its domestic monetary policy since it is at the mercy of the international market. Short-term capital movements, for example, help to balance out international accounts.

Regarding the entrepôt, the placing of foreign funds with non-resident investors, or lending to foreign borrowers capital owned by non-resident investors, does not impose an additional burden on the balance of payments, neither would it result in excess shortage of liquidity, increasing or decreasing the money supply. Here the Central Bank is happily relieved from the trouble of using its techniques of credit control. Only the interest differential earned on entrepôt transactions by residents falls under the control of the Central Bank as it enters the economic circuit. But within the limits of the entrepôt the Central Bank has no role to play. It could, however, help to facilitate the work of the entrepôt providing certain tax and reserve requirements exemptions as the BL has done when the Lebanese banking free zone was established. It was an encouragement to the development of the entrepôt and an incentive to attract non-resident foreign currencies. But the fact remains that the direct role of the Central Bank in the entrepôt is almost zero.

OPPORTUNITIES FOR AND RESTRAINTS ON THE BANK OF LEBANON

To the extent that Lebanon plays the role of a financial centre and a financial entrepôt, its Central Bank could exploit special opportunities, but could also simultaneously confront special restraints.

The opportunities

The special opportunities for the Central Bank in Lebanon, being in a financial centre and a financial entrepôt for a region larger than the country itself, are: the substantial increase in its official reserves; the profit to the economy from capital inflow (growth); and the export of capital, as an important instrument of international monetary co-operation.

Lebanon experienced a substantial increase in its official reserves. Statistics show that the official reserves were LL3,804 million in 1974; LL3,866 million in 1975; LL4,958 million in 1976; LL5,873 million in 1977; and LL7,477 million in September 1980.

Monetary reserves of both the banking system and the Bank of Lebanon became equivalent to LL5,757 million in 1974,[66] representing LL1,919 per person. In 1977 they reached LL9,077 million and LL9,642 million in 1978, to rise to LL14,474 million in September 1980. This increase in reserves was made possible despite an enormous trade deficit, mainly by the considerable amount of capital that entered the country.[67]

Lebanon's position as a financial centre attracted a great deal of funds from the neighbouring Arab countries in the post-war period. This capital inflow helped to promote the country's growth directly and indirectly through two channels. First, by flooding the banking system with liquidity it compelled banks in general to invest in different sectors of the economy, thereby helping these sectors to develop. Second, a substantial part of the funds that flowed into the country was invested in the construction industry, which proved to be the leading industry in Lebanon as far as its rate of growth was concerned.

As previously mentioned, the Lebanese banks, due to their ample liquidity in the 1970s, were looking for opportunities to provide medium-term and long-term loans in Lebanese pounds to other countries. Lebanon's direct investments abroad seem to be considerable. There have been some investments in such fields as contracting and construction in the neighbouring Arab countries, particularly in Syria, Iraq, Libya, Saudi Arabia, and the Gulf countries but no statistics are available on the size of these investments.

Also, with regard to capital exports for financing securities many deals have been effected, particularly during the last seventeen years, through foreign investments and brokerage houses such as Merryl Lynch, and also through agents of American mutual funds and through the banking system. Although no figures are available to indicate the volume of business they have done, their activity and publicity was very noticeable in the market. The law, however, does not authorise the Central Bank to grant credit to other countries. The Bank of Lebanon can sponsor issues by the government, or by a government agency, possibly with its own guarantee concerning convertibility, and possibly by promoting multi-currency issues.

In Lebanon, where money and capital markets are not yet developed, the part played by non-bank financial intermediaries is neither conspicuous nor acute, and the banking system continues to be the major potential source of loanable funds. An active, broad and well-developed capital market to absorb securities is needed, since Lebanon has had overall balance of payments surpluses year in, year out, reflecting its position as an entrepôt, and influencing the pattern and rate of growth of GNP, and directly or indirectly, the banking liquidity, affecting many sectors of the economy. In the absence of either control or direction from the monetary authorities, commerce and services emerged as the principal beneficiaries of this abundance of credit.

The importance of Lebanon's international role is seen in the part played by the Lebanese banking system with respect to Western money and capital markets. It has channelled foreign currencies from neighbouring Arab sources as well as from its residents. Beirut has become the centre of activities in the Middle East for foreign banks and their representative offices.

The restraints

In contrast to the special opportunities, the special restraints on a central bank in a financial centre are the dangers of inflation, and the fact that the conventional central banking instruments are rendered less effective. In Lebanon not all capital from the oil countries stays; partly because there are not many investment opportunities and partly because of the international character of the Lebanese banking system. The recent issues which have been made in the Lebanese market for accounts of foreign borrowers in Lebanese pounds have produced the fear that this might eventually lead to an internationalisation of the Lebanese pound which might in turn capture the attention of currency speculators. The Lebanese pound might consequently become the scene of speculative activity whenever an international currency crisis occurs, at a time when the Bank of Lebanon might not be capable of dealing adequately with massive capital flows. The experience of Switzerland in this regard, especially when it was forced to float (14 February 1973), and the repeated occasions when it has had to deal with speculative capital inflows, is certainly a lesson for Lebanon to ponder over before it goes too far in tolerating an internationalisation of the Lebanese pound.

The dangers of inflation

Lebanon, until 1973, has not been as exposed to the threat of inflation on account of capital inflow as Switzerland has been, mainly because a large part of the capital that the country received was offset by the enormous trade deficit, and in addition because capital exports were also substantial. This is not to say that Lebanon has been completely immune from inflation.

In 1973, as in previous years, the BL had to face substantial capital inflows and their consequences either with regard to the liquidity of the banking system, or to the external value of the Lebanese pound. Intervention in the foreign exchange market was threatening to cause dangers of excessive liquidity. On the other hand, leaving foreign exchange to the market forces would have caused a sharp increase in the external value of the Lebanese pound which was undesirable. In fact, the BL intervened buying dollars until it could not continue to ignore the resulting imported inflation. Total foreign exchange purchases in 1973 were equivalent to LL340 million.

This ample liquidity induced commercial banks to increase credit to the private sector, until a liquidity crisis appeared, due to the shortage of Lebanese currency. By the end of 1973 commercial bank credit to the private sector rose to LL4,588 million from LL3,204 million in 1972, i.e., an annual increase of 43.2 per cent in 1973 in contrast to 21 per cent in 1972. Real estate prices rose sharply accelerating the rise in the general price level. Thus, as well as imported inflation through rising prices of imported raw material, it could be said that a considerable part of the inflation was internal, namely excessive liquidity and credit increase by commercial banks.

In 1974 the rate of increase of capital inflow was more than the previous years, inducing more intervention in the foreign exchange market to reduce, as much as possible, the undesirable appreciation in the external value of the Lebanese pound. The unprecedented amount which the BL had to absorb was equivalent to LL1,780 million. Naturally, the result was excessive liquidity, part of which was frozen through the reserve requirements, whose rate was increased from 7 per cent (September 1972) to 8 per cent beginning from 1 July 1974, and to 10 per cent as from 1 October of the same year.

Central Bank instruments rendered ineffective

A huge inflow of funds and a high banking liquidity reduce the effectiveness of the central banking weapons. Perhaps it is due to the French influence that the discount rate was not used as a banking weapon in Lebanon until relatively recently.[68] A few months before the Intra affair, in 1966, the Central Bank considered raising the discount rate as a contractive measure to stablise the exchange rate of the Lebanese pound. It did not do so, on the grounds that contraction was not appropriate at the time because of its possible adverse effect on income and employment.

Since the Bank of Lebanon has been in its formative stage and the banking system undergoing radical reform, the instruments of monetary policy have not been used apart from what might be called the open-market operations in foreign exchange. The bank rate has stood at 3 per cent since the days of the BSL. Only during the Intra crisis did the Bank of Lebanon resort to different rates on the exceptional facilities granted to banks. The re-discount rate proper, then, remained the same at 3 per cent on first-class trade bills (with three signatures and ninety days' maturity).[69] The only change in the rates was imposed on advances other than the re-discount proper; this was a penalty rate of 7 per cent, to discourage unnecessary borrowing by banks.

In actual fact, re-discounting at the Bank of Lebanon has been resorted to only as a safety valve for the banking system in emergency situations, rather than as a tool of monetary control, but most local banks aspired to be given credit lines at the Central Bank. After the Intra failure, Lebanon as a centre and an entrepôt suffered a crisis of confidence, and the inflow of capital was slow. In this case the weakness of the centre made it easier for the Bank of Lebanon to regulate money and credit in the country. Consequently, the Bank of Lebanon could effectively vary the re-discount rate and thus influence the volume of banks' borrowing. But this is an exceptional case. Ordinarily, as in the Swiss case, easy market conditions render the re-discount weapon ineffective.

Even organised money markets, in highly liquid conditions, are not always automatically responsive to changes in the discount rates.[70] The legal powers governing the price of credit are adequate in the Bank of Lebanon, and the authorities were looking forward to the time when these weapons could be used to greater effect.

The reluctance which banks in Lebanon used to have in regard to borrowing from the BSL has tended to diminish since the Bank of Lebanon was established, and has all but vanished since the Intra crash forced a great number of banks to solicit help. There is ground for hoping that the re-discount policy can be applied effectively by the Bank of Lebanon in implementing its monetary policy.

As an example of the ineffectiveness of the discount rate in Lebanon, it could be observed that raising the discount rate did not result in contracting credit. The BL raised its discount rate from 5 per cent to 7 per cent, beginning on 1 June 1974, as a contractionary measure. But commercial bank credit in the third quarter of the year increased from LL5,070 million at the end of June to LL5,404 million at the end of September 1974, i.e., by 10.7 per cent, or by over 40 per cent annually. The BL, then, had to resort to direct action, imposing a ceiling on bank credit of 6 per cent, beginning from end of September to end of year (i.e., 24 per cent per annum).

The absence of the developed capital market in Lebanon limits the Central Bank's ability to conduct open-market operations. Thus, such operations in government securities or commercial bills were precluded in Lebanon by the absence of Treasury issues and of an active bill market. Active trading in commercial bills by specialised dealers of the kind existing, for example, in the London discount market, does not exist in Lebanon. Treasury issues have started, however, but so far they have not been intended for credit control. In fact, they were simply an internal loan needed by the Government. The Bank of Lebanon can issue its own securities, as Switzerland intends to do, for regulating the money supply, until a sufficiently advanced securities market develops.

Yet the Bank of Lebanon is capable of operating in the foreign exchange market with a view to influencing the volume of money and credit in the economy. However, such open-market operations in foreign exchange, are also limited by the fact that the foreign exchange market in Lebanon is thin, in the sense that it cannot absorb large transactions which the Bank of Lebanon might have to undertake, and by the fact that the internal stabilisation policy of the Bank of Lebanon, if implemented via the foreign exchange market, could induce undesirable tendencies in the foreign exchange rate of the Lebanese pound.

Reserve requirements seem to be the most potent instrument of monetary policy in Lebanon. When there is virtually no open market in which to operate, it is suggested that open-market operations could have a substitute in the weapon developed in America (1933), i.e., the variation of compulsory cash reserve ratios, and because there are such reserve requirements open-market operations can influence the willingness of the commercial banks to lend to their customers.[71]

When commercial banks have reserves greatly in excess of legal requirements, the customary instruments of credit policy, open-market operations and discount rates, are wholly ineffective. In this way open-market operations—a far more flexible instrument of credit policy than changes in reserve requirements—become once more an effective measure for exerting the Central Bank's influence on credit conditions.[72] This method of change in reserve requirements might be adopted either as an alternative to open-market operations where they cannot be undertaken extensively or effectively or as a supplement to them, in order to strengthen the technique of central banking control under highly liquid monetary conditions or, conversely, under conditions of severe credit stringency. 'When reserve requirements are increased some banks will be hit much harder than others'. Burgess concluded that 'despite these limitations the power to raise or lower the banks' reserve requirements is the most useful addition to the system's mechanism for credit control, especially as a means for dealing fundamentally with the large excess of reserves created by the extraordinary events of the depression emergency.'[73]

The imposition of higher cash reserve requirements reduces to zero the rate of return on a certain proportion of commmercial banks' assets that have hitherto yielded a positive rate of return. On the other hand, open-market operations reduce the total volume of commercial bank assets without reducing the proportion of earning assets to total assets. Thus the imposition of the higher reserve requirements has a more restrictive impact on commercial banks' income than the equivalent volume of open-market sales by the monetary authorities.[74]

A reduction in reserve requirements augments, immediately and simultaneously, the lending capacity of all member banks. In contrast, the Central Bank's purchase of Government securities affects, in the first instance, only the lending capacity of those institutions that are sellers of the securities bought by the Central Bank. It appears, therefore, that when faced with a downturn in economic activity, the Central Bank should prefer the reduction of reserve requirements to the purchase of Government securities. As monetary policy is generally deemed to be more potent in curbing inflation than in reversing recession, resort to the more spectacular measure of cutting reserve requirements seems particularly inviting.[75]

The difficulty the Bank of Lebanon faced in imposing compulsory reserves was that it was established at a time when the liquidity crisis was growing in the banking system. The Bank of Lebanon, especially after Intra, found itself unable to introduce such reserves, simply because the banks have not had enough liquidity to cope with such requirements, small as it might be to begin with. However, the Bank of Lebanon, as mentioned earlier, started such a requirement, beginning with a low ratio (2½ per cent), raising it to 5 per cent, and recently to 15 per cent, of which 7.5 per cent may be in Treasury bills. This instrument is rendered less effective in a financial centre, as could be observed in Lebanon when the BL raised the rate of reserve requirements to 8 per cent beginning from July, and to 10 per cent (Memorandum No. 143, 18 November 1974). Here commercial bank credit to the private sector was unaffected and continued to increase by 10.7 per cent in the third quarter of 1974.

Finally, among the conventional weapons of monetary policy, 'moral suasion', as one is tempted to think with Ascheim, is 'at best, a means of substituting words for actions; it is no safeguard against the perennially possible failure of words to affect the central bank's wishes'.[76]

Scope of action of the Bank of Lebanon

In certain respects the Bank of Lebanon, though in a liberal economy, is more equipped by law with the weapons of monetary control than is the Swiss National Bank. In practice, in the absence of a developed capital market, the Bank of Lebanon is unable to apply to advantage the weapon of open-market operations. However, as the Swiss National Bank is committed to a long tradition of fixed re-discount rate, one may consider that the Bank of Lebanon can use the re-discount rate more effectively as a policy weapon. The Bank of Lebanon may also impose mandatory reserves and use them as an instrument of monetary control.

There has been a positive development in the banking system in Lebanon. The credit market is becoming more and more dominated by the foreign banks, who have been the backbone of the Lebanese banking system. This is becoming more evident as many local banks are welcoming the participation of foreign capital. This constitutes an extra difficulty to monetary control with the ordinary weapons, mainly because of the foreign banks' close relations with their head offices and their dependence on them, a fact which puts monetary policy in the position of having to deal with banks having vast resources at their disposal.

The Bank of Lebanon may apply other restrictive devices for the purpose of controlling the money supply. According to Article 174 'The Central Bank shall, in particular, set and alter, whenever it shall deem it necessary, the management rules banks should comply with, to maintain their liquidity and solvency'.[77] Further, Article 175 states that in application of this the Central Bank may determine periodically the required ratios between: a bank's assets—classified by order of liquidity on the one hand—and its liabilities, classified in order of maturity, on the other; also the ratios of a bank's net worth on the one hand, and on the other, total deposits, total liabilities, acceptances, guarantees and accommodations. Further ratios were required between total credit granted by a bank to one person, real or personal, on the one hand, and on the other the total of its net worth and deposits.

As a new central bank the Bank of Lebanon has been empowered by the Money and Credit Law with powers which older central banks have gained with experience. Having a relatively more difficult task, the central bank in a financial centre is entitled to more discretionary power. 'The exercise of discretion is broader than the role of rules.' The very reason that central banks exist, as Sayers points out, is that there are no eternal rules applicable at all times and places; discretion, however, should be exercised in a responsible manner.

The amendments to the Money and Credit Law would vest the Central Bank with new potent instruments of monetary control.[78] The amendments introduced a new authority for the Central Bank to impose marginal and differential reserve requirements, and also to apply selectively, in case of need, reserve requirements on certain groups of assets. In a heterogeneous system like the Lebanese banking system, these powers are bound to prove exceedingly useful.

The scope of action of the Bank of Lebanon is, by law, wider than that of the Swiss National Bank. The Money and Credit Law left to the Central Bank authorities such discretion as they are entitled to in a financial centre. Even wider scope is provided by the recent amendments. The year 1974 provides a good illustration of how wide the scope of action of the Bank of Lebanon is. In the foreign exchange market the BL intervention was the heaviest; the amount of dollars purchased in that year was unprecedented (equivalent to LL1,780 million). That was due to the situation of the United States currency in world markets, the relatively huge dollar flows into Lebanon, and the internal liquidity crises.

The liquidity crisis worsened at the beginning of 1974 in both quality and quantity of bank credit to the private sector which had been excessive even before that. Inter-bank interest rates reached 35 per cent in January. The BL intervened, taking two measures to deal with this situation: firstly, it provided special credit facilities to banks through re-discounting and swap operations totalling about LL110 million by the end of January, and about LL169 million by the end of April 1974. Secondly, it authorised the banks to hold their reserve requirements at the Central Bank partly in foreign currencies (to the extent of 25 per cent, as from January 1974 and 50 per cent as from April on their engagements in foreign currencies). Simultaneously, the BL advised the banks not to finance construction and stock formation excessively. It is to be noted that the BL had previously imposed the same reserve ratio on all engagements, whether short-term or long-term, and in both Lebanese currencies and foreign currencies, but those reserves were to be absorbed only in Lebanese pounds.

But the commercial banks did not follow the suggestions of the Central Bank: they resumed their excessive investments as before. Further, the time came when the banks had to repay the facilities which they had had from the Central Bank. At that time (April) the liquidity crisis recurred, and inter-bank interest rates rose to 20 per cent. The BL in late March and April had to absorb dollars in order to limit the appreciation of the Lebanese pound, as well as to provide some liquidity to the banking system. It absorbed then an amount of foreign exchange equivalent to LL400 million.

To avoid the dangers which would have resulted from excessive liquidity in Lebanese pounds due to its dollar purchases, the BL adopted the following measures on 28 May 1974 (Circular No. 126): first, to raise the ratio of legal reserve requirements from 7 per cent to 8 per cent, as from 1 July 1974; second, to impose additional progressive reserve requirements as from 1 July on the increase of banks' advances as on 31 December 1973 as follows:[79]

(a) 5 per cent on the increase which does not go beyond 10 per cent of total advances as they were on 31 December 1973;
(b) 7 per cent on the increase above 10 per cent of total advances on 31 December 1973, and which is under 15 per cent;

(c) 10 per cent on the increase above 15 per cent of total advances on 31 December 1973, but not more than 20 per cent;
(d) 15 per cent on the remaining increase, i.e., on the increase over 20 per cent.

Those requirements had to be formed in Lebanese pounds. And banks specialising in medium-term and long-term credit were exempted.

Certain banks exploited the latter measure as an excuse to impose excessive interest rates on customers. Besides, the banks continued their excessive investment policy in the third quarter of the year, ignoring the suggestions of the Central Bank. For this the BL abolished the latter measure on 18 November 1974 and resorted to one of 'the other methods of credit control', i.e., to direct action, imposing a ceiling on bank credit to the private sector.[80] It limited credit in the last quarter of 1974 to a 6 per cent increase of total credit given on 30 September 1974, to an increase of 12 per cent on total credit given on 31 December 1974 for the first half of the year 1975.

And according to Circular No. 130, 4 June 1974, the re-discount rate was raised as follows:

(a) from 5 per cent to 7 per cent on re-discounting;
(b) from 5¼ per cent to 7¼ per cent on trade bills *en pension*;
(c) from 7 per cent to 9 per cent on current loans under Article 102 of the Money and Credit Law.

The above rates were to be implemented from the beginning of June 1974.

In the third quarter of the year, credit slowed down for a short period, then resumed to exert inflationary pressure threatening a new liquidity crisis. Thus, in the fourth quarter of the year, credit was absolutely limited and the Central Bank had to provide market liquidity of over LL1 billion through its dollar purchases.

An important circular (No. 145) was issued by the Central Bank on 15 January 1975, separating the local market from the foreign exchange market. It also limited the use of foreign currencies to finance foreign trade, trying to prevent speculation, and protecting its intervention in the foreign exchange market from being neutralised by commercial banks who would borrow dollars from abroad to sell to the Central Bank.

Thus the circular stated:

(i) banks are prohibited from keeping net over-bought foreign exchange positions beyond twice their paid-up capitals;
(ii) banks are also prohibited from keeping net over-sold foreign exchange positions;

(iii) maximum forward foreign exchange operations are limited to LL500,000. Banks cannot go beyond this limit except for foreign trade operations;

(iv) banks could give credit to non-residents in Lebanese pounds within the limits of their paid-up capital, provided the purpose of such credit is foreign trade operations;

(v) any increase in credit to residents in foreign currencies, occurring after 30 September 1974, would be subject to 20 per cent special reserve requirement constituted in foreign currencies; also the increase of credit in foreign currencies to non-residents occurring after 30 September 1974 would be subject to 20 per cent special reserve requirement constituted in foreign currencies in case that increase of credit is used inside Lebanon;

(vi) all increase in banks' liabilities in foreign currencies to the non-resident sector occurring after 30 September 1974, which does not have a counterpart in the foreign exchange assets at non-residents' banks or investments to non-residents outside Lebanon, would be subject to 20 per cent special reserve requirement constituted in foreign currencies.

Again the BL had to face post-war pressure on prices as well as on the exchange rate. It resorted to various restrictive measures: increases in the reserve requirements and the discount rate. Ceilings on bank credit were imposed and steps were taken against speculative conversion of the Lebanese currency into foreign exchange. On 31 March 1979, reserve requirements on deposits in Lebanese pounds were resumed at 5 per cent. On 10 May 1979 they were raised to 10 per cent; and they reached a level of 15 per cent by November 1979. Half of this could be held in Treasury bills. Then the re-discount rate was raised in November 1979 from 6 per cent to 8.5 per cent, then to 9.5 per cent on 12 January 1980, and to 10 per cent on 28 January 1980. It was lowered to 9 per cent on 9 July 1980, and raised again to 10 per cent on 3 December 1980. The fluctuations of interest rates abroad were responded to in Lebanon by adjustments in the domestic rates of interest as well as in the exchange rate.

With regard to speculative conversion of Lebanese pounds the BL imposed 15 per cent reserve requirements on deposits in foreign currency that served as collateral against loans in Lebanese pounds. The latter loans were also subject to 40 per cent reserve requirements. Moreover, banks were prohibited from holding net creditor positions in foreign currencies. Debtor positions were not to exceed twice the banks' capital. Ceilings on bank credit in Lebanese pounds to the private sector were imposed in June

1979. The limit was 20 per cent for each bank from the end of 1978 to 1979. In July 1979 it was raised to 25 per cent. For industrial and tourist sectors additional credits could be raised by 5 per cent. For 1980, the ceiling was 20 per cent. Excesses were subject to 50 per cent reserve requirements; however, at the end of 1980 those ceilings were cancelled.

Thus, it is necessary for a central bank in a financial centre to be given wide scope for action. In other words, more instruments are needed in these circumstances as conventional tools are rendered either less effective, or totally ineffective. It is not only more important to have wide powers and more instruments but also to use them wisely, conscientiously and intelligently, for the welfare of the country.

NOTES

1. Clarke, W. M., *Money Markets of the World: What the Future May Bring*, pp. 1–2.
2. Ibid., p. 3.
3. Einzig, Paul, *Foreign Dollar Loans in Europe*, p. 42. 'The term entrepôt in capital had its origin in the entrepôt trade in goods which originally means a commercial centre for import and export, collection and distribution' (*The Concise Oxford Dictionary*, 1959). 'It is also a name given in France and elsewhere to places analogous to the English "Bonded Warehouse", where dutiable goods can be stored free of duty until they are required for use, or until they are re-exported. These entrepôts are "réels" if the goods are really stored, "fictifs" if the owner is liable for the duty but retains the articles in his own possession' (Winton, J. R., *A Dictionary of Economic Terms*, 1960, p. 32). 'The entrepôt trade is defined as the trade of a country in the products of other countries; that is, the importing of such products with the intention of exporting them subsequently' (Taylor, Philip A. S., *A New Dictionary of Economics*, London 1966, p. 83).
4. Clarke, W. M., *The City in the World Economy*, p. 3. Also Einzig, op. cit., p. 42.
5. Ibid., p.1.
6. Clarke, *Money Markets of the World*, p.1.
7. Robinson, Roland, I., *et al.*, pp. 194–5.
8. Fehrenbach, T. R., *The Gnomes of Zurich*, p. 265.
9. Clarke, *Money Markets of the World*, p. 4.
10. Clarke quotes Powell, E. T., 'Evolution of the Money Market, 1385–1915', *Financial News*, 1915, Ibid., p. 7.
11. Ibid., p. 6.
12. Aschinger, F. E., *Zurich as a Centre of Finance*, pp. 7 and 8.
13. Ibid., pp. 12–14.
14. Ibid., p. 10.
15. Iklé, Max, *Switzerland, an International Banking and Finance Center*, p. 102.
16. Einzig, Paul, *The Euro-Dollar System*, London 1967, pp. x and xi.
17. Iklé, op. cit., p. 102.
18. Ibid., p. 101.
19. Ibid., pp. 102–3.
20. Ibid., p. 103.

21. Ibid., pp. 103–4.
22. Ibid., p. 105.
23. Ibid.
24. These were 1,508 million francs of foreign bills of exchange; 1,085 million francs of federal and cantonal bonds, including the money market bonds issued by the SNB; 4,266 million of domestic bills of exchange. Iklé, op. cit., p. 107.
25. Ibid., pp. 106–7.
26. Created as instruments of a war economy to finance inventories. They are being renewed each time they fall due. Iklé, op. cit., p. 106.
27. Ibid.
28. Aschinger, op. cit., p. 25.
29. Ibid., p. 27. Up-to-date figures all through this section on the capital market were privately secured by the author from reliable Swiss sources.
30. Ibid., pp. 32–3.
31. Iklé, op. cit., pp. 111–14.
32. Ibid., pp. 114–16.
33. Aschinger, op. cit., p. 35.
34. In 1968, the trade volumes of the European stock exchange expressed in billions of Swiss francs (both purchases and sales) were London, 335.6; Zurich, 41.5; Paris, 26.1; Amsterdam, 16.8; Milan, 9.9; (Frankfurt, 7.9; Düsseldorf, 7.9; only purchases); Brussels, 2.9; Madrid, 1.8. See Iklé op. cit., p. 118 (footnote).
35. Aschinger, op. cit., pp. 40–1.
36. Ibid., pp. 42–3.
37. Iklé, op. cit., p. 94.
38. Ibid., p. 97.
39. Aschinger, op. cit., p. 55. Figures brought up-to-date from reliable Swiss sources.
40. Ibid., pp. 56–7,
41. Ibid., pp. 60–3.
42. Unless otherwise stated, the information on Switzerland in this chapter was obtained by the author from Mr Alexandre Hay, Vice-President, and Dr Pierre Flückiger, Director, both of the Swiss National Bank (Berne). A particular debt is owed to the following: Alexandre Hay, Vice-President de la Direction Générale de la Banque Nationale Suisse, 'Les Moyens d'Action de la Banque Nationale Suisse et leurs extentions', conférence donnée à la Réunion des Cadres de la Caisse d'Epargne de Genève et du Crédit Foncier, Vaudois à Territot le 21 octobre 1967; M. Iklé, Member of the Directorium of the Swiss National Bank, Zurich, 'Switzerland's International Capital Relations', address delivered (in German) before the Basle Statistical and Economic Society on 27 February 1967; Ricardo Motta, Vice-President of the Board of Management of the Swiss National Bank 'Some Aspects of the Swiss National Bank's Policy', lecture delivered (in German) on 16 June 1962 to the International Conference of Commerical Bank Economists in Hertenstein (Lucerne).
43. These were bonds sold by the National Bank in the autumn of 1960 to banks to the amount of Sw.fr.400 millions. The Federal Government, for whom these bonds were issued, did not require the proceeds, but arranged with the National Bank to hold the proceeds in a special blocked account at the National Bank. The operation has thus depended on the co-operation of the Federal Government, Sayers, *Banking in Western Europe*.
44. Motta, op. cit.
45. De Kock, M. H., *Central Banking*, p. 180.
46. De Kock, op. cit., p. 184.
47. Ascheim, *Techniques of Monetary Control*, p. 12.
48. 'The proposal to extend the powers of the Central Bank bear exclusively on the limitation of an exaggerated growth of banking liquidity and credit, and are full

of clauses which prohibit the use of new instruments that bring about deflation . . . the National Bank abstains from creating money in order to hinder an unhealthy growth of credit.'

49. See Banque de Syrie et du Liban, 'Rapport relatif aux propositions de révision de la loi fédérale du 23 décembre 1953 sur la Banque Nationale Suisse' (Extension des moyens d'action de la banque d'émission), p. 20.
50. Swiss Bank Corporation 'The New Swiss Agreement on Minimum Reserves and Credit Restrictions', *Prospects* (Business News Survey), No. 123, October 1969.
51. Ibid.
52. Ibid.
53. Swiss Bank Corporation, 'Restrictive Measures to Check the Inflow of Foreign Capital', *Prospects* (Business News Survey), No. 140, August 1972.
54. Einzig, *The History of Foreign Exchange*, p. ix.
55. Taylor, *A New Dictionary of Economics*, op. cit., 1966.
56. Robinson, R. I., *et al.*, (eds.), *Financial Institutions*, pp. 193–4.
57. Previous regulations: Decree No. 233, see Chapter 5.
58. The figures for 1972 are given by Hoss, Salim, 'The Banking System since 1966', *The Banker*, January 1972, pp. 15–17 and 28–9.
59. Demand deposits + time deposits + Government deposits.
60. See Chapter 3, p. 59.
61. Liquidity = commercial banks' reserves at the central bank + central bank claims on commercial banks. Here the expansionary as well as the contractionary factors affecting the liquidity of the banking system are: changes in the *net foreign assets of the banks, currency outside banks, net Government deposits*, and *other items net*.
62. Other items are added, amounting to over LL100 million.
63. See the section on the Swiss money market earlier in this chapter.
64. Einzig, *The History of Foreign Exchange*, p. 43.
65. Idem.
66. It is to be noted that the gold reserves of the Bank of Lebanon have been estimated ever since the end of 1973 at $42.2222 the ounce.
67. Incidentally, the net profit of the Bank of Lebanon in 1974 was LL158.5 million. According to Article 113 of the Money and Credit Law, 80 per cent of this amount was given to the Treasury which was LL126.8 million, and 20 per cent went to the Central Bank, i.e., LL31.7 million. This profit was mainly the result of investing the foreign exchange reserves of the Central Bank. In 1980, the net profit of the BL was LL621.9 million.
68. 'In general, the Bank of England stood at the one end, with the greatest frequency and the widest range of changes in rates of discount, and the Bank of France stood at the other end, with the smallest frequency and the narrowest range', De Kock, op. cit., p. 150.
69. Amended to 180 days.
70. De Kock, op. cit., p. 166.
71. Sayers, *Central Banking After Bagehot*, p. 129.
72. De Kock, op. cit., p. 233.
73. Ibid., p. 239.
74. Ascheim, op. cit., p. 23.
75. Ibid., p. 30.
76. Ibid., p. 12.
77. The Money and Credit Law.
78. See Chapter 3, p. 61.
79. In accordance with the amendment to Article 76 of the Money and Credit Law, the Central Bank was given wider scope and flexibility with regard to the

weapon of legal reserve requirement. It could impose 'special minimum reserve requirements' on a given group of assets defined by the Central Bank.

80. Article 79 (new) of the Money and Credit Law, empowers the Central Bank to limit any kind of credit, or credit granted to certain purposes of certain sectors. 'Direct action embraces, among other things, those cases where the central bank decides to take such coercive measures . . . to issue directives to banks generally concerning their lending and investment operations under special statutory authority.' De Kock, op. cit., p. 225.

7. Central banking in a financial centre and a financial entrepôt in wartime (Lebanon)

This chapter examines wartime monetary policy in Lebanon (1975–80), in order to see whether the Lebanese centre and entrepôt survived and contributed to the economic viability of the country. It is imperative here to indicate that the Lebanese pound withstood all national perils on its own without the authorities being obliged to resort to any exchange control. The new structure of the Lebanese economy, with its increased dependence on the outside, is revealed by the balance of imports minus exports which represented 15 per cent of total resources (goods and services), before 1975 and which became over 25 per cent in 1977.

GOVERNMENT SUPREMACY: SUSPENSION OF CENTRAL BANKING, AND THE EXCEPTIONAL CASE OF LEBANON

This section first describes Lebanon in wartime, and then examines the role of the Government and the Central Bank in Lebanon and elsewhere.

The war in Lebanon

Since early independence Lebanon has experienced various crises. The Intra crisis was certainly serious, but the war proved overwhelming. Not only was it another sad experience for the central banker, but also a dangerous and a fearful one in which the ghost of death and destruction reigned over the whole vulnerable country. The economy was adversely affected; many banks were closed, looted and destroyed and many of their clients were ruined. Industry was almost paralysed, tourism vanished, and the trade sector was stagnant. But illegal trade and smuggling became active once the port of Beirut was closed. Illegal authority became the effective authority, and there was a *de facto* political partition.

Many Lebanese citizens emigrated, thus contributing to the endless losses of the economic sectors. The Central Bank and the central banker, like everything else, were at the mercy of shellfire from rockets; it was a state of anarchy, uncertainty and despair. The Lebanese, indeed, suffered much hardship. They were liable to lose their homes, trade and lives. Both people and institutions were shattered as a result of the bombing, sniping and kidnapping. Those who did not fight stayed in their houses or shelters, sometimes for weeks, with almost no contact with the outside world except through radios or perhaps newspapers. There was a terrible lack of public services: for a relatively long time there was no electricity and therefore no lifts or refrigerators; telephones were cut and water pipes were damaged; foodstuffs and petrol were short and naturally at very high prices.[1] Heaps of rubbish lay everywhere. This picture was further aggravated by the bombing and then the closing of Beirut International Airport, just as the port of Beirut had been bombed and closed earlier. Lebanon was isolated from the rest of the world. It was a savage war, but the Lebanese proved to be most adaptable, surviving in spite of considerable deprivation. All kinds of devices were pressed into service: for lighting, camping gas, kerosene or candles were used; some could get their own electric motors; water was drawn from wells, and rubbish was burned whenever possible . . .

However, in January 1977, as the political and security situation improved the banks resumed work. Deposits in the banking system increased rapidly as banks proved safer than private vaults. The Central Bank loan to the Government of about one billion Lebanese pounds was another reason for the increase in deposits. Legal or illegal profits during the war were also deposited in banks. Further, the Lebanese who emigrated to the countries of the Arabian Gulf transferred their money into the Lebanese banking system. Finally, the banking sector was gaining momentum as it anticipated an influx of reconstruction funds. The great and rapid increase in bank deposits was a sign of confidence in the country and its banking system. There was, however, a negative side to this increase. Perhaps a considerable part of the increase in deposits was the result of banks refraining from investment due to the absence of minimal security and certainty.

The second explosion of war (October 1978) aggravated the picture and the economic future looked gloomy as most economic targets were hit. Destruction of industry was resumed, the port of Beirut closed, and hostilities in the already ruined commercial centre were renewed. Some institutions were preparing to leave and the stock exchange closed. Prices rose considerably as security deteriorated. Many workers were considering emigration. For the first time the viability of the Lebanese economy was in question.

The Lebanese became less hopeful, no longer asking when their country would return to normal. This loss of confidence in recovery was more detrimental than the material damage. Pessimism as well as optimism were expressed at various intervals by leaders of the economic sectors. In October 1978 Dr Fuad Abi Saleh,[2] a leading industrialist, exposed the serious difficulties facing Lebanese industrialists who, he said, might not be able to honour their commitments to outside markets, and the danger that the link between Lebanon and foreign markets would be cut. Mr Georges Asseily was no less pessimistic.[3] To Mr Georges Sakr,[4] leader of the Trade Unions Federation, it appeared that the workers suffered most in the war and Lebanon needed a miracle to rescue it. As for Mr Kassar,[5] President of the Beirut Chamber of Commerce, the picture at the time was neither bright nor gloomy, but he saw signs of economic recuperation. In June 1979 both Dr Abi Saleh and Mr Victor Kassir drew a very gloomy picture and expressed anxiety about the fate of the country itself.[6]

Optimism, however, was revealed by the Governor of the Central Bank as early as December 1978.[7] He stressed the dynamism of Lebanese private initiative, particularly in the banking sector, which he expected to share in the reconstruction and rebirth of the economy.

A positive picture was revealed by Dr Assaad Sawaya, Chairman of the Lebanese Bankers Association, in November 1979.[8] He considered the ability of the banks to continue their business during the war period enough proof that there was no alternative to Beirut as a financial and commercial centre in the region. Naturally, he said, there were difficulties but also there were solutions. He appreciated the great understanding and co-operation of the authorities and the Central Bank with regard to banking conditions.

The Governor of the Central Bank, Cheikh Michel El-Khoury, once again expressed great admiration for the banks' ingenuity in the difficult circumstances.[9] To him, the situation was not all negative. There were positive points, such as their new experience, which contributed to the efficiency of the banks. Most important was the confirmation of confidence in the Lebanese banking and economic systems.

Suspension of central banking

In wartime governments dominate central banks, but the case of Lebanon was different. The experience of the United Kingdom and the United States may be drawn on here as examples of central banking in wartime. In both countries the central bank during the world wars was subject to the financial policy of the government which was in a powerful position. The ultimate objective was to win the war. Given this objective, the next problem was how to manage war conditions so as to satisfy the needs of the economy and to provide the required funds, and at the same time, to safeguard money and banks.

In the case of Lebanon, there was nothing to stop the Central Bank from using its powers and instruments to the extent permitted by circumstances. It was a civil war, where government authorities lost their sovereignty to impose the law. However, in periods of relative calm there was some revival of the authorities' power, but it vanished again with the disappearance of security. In contrast to the weak position of the Government, the Central Bank, accorded privileged status by belligerents on both sides, was left unharmed, and the Lebanese currency remained a common denominator to all conflicting parties. Thus, the Bank of Lebanon (BL) was able to maintain its operations most of the time as the bank of issue and the lender of last resort. It worked just as if there were a sovereign government. It had to do its best in order to save as much as possible of what was left of the economy, or more particularly, of the banking system. It also had to take the initiative, playing a leading role in the economic rebirth of the country and its institutions. The responsibility of the Central Bank was of crucial importance since the Government was paralysed.

The classical models of the great world wars show governments in strong positions, dominated by central banks, as has been referred to by well-known economists. Geoffrey Crowther, for example, mentioned that 'the chief objective of financial policy in wartime should be to see that nothing is ever decided on financial ground. There must always be money for everything.'[10] He added that the economic problem of wartime is to provide the government with command over all. And all must be devoted to the insatiable demands of the war.

When Sayers presented the British and American experience in the early post-war years, he introduced his work as follows:

> In time of war central banking, like so many other things, is pushed aside or at least loses all its virtue. Under the impulse of war finance, the technique of the central bank, is manipulated so as to conform to events rather than used to control them. Central bankers become the slaves of deficit finance.[11]

As far back as 1919 Benjamin Strong referred to the subordination of the central bank to the government and to the great temptation of the secretaries of the treasury to borrow cheap money at the expense of sound monetary conditions and of the price level.[12]

Moreover, Chandler expressed the same idea, saying that during the First and Second World Wars the Federal Reserve became 'a servant of the Government's fiscal policy'. He added that 'The most important of the consequences of this passive open-market policy were that the Federal Reserve thereby abandoned control over its volume of Government holdings, the volume of bank reserves, and the money supply'.[13]

In the words of Hawtrey:[14]

> In the face of the exigencies of war, no reliance can be placed on an independent central bank to resist demands from the Government. At such a time, the government is accepted by public opinion as the sole authoritative exponent of the national needs.

Governments and war expenditures

Unlike the Lebanese case of a free economy and a paralysed government, the British Government in the Second World War assumed all responsibilities, including command over the economic process and monetary procedures. It restricted civilian standards as a part of the war effort. It subsidised and controlled supplies, whether domestic or imported. Increased consumption was prevented by rationing, and the cost of living was kept down.[15]

Direct wartime controls were also imposed in the United States to prevent consumers and business from spending as much as they wanted and could afford.[16] A series of direct controls was established: price ceilings were imposed on all sorts of output, wages and rents; there were also controls on production, distribution and use of output; and the country was in a state of supressed inflation. War expenditure had to come from increases in taxation, borrowing the savings of the public, or borrowing from the banking system and the central bank. In 1917 the United States' national debt was less than $1,000 million. Federal expenditures had risen to $18,500 million—about twenty to twenty-four times what it had been before. In the Second World War federal expenditure increased by $9 billion in mid-1940, and by an annual rate of over $95 billion in 1944—or ten times. Total expenditures were $383 billion between mid-1940 and mid-1946. It amounted, therefore, to more than twice the federal expenditure during the preceding one hundred and fifty years, to about a hundred times as much as that during the Civil War, and to ten times that during the First World War. The deficit was huge, totalling $187 billion in the six years following mid-1940. Investment, then, consisted almost exclusively of contributions to government loans. Non-bank investors were sold Treasury obligations for $109 billion. Commercial banks holding Treasury bills increased by $68.3 billion, and those of the Federal Reserve banks by $21.3 billion.

Treasury financing by the Federal Reserve was different in the Second World War. While in the First World War it bought very few Treasury obligations and lent very little to banks, in the Second World War it had to stand ready to buy directly all securities offered to it at selected levels of prices and yields. Interest rates were not allowed to rise at all. This willingness to buy all securities without limit, monetising Government debt, meant that the Federal Reserve surrendered its control over the money supply. That policy has robbed its other instruments of all or almost all of their effectiveness for restrictive purposes.[17]

The Federal Reserve System, unlike the Bank of England, had large resources compared to the total United States' national debt. It could therefore afford to monetise the national debt, creating that much money.

Again, unlike the smooth relations between the BL and the Lebanese Government, a controversy began between the Federal Reserve and the Treasury late in 1949. The Federal Reserve wanted to restrict credit, while the Treasury insisted on low interest rates. This controversy came out into the open in August 1950. The President and the Council of Economic Advisers were on the side of the Treasury, and there were heated discussions in Congress. However, a settlement was reached in March 1951, on a common purpose reconciling successful financing of the government's requirements and minimum monetisation of public debt.[18] And the Federal Reserve regained its freedom to refrain from purchasing all securities offered to it, to limit its creation of bank reserves, and to restrict credit when necessary to prevent inflation.[19]

In Lebanon the cost of the war resulted in a public debt of about LL4 billion. Almost half of this was a Central Bank loan to the Government and the rest came from Treasury bills sold mainly to commercial banks. The external Government debt was LL302.7 million at the end of 1979 and an estimated LL853.2 million at the end of 1980. The sources of the external debt were mainly the World Bank and the United States and Kuwait Governments. The budget deficit in 1973 was only LL38.4 million and it was reversed to a surplus of LL51 million in 1975. The deficit started again in 1976 at LL222.7 million, and LL490.2 million in 1977. The estimated budget deficit for 1978 was LL624.7 million, for 1979 LL992.9 million, and for 1980 LL1,366.5 million. The total budget for 1980 was set at LL3,868.5 million, and total revenues were estimated at LL2,502 million. It should be noted here that the Gross Domestic Expenditure for 1980 was expected to be LL18.5 billion. But whatever the Gross Domestic Product or Expenditure, the Government was still unable in 1980 to collect all the revenues due, especially customs duties. There were so many imports through illegal ports that it was said that the Lebanese were getting richer while their Government was getting poorer.

Vietnam

In addition to comparing the Lebanon in wartime with great financial centres such as the United States and the United Kingdom in similar circumstances, it is profitable to look at the example of a developing country, Vietnam, which passed through similar difficult times of war.[20]

The Vietnam War picture was in certain respects not very different from that of Lebanon. The damage and destruction were almost the same, and so was the dislocation of people and institutions. There was very little investment in productive enterprises, due to the risk to capital, and the fact that there were quicker avenues for making money—some of them illegal. In Vietnam economic collapse was prevented by French military expenditure.[21] In Lebanon also economic collapse was prevented to a great extent by those who paid for the war industry, which was the great source of productivity and income.

Monetary policy had to face the classical problems of a war economy, such as inflationary pressures, a distorted pattern of spending, settling refugees, and disruption of agricultural production. In both Lebanon and Vietnam it was decided to strengthen the economy during the war in order to ease post-war problems since post-war objectives are largely dictated by wartime conditions.

It is worth noting that even during a period of bitter and destructive warfare, the authorities agreed that it was timely to prepare for post-war developments. In Vietnam direct regulations of economic activity were to be replaced by more normal fiscal and monetary measures as monetary and fiscal policies were considered the key to the successful transition of the economy. It was also envisaged to strengthen the financial sector in order to mobilise savings and capital, and to expand commercial banking. Interest rates were to be increased so as to raise the level of loanable funds or bank credit for investment and economic activity which might need to rise by five to fifteen times. Cash holdings would then be encouraged to shift to deposits. Finally, a money and capital market as well as a secondary market was to be developed, and the overvalued currency unit was to be adjusted. The same approach was revealed in Lebanon.

The financial sector in Vietnam was underdeveloped by most standards. In 1967 it had twenty banks and a total of thirty-seven banking offices, serving 440,000 persons per banking office. The Government of Vietnam had taken some steps, via tax concessions, to make it more attractive to establish branch banks in the provinces. Lebanon, in comparison, had eighty-nine banks (February 1981) with over 382 branches, i.e., over 471 banking offices, serving about 7,500 persons per banking office. Lebanon thus ranks higher than Japan, which served 15,000 persons per banking office in 1967. Moreover, Lebanon is not very far from highly developed countries such as the United States which served 6,000 persons per banking office in 1970, and the United Kingdom which served 4,200 persons in 1966. Switzerland, however, seems to rank first, serving 1,400 persons per banking office in 1968.

Before war broke out, the banks in both Vietnam and Lebanon concentrated primarily on the financing of imports. After the war the volume of imports could be expected to drop, and the banks would have to finance industry, agriculture and commerce.

The percentage of bank credit in relation to GNP in Vietnam was relatively low—never more than 12.1 per cent in the period 1960–7. In 1967 it was 7.8 per cent. In Lebanon this percentage is much greater. The composition of the money supply and its relationship to the GNP suggests other structural problems. In Vietnam the money supply was 20–25 per cent of GNP in 1967. It has been suggested that the percentage was higher than it should be. In Lebanon, on the other hand, the percentage of money supply to the GNP in 1977 was 61.73 per cent, which can be considered very high.[22] That percentage has always been high in Lebanon, even before the war.

Further, the percentage of currency in relation to money supply in Vietnam was exceedingly high in 1967 (75 per cent). That indicated the relatively low growth in demand deposits as well as in time deposits. In Lebanon that percentage was 66.9 per cent in 1976 and 57.74 per cent in 1977.

Interest rate reforms were suggested for Vietnam and for Lebanon in order to help to control inflation in the short run, and for development requirements in the long run. In Vietnam the maximum allowable rate on time deposits was only 6 per cent and on savings deposits 4 per cent. The real rate of interest was therefore highly negative as the increase in prices in the years 1966–8 was 30 per cent to 60 per cent. In Lebanon, on the other hand, interest rates were lowered at the beginning of the war to about the same level as that allowed in Vietnam, but raised in November 1979.

An interesting example of an attack on inflation was that mounted by Taiwan in 1949 and early 1950. The Government paid high interest rates on time deposits. Certificates of deposits were first issued for one month maturity at a rate of 7 per cent, or 125 per cent annually. Time deposits, accordingly, grew eighteen-fold in five months and price increases stopped at least for a time. Another example was that of Korea in 1965 when the rate on time deposits was raised from 3.6 per cent to 12 per cent and rates on all other types of deposits were similarly adjusted. So were loan rates.

As in the case of Lebanon, the creation of a money and capital market was also suggested for Vietnam to strengthen the hand of the central bank. The money market was envisaged as a means through which the National Bank could market the wide variety of government securities.

Finally an exchange rate policy was proposed for Vietnam for the future. It was considered the responsibility of the monetary authorities to maintain a reasonable equilibrium in the balance of payments through exchange rate policy as well as through credit and fiscal measures. In 1967 accounts in Vietnam were badly unbalanced, owing to the war. Exports had dropped to very low levels, while imports had risen greatly. Imports were about twenty-five to thirty times that of exports. The large deficit in the trade balance was met by services (spending on troops and contractors, and external aid). Imports were used as an anti-inflationary measure to absorb purchasing power, holding down prices.

The real exchange rate[23] in Vietnam deteriorated after 1966: thus the real rate at the end of 1968 (with a wholesale price index of 405) was only about thirty. Such a rate stimulated more imports. As devaluation was considered to be a painful course of action, and as the policy of freely-fluctuating exchange rates would increase speculative activities, and as the so-called 'creeping peg' required monetary management—delicate and difficult to achieve in Vietnam—the policy of fixing a rate which could be maintained for a time was preferred.

The exchange rate of the Lebanese pound seems to have moved parallel to that of Vietnam and in March 1981 it seemed less over-valued than that of Vietnam. The trade balance deficit was more than offset by capital inflow. With regard to the balance of payments, banking statistics indicated a surplus in 1974 of LL1,493 million. It dropped to LL351 million in 1975, then resumed its increase to LL508.5 million in 1976, and LL2,404 million in 1977. But in 1978 it dropped to LL554 million, to show another high increase of LL2,074 million in 1979 and LL3,124 million in 1980.

These fluctuations follow a pattern such as might be found in a case study in an international economics textbook. Foreign capital inflow stabilises the foreign exchange rate higher than would have been the case. Here the currency is overvalued in the foreign market relative to the domestic market. Here also consumers expect higher prices and lower exchange rates, spending their income as quickly as they can. This pushes the level of internal prices up, accelerating inflation, and the exchange rate is pushed down as capital flight begins when domestic holders of local currency sell it for foreign exchange.

In Lebanon monetary controls or financial measures seem to have been adequate to avoid explosive hyper-inflation, and the rate of inflation could be kept at about 20 per cent, while the exchange rate of the Lebanese currency did not decrease to that extent, due to capital inflow. It seemed that the Lebanese pound was overvalued relative to the US dollar, judging by the purchasing power parity theory. While the rate of inflation in Lebanon in 1978–81 was roughly double that of the United States, the exchange rate of the Lebanese pound was not halved during that time.

THE CENTRE AND THE ENTREPÔT

The centre

A financial centre in wartime could count more on its foreign sector to compensate for internal stagnation, if it were well-established internationally.

Clarke's definition of a financial centre mentioned at the beginning of Chapter 6 fits Lebanon to some extent. Both domestic and international money has been constantly flowing freely in and out, or deposited in banks inside the centre (protected, if need be, by the Banking Secrecy Law), or provided for trade and industry. Lebanese financial institutions were relatively adequate, experienced and efficient, and above all well-established outside. The currency, as well as the public, inspired confidence. Taxes were not excessive, neither were official borrowings before the war. Monetary policy was reasonable.

Lebanon was not only located at a global crossroads, but it was also a neighbour of the huge world sources of wealth in the Arab oil-producing countries. Except in crises, it enjoyed relative stability and a satisfactory infrastructure. It proved to be a financial centre and a financial entrepôt which, though on a small scale, was so strong that even the war could not destroy it. (In this study, the 'centre' is considered to be the whole pool of monetary resources or almost the total assets of banks.)

As mentioned previously, as a general rule, in time of war, power, or to be exact, exceptional power, rests in the hands of the government to which the central bank is subject. In Lebanon it was the Government, not the Bank, that lost almost all power as well as most of its institutions. Official laws, regulations and sanctions disappeared as courts of law closed and prisons were destroyed. It was a civil war. The Central Bank kept functioning most of the time, providing for the needs of the government and the banks. The belligerents apparently refrained from shelling it, though this may have been sheer luck. Besides, when the Governor became President of the Republic on 8 May 1976, it became a kind of family relationship between the Central Bank and the Government.

The anarchy of civil war did not greatly affect banking because Lebanon has all along adopted a free economy and a free foreign exchange system. The Lebanese people were adaptable to any situation, however difficult. The fact that it was a financial centre with good international relations was a great help to it as a country providing financial services.

With regard to monetary policy there was full understanding between the Bank and the Government. The role of the former was not restricted to safeguarding money and banks, it also safeguarded the state and its institutions. It continued to pay government employees (even those who were not working). Its aim was the continuity of the administration.

The Bank was working within the framework previously envisaged by the Government. Though the daily work of the Bank continued most of the time with many fewer employees, meetings of the Bank Council were not as frequent as they had been in peacetime. Early in November 1975 the situation was so difficult that the Bank Council could not notify all its members for a meeting. The monetary and banking situation was also difficult. Rumours spread of transfers of funds outside the country, as well as withdrawals of deposits due to fear of the political and economic situation worsening. In fact, it was an unusual situation which necessitated precautions and planning for exceptional measures by the Bank of Lebanon in order to contain both adverse effects and future consequences. Accordingly, the Bank considered providing credit facilities to banks and buying foreign exchange.

With regard to the first point, the Bank discussed the text of Articles 76 and 77 of the Money and Credit Law, on influencing bank liquidity and the volume of credit, and Articles 100, 101 and 102, on its operations with banks with regard to credit facilities. It decided, under the circumstances, to inform the banks temporarily and until further notice:

(i) That the Bank should not apply the penalty on the deficiency of reserve requirements mentioned in Article 77, beginning 1 November 1975. Thus, the reserve requirements were actually suspended.

(ii) That it will be possible for banks in exceptional circumstances to surpass the previously determined re-discount ceilings, as well as the total amount of facilities given to them, provided necessary justifications could be presented to the Banking Control Commission.

(iii) The Central Bank would be prepared to provide all operations stated in Articles 100, 101 and 102 of the law. It also approved the application of the text of the third paragraph of Article 102 which included granting exceptional credits but with whatever collateral possible in real guarantees. For that, banks were requested, if they needed to benefit from the above-mentioned exceptional facilities, to prepare themselves beforehand, taking the necessary measures to get such facilities when the need arose.

With regard to the second point under discussion, the Central Council decided to purchase foreign exchange from the local market with a view to providing the necessary liquidity. Early in February 1976 the Central Council (with a minimum quorum) discussed the general banking situation in the light of the decision taken by the Council of Ministers on 12 November 1975. To do his best to ensure the safety of the banking sector at the time, and to ask the Bank of Lebanon to supply commercial banks on Government responsibility, with the needed liquidity against available collateral, in order to protect the economy in general, the Prime Minister—who was also the Minister of Finance—was empowered to take all measures appropriate to the general financial situation. Decisions taken in this respect would be settled later on by legislation.

The departments concerned at the Central Bank had already prepared a draft form of credit contract on current account to banks according to the last paragraph of Article 102. At the same time commercial bankers embarked on the necessary measures to mobilise to the Central Bank collateral for their debts. That was to be taken on their personal, civil and penal responsibilities.

Thus, the Bank was working in conformity with the framework envisaged by the Council of Ministers. The Bank Council, however, had felt the necessity to act this way earlier, on 6 November 1975. It seems therefore that the views of both the Council of Ministers and the Bank of Lebanon were parallel, and that there was complete understanding and co-operation between the Bank of Lebanon and the Government which was then very much concerned about the monetary and banking systems. Such co-operation came as no surprise when the Governor of the Bank of Lebanon became the President of the Republic on 8 May 1976. Thus, over and above the common purpose, the head of the Bank of Lebanon's family became the head of the Council of Ministers, i.e., the President of the Republic.

On 23 February 1976 the Bank took a more accommodative stand in the light of the current conditions. It decided the following reductions in interest rates and discount rates beginning 1 March 1976:

(a) to reduce the re-discount rate from 7 to 6 per cent;
(b) to reduce interest rates on purchasing trade bills *en pension* from 7¼ to 6¼ per cent;
(c) to reduce interest rates on loans given under paragraph 3 of Article 102 (exceptional facilities) from 9 per cent to 7 per cent.

An interest rate of 2 per cent was envisaged as penalty on delays in repaying BL loans.

Also in February 1976, the Treasury situation was considered by the Bank of Lebanon. The credit account of the Treasury was decreasing, while Government obligations were increasing. During that eventful period Government borrowing from abroad was not a feasibility. Also, the possibility of borrowing from local banks was not desirable as it was preferable to leave the funds available for banks to help the private sector, satisfying demands of depositors and debtors. Therefore, it appeared to the Bank of Lebanon that there was no escape from granting credit to help the economic sectors in that difficult period, via the National Bank for Industrial and Touristic Development.

In early March 1976 the situation got worse.[24] As the Governor was elected President of the Republic on 8 May 1976, the first Deputy-Governor became an Acting-Governor. Naturally then, the link was stronger between the Government and the Bank. On 20 July 1976 the Bank discussed granting the Treasury drawing facilities according to Article 88. Such facilities were not to exceed 10 per cent of the average receipts of the ordinary state budget over the preceding three closed fiscal years, and for no longer than four months. Articles 89 and 93 were also considered in this regard. According to the former Article Government recourse to the drawing facilities is authorised when it becomes evident to both the Ministry of Finance and the Central Bank that the Treasury's balance at the Bank is inadequate to meet the state's immediate obligations . . . Thus, in view of the demand of the Ministry of Finance and the Treasury's balance (Account No. 36) at the Bank, a drawing facility was granted at the beginning, amounting to LL80 million. The principle was that the state must not stop payments and consequently the Bank was asked to provide the required finance necessary to pay salaries and wages, as well as to provide the country with the basic consumer goods, and to help hospitals to continue their services.

The Central Council thought that should the Government stop payment it would have been most harmful, with far more dangerous consequences than the potential damage due to borrowing from the Central Bank. It also appeared impossible in the circumstances to apply the text of the law with regard to granting credit to the public sector. Because of this impossibility, and the need to provide the Treasury with continuous payments, the Bank approved in principle the provision of the required Government financing, provided that the necessary legislation was enacted as soon as possible. Accordingly, the Central Bank loan to the Government started with a credit line of about LL200 million.

Late in July 1976 the Bank realised that it could not make a thorough appraisal of the banking situation as it was short of the basic statistics. Ever since July 1975 banks had been unable to submit their usual monthly statistics to the Bank of Lebanon. The Bank could not tell what banks had closed since that date, nor did it know everything that the banks were doing, whether they operated in the eastern sector of Beirut, the western sector, or abroad. Clearly also, the duration of the tragedy was unknown. What was known was the amount of destruction of the means of production as well as the number of Lebanese who had left the country. With regard to the banks which had special facilities early in 1976, their collateral presented had lost much of its value[25] so that most of the credit given to banks could have been considered short of enough collateral.

Commercial banks' total deposits at the Bank of Lebanon decreased by LL25 million between 1 March and 22 July 1976. Also, while the deposits of local banks at the Central Bank decreased, those of foreign banks increased.

According to Article 71 of the law, the Bank, as the Government adviser, discussed the subject of Government subsidies for certain consumer goods. It felt that such subsidies were costing the Treasury large amounts every year and that they should be reconsidered with a view to cancelling them for certain goods and reducing them for others. The post-war efforts of the Central Bank were also important. For example, in an emergency meeting the Central Council, on 24 February 1979, discussed the economic situation in the light of the sudden fluctuations in the foreign exchange rate and active speculation against the Lebanese currency. It seemed as though the red line was not yet reached, using the purchasing power parity theory and, therefore, that the Lebanese currency was somehow overvalued. Internally, the purchasing power of the Lebanese currency was being eroded by an inflationary rate of about 18 per cent annually. The Council, however, took a series of measures to reduce the liquidity of the banking system, discouraging bank-lending for speculation against the Lebanese pound.[26]

Moreover, the institutional changes which took place during the war period were, as mentioned previously: the increase in commercial bank branches, which was regulated in June 1978; the abolition of the ban on establishing new commercial banks; and the suggested National Financial Institution to regulate the issue of government bonds and other securities. In addition, the legislation of the banking free zone was enacted in March 1977.

Table 7.1. Monetary statistics (LL Millions)

	1974	1975	1976	1977	1978	1979	1980
BANK OF LEBANON							
Gold	888	946	1,140	1,168	1,170	1,268	1,420
Foreign exchange	2,916	2,913	3,810	4,696	5,505	4,974	5,765
Claims on Government	306	151	811	900	853	1,487	1,954
Claims on private sector	38	45	45	33	76	110	129
Claims on commercial banks	68	98	158	98	76	72	60
Special claims; law No. 28/67	3	11	6	3	1	1	–
Unclassified assets	61	129	56	251	159	199	178
Assets = Liabilities	4,280	4,293	6,026	7,149	7,840	8,111	9,506
Currency outside banks	1,353	2,241	3,084	2,729	3,286	3,506	3,982
Currency in commercial banks	126	166	198	194	382	212	238
Bankers' deposits	1,649	758	929	1,795	1,692	1,465	1,961
Private sector demand deposits	2	7	18	33	24	26	16
Quasi-monetary liabilities	2	2	3	2	3	2	2
Government deposits	978	902	1,491	1,841	1,716	1,829	2,053
Foreign liabilities	7	7	58	65	75	71	81
Capital accounts	90	126	161	213	213	278	370
Unclassified liabilities	73	84	84	275	449	722	803
Escompte & *en pension*	(5)	(36)	(13)	–	–	–	–

COMMERCIAL BANKS							
Reserves	1,667	808	1,074	1,898	2,031	1,390	2,168
Foreign assets	3,980	5,112	4,524	5,770	6,063	9,379	13,401
Claims on Government	36	16	10	475	982	1,066	2,027
Claims on private sector	5,649	6,723	7,141	7,919	9,881	13,029	16,004
Porfolio-securities	79	96	93	112	129	135	162
Unclassified assets	902	734	1,007	1,124	1,376	2,157	3,435
Assets = Liabilities	12,313	13,489	13,849	17,298	20,462	27,156	37,197
Demand deposits	1,642	1,588	1,804	2,300	2,838	3,152	3,668
Time deposits	6,578	6,814	6,299	9,309	11,078	15,182	21,158
Government deposits	344	407	419	490	517	585	586
Foreign liabilities	2,027	2,863	2,807	2,558	3,096	3,909	5,752
Capital accounts	496	551	583	619	683	878	1,180
Unclassified liabilities	1,226	1,266	1,937	2,022	2,249	3,315	4,853
MONETARY SURVEY							
Foreign assets (net)	5,750	6,101	6,609	9,013	9,567	11,641	14,753
Claims on Government (net)	−980	−1,142	−1,089	−959	−399	139	1,342
Claims on private sector	5,692	6,804	7,199	7,952	9,905	13,004	16,133
Special claims; law No. 28/67	3	11	6	3	1	1	–
Total	10,465	11,774	12,725	16,009	19,074	24,785	32,228
Money	2,998	3,836	4,905	5,062	6,148	6,684	7,666
Quasi-money	6,580	6,816	6,302	9,311	11,080	15,184	21,160
Other items (net)	887	1,122	1,518	1,636	1,846	2,917	3,402

Wartime highlights

According to Table 7.1, Central Bank claims on the Government increased from LL151 million in 1975 to LL811 million in 1976, to LL900 million in 1977, dropping to LL853 million in 1978 and rising to LL1,954 million by the end of 1980. Commercial banks claims on the Government were negligible during the years of fighting. Treasury bonds were only LL16 million in 1975 and LL10 million in 1976. Their issue was re-activated in 1977, reaching LL475 million, and LL2,027 million at the end of 1980. Thus, the impact of the public sector operations became cxpansionary as a result of the increased recourse to the banking system to finance budget deficits. And by the end of 1980 the public debt both to the Central Bank and the commercial banks stood at LL3,981 million.

With regard to Central Bank claims on the private sector, the LL38 million in 1974 increased only to LL76 million in 1978 and to LL129 million in 1980.

The Central Bank claims on commercial banks were at their maximum in 1976—LL158 million. But commercial banks' deposits at the Central Bank decreased in 1975 to LL758 million, i.e., by LL891 million. They continued rising in 1976 to LL929 million, and to LL1,795 million in 1977. They decreased to LL1,692 million in 1978, and to LL1,465 million in 1979, to increase again and reach LL2,120 million in June 1980 and LL1,961 million at the end of 1980. The same table shows further that the reserves of the commercial banks have decreased in 1975 by LL859 million, reaching LL808 million. In 1976 it started to increase to LL1,074 million, in 1977 to LL1,898 million, and to LL2,031 million in 1978. In 1979 it stood at LL1,390 million, and at LL2,168 million at the end of 1980.

Commercial banks' claims on the private sector increased in the period 1975–8 by LL3,158 million, or by about 47 per cent. In 1979 they stood at LL13,029 million, i.e., increasing by 30 per cent over 1978. It was a big increase for one year—over three billion Lebanese pounds—and in 1980 it was LL16,004 million. In actual fact, the private sector demand for credit weakened, due to the outbreak of hostilities in 1975–7. However, the increase in deposits induced banks to extend credit rather than keeping idle money.

Money (M1) increased (Table 7.2) in the period 1975–80, from LL3,836 million to LL7,666 million, i.e., by LL3,830 million, or 99.8 per cent. In 1979 M1 increased by LL536 million, or by 9 per cent. In 1980 it increased by LL982 million, or 14.6 per cent. The increase in the money supply before the war was due to the increase in net foreign

Table 7.2. Money and quasi-money, 1974–1980 (LL Millions)

	Money	Net change	Percentage change	Quasi-money	Net change	Percentage change
1974	2,998			6,580		
1975	3,836	838	28	6,816	236	4
1976	4,905	1,069	38	6,302	−514	−8
1977	5,062	157	3	9,311	3,009	48
1978	6,148	1,085	21	11,081	1,770	19
1979	6,684	536	9	15,184	4,103	37
1980	7,666	982	14.6	21,160	5,976	39.3

assets as well as to the increase in credit to the private sector. Moreover, the balance of payments was in surplus and the private sector demand for credit was strong. Budgetary surpluses reflected the contractionary impact of the public sector operations. Naturally the picture has been changed by the war: the balance of payments was not as favourable and, as mentioned previously, economic activity stagnated since there was no demand for credit by the public, and banks in their turn were not keen on risking domestic investment. The recourse of the Government to the banking system to finance budget deficits was expansionary and inflationary.

Quasi-money, on the other hand, decreased in 1976 by LL514 million to LL6,302 million, but returned in 1977 to LL9,311 million and LL11,081 million in 1978, and LL21,160 million in 1980, or 39.3 per cent over the previous year. It reflects the fact that the shift from savings accounts into currency during periods of fighting shifted back to savings deposits when conditions returned to normal.

The figures confirm the advantages of the centre in peace as well as in wartime. Naturally, it is more profitable to extend economic and financial activities beyond national boundaries than to restrict activities inside the homeland. The importance of the centre is therefore not limited by the strip of land of the country itself, but stretched to limits determined by the efficiency and ingenuity of the people and the banking system. The small area of Lebanon did not confine the ambitious Lebanese: it is said that there are more Lebanese abroad than at home. The Lebanese foreign ministry is called 'The Ministry of Foreign Affairs and Lebanese Overseas'. For the same reason, the Lebanese World League has also been established.

Financially, therefore, the growth of the balance sheet of the Lebanese banking system depends on the skill of the Lebanese people, bankers and authorities. The figures also reveal that the centre was of greater importance to Lebanon in wartime, as all domestic sectors were hit, and it had to rely more on the foreign sector. The same can be said of the entrepôt.

The entrepôt

Theoretically, the entrepôt is that part of the banking centre which consists exclusively of foreign or non-resident money. It is completely external to and not included in the money supply of the country. Moreover, those funds could be utilised by the country if needed. Here, they leave the entrepôt to get into the economic circuit of the centre. It is an extra earning function or service the size of which is determined mainly by the efficiency of the banking system. The *raison d'être* of the entrepôt is to reduce dependence on domestic sources of funds, and to exploit foreign sources. It was of real need in the Lebanese War as domestic credit and investment were scarce. Other advantages are the commissions earned, the possible purchases of goods by the proceeds of the loans in the country of the entrepôt, and the contribution to the integration of capital markets.[27] The entrepôt was recognised officially in Lebanon when the free-zone banking legislation was enacted in March 1977. Reserve requirements on non-residents' deposits in foreign currencies were prohibited. Also, the 10 per cent withholding tax on interests paid on these deposits and the fees for deposit insurance were abolished.

Observers noted that much of the capital and most of the international corporations that had left the country due to the war were believed to be willing to return if normal conditions were re-established. Other centres in the region have not been able to replace Beirut fully. The figures show that the Lebanese banks could count on their foreign business more than on domestic activity during the war.

Statistics of commercial banks indicate (Table 7.3) that foreign liabilities decreased from LL2,863 million in 1975 to LL2,807 million in 1976, and to LL2,558 million in 1977. Then they rose to LL3,096 million in 1978, and to LL5,752 million in 1980. Here it is noted that the decrease in foreign liabilities was relatively small and took place only in 1976 and 1977. But with improving conditions, the increase was resumed, indicating that the decrease was a temporary matter and the entrepôt had survived. Also, it is noted that the banks' foreign assets did not decrease except in 1976, after which they soon resumed their increase. Such a decrease in both foreign assets and foreign liabilities seems unimportant relative to the hard time Lebanon has been subject to. Moreover, the fact that foreign assets as well as foreign liabilities began to increase again after 1977

Table 7.3. The variation in foreign flow, 1969–1980 (LL Millions)

Year	Foreign assets	Change	Foreign liabilities	Change
1970	2,087	446	909	75
1971	2,597	510	1,048	139
1972	3,178	581	1,174.2	126
1973	3,624	446	1,520.2	346
1974	3,980	356	2,027.1	507
1975	5,112.2	1,132	2,862.8	835
1976	4,524.5	−588	2,806.8	−55
1977	5,770.4	1,246	2,557.6	−249
1978	6,063.0	293	3,096.0	538
1979	9,379.0	3,316	3,909.0	813
1980	13,401	4,022	5,752	1,843

is clear evidence that Beirut did not lose its role as a financial and banking centre.

In the dark years of fighting, 1975 and 1976, it was naturally the entrepôt that had grown most. The ratio of non-resident foreign liabilities to total resources of the banking system was 24.5 per cent to 24.8 per cent (see Chapter 6, Table 6.6). When relative peace came in 1977 this ratio fell to 17.5 per cent as foreign liabilities decreased by LL249 million, while total resources increased by LL3,328 million.[28] It should be noted that the bulk of the increase in total resources was in time deposits.

Considering the foreign sector, and relations between the banking system and non-residents (Table 7.4), it can be seen that the ratio of foreign liabilities to foreign assets increased during periods of hostilities in the country. For example, it was highest during 1975 and 1976, where it was 56 per cent and 62 per cent respectively. Even in 1978 it had increased. It is evident that this ratio had started to increase ever since 1973, due to internal troubles. In other words, the degree of capital inflow in this case is greater than that of capital outflow. In 1977, a year of relative peace, this ratio dropped, to resume its increase in 1978 as a result of the October fighting that year. The figure for 1979 is 41.68 per cent, a decrease of 9.4 percentage points in that relatively peaceful year. The increase in foreign liabilities was automatic, i.e., without the intervention of the Central Bank. The relative inflow, further, is the factor that has contributed to the relative strength of the exchange rate of the Lebanese pound.

Table 7.4. The ratio (L/A) of non-resident foreign liabilities (L) to non-resident foreign assets (A), 1969–1980

1969	50.82%	1975	56.00%
1970	43.55%	1976	62.03%
1971	40.35%	1977	44.33%
1972	36.94%	1978	51.06%
1973	41.94%	1979	41.68%
1974	50.93%	1980	42.09%

On the other hand, foreign assets increased normally in the pre-war period (1969–74). But in 1975 it was a sharp increase, an indication of great capital outflow. The increase in the simultaneous inflow rose from LL507 million in 1974 to LL835 million in 1975 (Table 7.3). This was abnormal since capital is usually expected to escape in such conditions.

During the period of heavy fighting (1975–6) both foreign assets as well as foreign liabilities decreased, perhaps due to the difficulties in communications. The decrease in foreign assets was LL588 million and in foreign liabilities, LL55 million. The decrease in foreign assets might be considered a positive sign, indicating the absence of capital flight. Foreign assets seem to have increased at the beginning as well as at the end of the war. For example, the increase was LL1,132 million in 1975, and LL1,246 million in 1977.

The decrease in foreign liabilities by LL249 million in 1977 might have been because banks which had borrowed during the war repaid their debts, or part of their debts. The change in foreign liabilities relative to that of foreign assets was about 56 per cent in 1975 and 62 per cent in 1976 (Table 7.4). It meant that the banking system profited from the entrepôt during 1975 as well as in 1976. Further, the importance of the entrepôt was clear in 1976, when both foreign assets and foreign liabilities decreased, but the decrease in the former was much greater than it was in the latter.

At the end of 1979 there was also an increase in foreign assets of LL3,316 million. But here liabilities have increased by only LL813 million, proving that the entrepôt played a smaller role in this year of relative peace. Table 7.4 again indicates the ratio of the retreat of the entrepôt which had decreased by 9.4 per cent to reach 41.68 per cent in 1979 and 42.9 per cent in 1980.

Even in peacetime the role of the Central Bank in the entrepôt is non-existent. In wartime, therefore, nothing changes as far as the Central Bank's role is concerned, as it is discharged from its task of credit regulation in the entrepôt and even in the centre. However, as it is the head of the banking system whose efficiency determines the importance of the entrepôt, the Central Bank is indirectly involved since one of its tasks is to aid in the banking system's development as well as the development of a capital and a money market. The entrepôt is an extra support to a nation under stress.

INFLATION AND MONETARY TARGETING

Inflation

Inflation is inevitable in wartime and it is the worst of the war legacies to the economy. Any destructive force—whether a national war, or an internal civil war, a revolution or even an earthquake—breeds inflation. In such situations, more money is printed than units of production are created. It is the responsibility of the central bank, when the crisis ends, to start a new war on inflation, the new disguised and destructive enemy.

In Lebanon consumer prices rose tremendously during the war period, to slow down in 1977 and in the first half of 1978. Then there was an even greater rise after the events of October 1978. In 1977 the average price level was over 70 per cent higher than its 1974 level. That represented an average annual increase of 19.1 per cent for the three years ending 1977. During the troubles the price index changed from an average of 158.4 per cent in 1974 to 305 per cent in March 1977, to recede to 275.5 per cent in September of the same year.[29] After relative stability in early 1978, food prices rose sharply again from October until the price index reached an average of 323.5 per cent in December. In both 1979 and 1980 the average rise in consumer prices was 23.6 per cent. The official figure, however, was 15.5 per cent, as a different method of calculation was used.[30]

In the United Kingdom over the nine years 1938–47, the index of M1 increased from 100 to 260. The national income, however, has not increased in the same proportion, its ratio rising from 100 to 189.[31]

The United States was in a state of suppressed inflation during the Second World War. As the war progressed direct controls were set up to curb consumer and business spending. At the end of 1945 the percentage increase above levels of six years earlier was 31 per cent for consumer prices, and 39 per cent for wholesale prices. Money balances of the private sector rose by 183 per cent and total holdings of liquid assets of the private sector rose by 230 per cent.[32]

As direct controls were eased, and then removed in 1946, prices immediately rose. Wholesale prices during 1946 rose more than they had done during the entire war period, and the cost of living increased by two-thirds. That showed a large inflationary potential in increased private spending.[33] In 1948 wholesale prices had risen 120 per cent and the cost of living 76 per cent since 1939. Two-thirds of the total rise of wholesale prices and three-fifths of the increase in the cost of living had occurred after the end of the war. The inflation which began in 1946 was sharp and painful.[34] The purchasing power of the dollar declined at the end of 1949 to about 60 cents, compared with its value before the war. About half of this shrinkage occurred in the post-war period.

Deficits arising from wars are beyond the control of fiscal or monetary authorities. They should be met as far as possible from taxation so as to reduce public demand for goods and transfer the buying power to the government. Creating additional buying power at such a time cannot increase output but can only result in a rise in prices.

The proper response in such a situation is to raise as much of the needed funds as possible by tapping current income, i.e., conducting bond-selling campaigns aimed at money which is otherwise likely to be used for current consumption. Tapping existing savings would not be so effective, as it could activate idle funds and thus add to the income stream. If sufficient funds could not be raised by taxation and borrowing from current income, the government would be forced to create money.[35] Raising the bank rate is no solution because the government is the main borrower. Nevertheless, this instrument has been used in Lebanon. What is required, according to Hawtrey,[36] is an extinction of a substantial part of the government indebtedness. Higher taxation helps, but works slowly and there are limits to what the fiscal machine can accomplish and the taxpayer will tolerate.

Targeting

On 11 December 1978 the author suggested a practical procedure on the conduct of monetary policy, taking into consideration objectives and operating guides. It was the method applied in the United Kingdom and the United States to control the growth of monetary aggregates. Naturally, this is to be conducted in the post-war period, since during a war monetary policy is suspended.

Central bankers have to develop operating guides for policy action in order to reach ultimate objectives such as real output, employment, price levels or the balance of payments. Operating guides are interest rates, money supply, total bank credit and the reserve position of the banking system.[37]

Although growth is the primary and real ultimate objective, priority since the late 1970s has been given to price stability as the specific proximate objective, on account of inflationary pressures. The world, therefore, has taken up Jacob Viner's view that the sensible and suitable single goal of a central bank is to maintain the stable purchasing power of the national monetary unit.[38] Low rates of economic expansion in the three years ending 1978 were adopted by almost all industrial countries with a view to limit inflation, and inflation rates have fallen.[39]

Milton Friedman proposed the behaviour of the money supply as the only operating guide, increasing it at a fixed and steady rate equivalent to the rate of potential real output, which was about 3 to 4 per cent a year. It should be noted that Friedman included time and savings deposits in his definition of money supply. Though Federal Reserve officials looked to the behaviour of the money supply as one of their policy guides, it was not the only one they took into account.[40]

However, Congress Resolution No. 133 of March 1975 stated that the Federal Reserve Board should 'Maintain long-run growth of the monetary and credit aggregates commensurate with the economy's long-run potential to increase production'. Simultaneously the resolution called on the Federal Reserve to 'consult with Congress' periodically on its 'objectives and plans with respect to the ranges of growth or diminution of monetary and credit aggregates in the up-coming 12 months.' It was, according to Mr Paul A. Volcker, then President of the Federal Reserve Bank of New York, the first normal congressional recognition of the importance of quantifying monetary objectives in terms of monetary aggregates for a period of time ahead. That gave rise to the present systematic procedures on projected money growth ranges, or targets.[41]

The essence of the procedure is as follows:

(i) broader definition of the money supply, including time and savings deposits, as the most important monetary aggregate, and used as a target and at the same time as an indicator of monetary policy;
(ii) projections of monetary growth;
(iii) establishment of appropriate targets, ranges or single points, for the growth of monetary aggregates.

Volcker supports the use of monetary targets with a different perspective from the 'monetarist' view. To him it does not imply that inflation can be explained almost entirely by monetary factors. But in the longer run there is a general parallel between monetary performance and price performance. He adds that 'the core of truth about the relation of money to inflation is that the latter cannot proceed for long without sufficient rapid monetary growth to accommodate it. It follows therefore that inflation cannot be eliminated for any significant period without a corresponding elimination of monetary excesses'. To reduce or eliminate inflation over time, monetary growth rate will have to slow down. 'As inflation has drawn attention to monetary objectives and behaviour, it has also tended to undermine the usefulness of interest rates as guides to central bank policy. There is no sure way to estimate the inflation component in nominal interest rates today, i.e. the "real" level of interest rates.'

The United States, Canada and other key countries have started to specify quite precisely the growth ranges, projections, and targets for certain monetary aggregates over a period of a year or so ahead.[42] Monetary targeting is a useful tool of communication with the public. Volcker views the 'monetary targeting' approach as an effort to adopt a new, and in many ways, more sensible and comprehensible symbol of responsible policy. He adds: 'The day is past when any instrument of Governmental policy, including monetary policy, can expect to be effective without exposing the objectives and policies to public scrutiny. Monetary targets lend themselves to such scrutiny.' Finally, he stresses the importance of targeting as a discipline on monetary authorities.

But monetary targets do not in themselves alter the real problems and hard choices imposed by the economic structure itself. To expect that approach to carry the whole burden therefore is to expect too much.[43] To the Federal Reserve the right path for monetary targets would be one of gradual reduction; in this way the gradual reduction in inflation would be consistent with continuing recovery.

Germany and Switzerland set annual targets as single points for monetary aggregates. Germany uses Central Bank money—a variation on high-powered money or the monetary base—as the primary target of its operations. Switzerland and Canada use M1 as their single target. The British Government has gradually been drawn into setting a monetary target. France announced a target for M3 in 1966, and Japan appeared to follow suit.

The United States

Regarding the procedure for setting monetary targets, the Chairman of the Board of Governors of the Federal Reserve System announces once each quarter in congressional testimony 'targets' for each of the three monetary growth measures—currently the narrowly defined money supply (M1), and two broader definitions (M2 and M3).[44] M1 is currency plus private demand deposits adjusted. (It is the same as the UK M1.)

M2 is M1 plus bank time and savings deposits adjusted, other than large certificates of deposit (CDs). (It is the same as the UK M3, except that the US M2 excludes large negotiable certificates of deposit.)

M3 is M2 plus deposits at mutual savings banks and savings and loan associations and credit union shares. M4 is M2 plus large negotiable CDs. M5 is M3 plus large negotiable CDs.

The targets are ranges measured in terms of percentage growth from the level of the previous quarter to the level four quarters hence. The ranges themselves are defined in terms of upper and lower limits for growth rates in three definitions of the money supply, as measured from the most recent quarterly average levels to the prospective levels four quarters ahead. The procedure for setting monetary targets is the result of a vote by the Federal Open Market Committee (FOMC). The Committee members vote for that set of target numbers they think is most likely to produce good results for the economy over the coming year, given the information at hand. They choose between alternatives. The economists at the Board of Governors of the Federal Reserve System and at the reserve banks assist, trying to project the consequences for the economy of alternative target ranges. These projections range from the use of econometric models to purely judgemental projections, with various combinations in between.

There are many other problems connected with monetary aggregate targets—problems in setting the targets, in hitting the targets, and indeed limits to what the approach can accomplish in improving the performance of the economy. Targeting is not a rigid mechanical process: it requires judgement in determining the levels of the targets, and the way to set and change them.

When the aggregates grow strongly the committee begins limiting the extent to which it accommodates the demand for member bank reserves. As the rate of economic expansion is moderated, the committee gradually shifts emphasis to promote a step-up in the growth of the aggregate through a more accommodative approach to the provisions of reserves. The committee continues to focus on a one-year time horizon and also adopts short-run instructions, prescribing a trading-desk response, through open-market operations, to indications of undesired strength or weakness in the monetary aggregates.

At each meeting the committee specifies conditions for bank reserve availability as measured by the federal funds rate. It also specifies for changing that rate within designated limits when projections in the aggregates indicate significant weakness or strength relative to the ranges specified for the two-month period covering the month of latest meeting and the following month.

Following each FOMC meeting, the account manager seeks to achieve the committee's current objectives through operations in Treasury and Federal agency securities and bankers' acceptances. Decisions about the size and type of operations and their timing are based partly on projections of reserve availability. The manager of the open-market account looks to the behaviour of the Federal funds rate for additional information on factors affecting the supply of, and demand for, bank reserves.[45]

Despite some disappointments, Davies considered that the kind of chronic inflation in which the United States found itself for nearly ten years prior to 1978, made a powerful case for the value of monetary targets:

(a) as a measure of the performance of policy;
(b) as a general guide to the strategic direction policy must take;
(c) as a useful device (to the extent credible) to help contain and reduce inflationary expectations;
(d) as a rallying point for support of prudent monetary policy;
(e) finally, in the form of targeted reductions in monetary growth, as a necessary, though perhaps not sufficient, substantive contribution to reducing inflation.[46]

The United Kingdom

It seems that the United Kingdom has adopted almost the same procedures and principles as those used in the United States. On 9 November 1978 the Chancellor announced that the target for the growth of sterling M3 for the year to October 1979 would be 8 per cent to 12 per cent. He announced the monetary target for 1978–79 in the budget speech, indicating that the target would be reviewed and rolled forward at six-monthly intervals. On the same day, the minimum lending rate was increased from 10 per cent to 12 per cent.[47]

It seems that the procedure for projecting, targeting and controlling the growth of monetary aggregates was successful in the United Kingdom. The Governor of the Bank of England referred to this in 1978, and expressed the opinion that monetary policy was and must be basic to the suppression and abolition of inflation. He added that they had been working for this for years. In fact, the emphasis in the Bank of England has been to continue to consider it as a specific proximate policy target since 1973. It constituted an internal aim until 1976, when it became a publicly-declared quantitative target.

It was not entirely accidental that the growth of sterling M3 amounted to about 10 per cent during each of the three years ending in 1976.[48] It was a rate below that of the expansion of the national income at current prices. What is worth noting is that that was achieved during a period in which inflation, though declining, was still at a high rate, and the financing requirement of the public sector increased notably.[49]

'Monetary policy cannot or should not be left to fight inflation single-handed', the Governor of the Bank of England is quoted as saying. To him, the essence of monetary management was to act to offset divergences from forecasts in the sources of monetary expansion. So long as it is possible to correct such divergences within a few months so as to return to the charted path, it is not important if monetary growth goes temporarily off course. Monetary developments, however, should not be allowed to diverge for too long from the norm. The need is to have clear and simple targets, and the Governor showed satisfaction in selecting M3. In conclusion, he explained that they had not adopted a monetarist philosophy in its entirety but enough of it to fulfil Volcker's definition of 'practical monetarism'.[50]

Lebanon

A broader definition of the money supply seems more appropriate in Lebanon than in either the United States or the United Kingdom. The distinction between demand deposits and time deposits in Lebanon is less precise. A depositor can sometimes ask to withdraw his time deposits even before maturity and the banks may acquiesce, considering a positive response a matter of prestige.

Also, with regard to foreign exchange deposits, the Lebanese free foreign exchange system makes them, in practice, virtual deposits in Lebanese currency. In fact, it has been the practice of commercial banks to make use of their foreign assets as a reserve of liquid resources for the creation of credit (see Chapter 1). The net inflow of funds into Lebanon in any foreign asset would offer the banking system an opportunity to increase lending in the domestic market, whereas a reduction in those foreign assets would reduce banks' capacity and willingness to lend or to create credit. Commercial banks can convert foreign assets into Lebanese assets in the free money market of Lebanon. Thus, they can meet claims of depositors by converting some of their dollar assets into Lebanese pounds, should their liquid reserves be inadequate. However, the fear of exchange fluctuations and losses in the conversion of foreign exchange into Lebanese pounds and vice versa is a constraint.

Thus, one cannot but suggest for Lebanon a broader definition of the money supply, in addition to the recent procedures in executing monetary policy such as projections and targeting, in controlling the growth rate of the monetary aggregates. There is no reason why the Bank of Lebanon should not plan the right path even if it cannot immediately walk on it.

It can try such a procedure and see how applicable and effective it would be. The Bank of Lebanon could adopt M2, which is almost the same as that used in the United States but equivalent to sterling M3 in the United Kingdom. It would include paper notes and coins plus demand deposits and time and savings deposits in Lebanese currency for Lebanese residents in the private sector. It is sufficient to adopt M2 in Lebanon as it is possible to control its component parts. Lebanese M3 should be used only for analysis because the free foreign exchange system means that it includes foreign exchange in Lebanon.

The proximate or immediate objective is price stability. And it is worth closing the door against even illiquid kinds of money. Here the door is being closed against the component parts of the aggregate, such as time and savings deposits, since they carry the potential of being made liquid.

After adopting the broader definition of money (M2 = M1 + savings and time deposits in Lebanese pounds of the private sector residents), the method of projection is decided upon. As a basis, certain previous years are chosen. There is then the possibility of reducing rates of growth within a target range between the upper and lower limits. (This is known as targeting.)

There are various means that can influence the rate of growth of these monetary aggregates, which might be appropriate to the needs of the Lebanese economy. In the United Kingdom supplementary special deposits have been used to influence the structure of interest rates. The bank rate has been used in a more flexible way to influence short-term rates. In the United States both variations in the minimum reserve assets ratio and special deposits have been used to influence the structure of interest rates, rendering this control more efficient. The control operation is performed through the use of the Federal Funds Rate, week-to-week on the basis of the fluctuation in banks' reserves.

In Lebanon it is possible to use M2 and to attempt to control its component parts or some of their counterparts with the Bank of Lebanon's credit control weapons. Also, the Bank of Lebanon can take into consideration the factors which influence demand for money in the particular circumstances of the country.

Table 7.5 illustrates the development of the money supply in Lebanon under its various definitions. Further, the table groups the years under study (1974–80) into three periods in an attempt to produce averages as near as possible to the real world. It could be seen that in the first period the rate of growth of M1 was only 3.4 per cent, which was roughly the rate of inflation. It seems, further, that the rate of inflation was felt more in the second and third periods when again it was very near to the rate of growth of M1.

Table 7.5. Developments of the monetary aggregates, 1964–1980 (LL Millions)

End of Year	MO	%	M1	%	M2	%	M3	%
1964	500		1,390					
1965	547		1,510	8.63				
1966	645		1,541	2.05				
1967	786		1,570	3.97				
1968	834		1,759	1.88				
1969	868		1,657	12.04	2,840		3,719	
1970	845		1,676	5.80	3,254	14.58	4,268	14.76
1971	919		2,034	1.15	4,406	35.40	5,370	25.82
1972	1,033		2,275	21.36	5,311	20.54	6,382	18.85
1973	1,226		2,619	11.85	6,196	16.66	7,733	21.17
1974	1,353		2,998	15.12	7,686	24.08	9,578	23.86
1975	2,241		3,836	14.47	8,565	38.23	10,652	11.21
1976	3,084		4,905	27.95	9,425	10.40	11,207	21.03
1977	2,729		5,062	3.20	11,778	24.96	14,373	28.25
1978	3,286	20.4	6,148	21.5	14,533	23.4	17,229	20.0
1979	3,506	6.7	6,684	8.1	16,262	11.9	21,868	26.9
1980	3,982	13.6	7,667	14.7	19,830	21.9	28,826	31.8

Selected periods	%	%	%	%
1964–70	9.8	3.4		
1970–74	12.3	14.2	20.6	19.8
1974–78	19.6	16.9	15.9	14.7
1974–76	(51)	(27.9)	(10.7)	(8.2)
1976–78	(3.2)	(11.8)	(24.1)	(23.7)

Notes: Lebanese M2 = M1 + time and savings deposits in Lebanese currency by residents in the private sector. Lebanese M3 = M2 + foreign exchange deposits by residents in the private sector.

The growth of M1 until the end of 1979 was projected on the basis of its annual rate of growth during the period 1976–8, which was 11.8 per cent, or even 12 per cent. The target range of the growth here was established between 10 and 15 per cent.[51] It seems that the percentage change in the growth rates of M1 was highest in 1976 (27.9 per cent), and only 3.2 per cent in 1977. This is typical of a war year followed by relative peace. On the same basis, projections and target ranges for the rates of growth of M2 and M3 were calculated for the year ending 1979. The rate for M2 was 24.1 per cent with a target range between 20 and 27 per cent. M3 was 23.7 per cent with a target range between 18 and 25 per cent.[52]

In fact the growth of M1 until the end of 1979 was 8.9 per cent. Such a modest growth was due mainly to the decrease in the rate of growth of sight deposits in Lebanese pounds. Also, the actual rate of growth of M2 was 12 per cent, i.e., it was within the projected range. M3 actually increased to 27 per cent due to the increase in foreign currency deposits, resulting from the increase in the interest rates in the Euro-market during 1979.

'Practical monetarism'

Monetary aggregate targeting is a scientific procedure which every serious central bank must use. Policy must be developed in the light of the monetary aggregates, or any combination of their component parts or counterparts. But this refers only to controlling the growth rate of the money supply. There remains the rest of the process, from controlling the money supply M to controlling the general price level P where M alone is not enough. Here lies the crux of the whole problem, and this is why both Paul Volcker (the President of the Federal Reserve Bank of New York) and the Governor of the Bank of England took a different view from that of the purely monetarist philosophy, adopting instead what Volcker has called 'practical monetarism'.

It is fascinating to compare the views of Volcker with those of Benjamin Strong, Governor of the Federal Reserve Bank fifty years earlier. Governor Strong was a Keynesian before Keynes, in fact Keynes quoted Strong in his argument against the quantity theorists. Keynes asked whether it was within the power of a central bank to fix the value of money at any prescribed level.[53] To him, the water-level in a reservoir depended not only on pouring enough water into it, but also on other factors such as 'the natural rainfall, evaporation, leakage and the habits of the users of the system'.

Keynes became sympathetic to 'some of the doubts and hesitations well expressed by Governor Strong in 1927 before the Committee of the United States Congress on Stabilization'. Governor Strong, then, expressed reasonable doubts towards a proposed amendment to the Federal Reserve Act to lay upon the Federal Reserve Board the duty 'to promote a stable price-level for commodities in general'.[54] He said: 'the tendency to look at the price-level as though it operated up and down against a counterweight of credit' is an over-simplification of price problems. There are sometimes situations where the relation of prices to other elements presents 'a real practical puzzle of management'. For example, the introduction of credit or the lowering of the interest rate might well correct prices, but might at the same time have adverse consequences for the amount of credit employed in support of speculation in stocks. 'There you are between the devil and the deep sea . . .' Sometimes there are many other factors far beyond the influence of the volume and cost of credit on the price-level, such as the needs of the people. 'Human effort and human consumption (producers and consumers) are the ultimate matters from which alone economic transactions are capable of deriving any significance.'[55]

Governor Strong added another possibility that has always struck him 'as inherent in any recognition of a power to regulate prices, i.e., the everlasting contest that takes place within all humanity between the producer and the consumer . . .' It seems to him that if the Federal Reserve System were recognised as a price regulator, it would be 'in the position of the poor man who tried to stop a row between an Irish man and his wife. They both turned in and beat him.'[56] Here Keynes concluded: 'these are reasonable doubts expressed by persons of great experience. They cannot be dispelled merely by pointing to the truism of a Quantity Equation'.[57] 'The relationship of the purchasing power of money (or price-level of consumption goods) and the price-level of output as a whole to the quantity of money and the velocity and circulation is not of that direct character which the old-fashioned quantity equations might lead one to suppose.'[58]

In his Treatise Keynes has claimed to prove that 'the price-level of output' depends on:[59]

— the level of money-incomes relative to efficiency;
— the volume of investment (measured in cost of production) relative to saving; and
— the 'bearish' or 'bullish' sentiment of capitalists relative to the supply of savings-deposits available in the banking system.

Keynes claimed also that the banking system can control the supply of savings-deposits, and by the terms of credit influence, can control the volume of investment. It can also control the money offers which entrepreneurs make to the factors of production by the indirect effects of the volume of investments. But the banking system, he said, cannot produce any of these effects instantaneously, and cannot be expected always to foresee the operation of non-monetary factors in time to take measures in advance to counteract their influence on prices.[60]

To Keynes, 'the banking system has no direct control over the prices of individual commodities or over the rates of money earnings of the factors of production. Nor has it, in reality, any *direct* control over the quantity of money . . .' The control of prices is exercised indirectly through the control of investment; there is nothing that the central authority can do except to influence the rate of investment. Thus, the art of the management of money is to possess enough knowledge and powers of prognostication to devise technical methods to exercise a sensitive control over the rate of investment.[61]

One could perhaps explore further into monetarism, realising the limits of the quantity theory and consequently the limits of monetary policy. One could therefore monitor the progress of money in its journey to control *P* (price level), rather than being satisfied with only controlling its growth rate, leaving it single-handed in the economic jungle. One should not ignore the interaction of money with other economic variables, or to what takes place in the economic 'haze' where, in the words of Keynes, 'nothing is clear and everything is possible'.[62] One must not take the easiest way out, going back to the classical position, satisfied to consider *M* as the dominant factor. The matter should not be left to the invisible hand described by Adam Smith—science does not recognise anything invisible. Surely Professor Milton Friedman realises that the matter is not that simple: visible hands rather than the invisible must strive to explore and contribute to the interaction of money in the economy.

It seems then preferable to proceed from the Keynesian analysis either to extend central banking techniques to touch on other variables, or to set up a *central economic institution* with enough powers to deal with those variables even if they are outside the monetary field, wherever that might lead to.

Sir Roy Harrod refers Milton Friedman (as a quantity theorist) to the Keynesian analysis of liquidity preference, which explains why the velocity of circulation (*V*) in the Fisher sense is very plastic for a long time.[63]

The limits on monetary management or monetary policy are, in other words, limits upon the whole science of central banking in order to deal with the economy and even to safeguard the value of the monetary unit itself. The magisterial work of Keynes shifted the emphasis from the supply side (where the classical economists put it) to the demand side. More recently, Friedman has come to regard money 'as an important field where economics is proved to be an empirical science with fundamental regularities'.[64] However, according to Lawrence Harris, recent empirical studies in the United States (1967) suggest that there are important systematic relationships between money and other economic variables. But there is no agreement on how monetary policy affects the economy.[65]

Growth which contributes to the increase of real output is theoretically a great limit on inflation in offsetting the increase in the money supply (*M*). To safeguard *M*, therefore, the central bank must either limit the growth rate of *M*, or contribute to economic growth. According to the monetarist approach, prices rise with the growth of *M* and with a rise in the velocity of circulation V, but fall with real growth (P $M + V - Y$). Thus, the central banker must be growth-minded, since increasing productivity and real output is as important in limiting inflation as controlling the growth rate of the money supply. Again, in the words of Sir Roy Harrod, inflation and growth conflict with each other. 'Price inflation', says Harrod, 'is bad for growth because it reduces the incentive to save, because it erodes amortisation funds, and because it blurs the criteria that are required to guide investment decisions.'[66]

It so happened that during the Lebanese War and post-war period the rate of inflation was parallel to the substantial increase in the growth rate of the money supply. This makes the quantity theory of money more attractive. Here it may be expedient for a central banker to make up his mind with regard to the all-important question of whether he is a Keynesian, a quantity theorist, or a practical monetarist. Being a quantity theorist or a monetarist is implied by his field of operations. Over and above this, he should be a practical monetarist because, while realising the overwhelming importance of money in the economy, he is also aware that monetary policy cannot fight inflation single-handed. There must be constructive co-ordination between monetary, fiscal and perhaps other policies. Keynes' thinking was entirely responsible for the inclusion of 'fiscal' in the now widely-used phrase 'monetary and fiscal policies'.[67]

In his fundamental equations Keynes does not use the money supply as a direct determinant of the price-level.[68]

$$P = \frac{E}{O} + \frac{I' - S}{R}$$

$$= \frac{W}{e} + \frac{I' - S}{R}$$

$$\pi = \frac{W}{e} \quad \frac{I - S}{O}$$

The money supply is implicit in the equations, as for example E, which is the money income on earnings, is equal to MV or to GNP in money terms. Here Keynes shifted the emphasis to the demand side. The price level P is here influenced by the ratio of total money income of the community E to the total output of goods O. Further, the price level of consumer goods is influenced by the ratio of the difference between savings S and cost investment I' (or the windfall gains or losses on consumption goods),[69] to the output as a whole (or the volume of consumption goods and services), R. Again, P is influenced by the rate of earnings per unit of human effort (or cost per unit of goods, or wage rate) W, in relation to the coefficient of efficiency (output per unit of effort) e.

Further, in the final form of the fundamental equations the price level of output as a whole π is also influenced by the wage rate W in relation to the coefficient of efficiency e plus value of investment I minus savings S (or total windfall gains or losses on consumption goods as well as on investment goods) over the total output of goods O.

The price level π is indirectly affected since it can affect one of the variables on the right-hand side of the equation and hence affect price indirectly. For example, if M is increased, interest will fall, I will rise, hence π will rise. But for this to happen, the change in interest ought first to affect I. Also, if W rises more than e, then π will rise, i.e., if wages rise more than productivity, cost inflation will occur.

Looking at the numerators and denominators in the equations, they appear as ratios of money units to units of productivity or real output—wage rate or cost per unit W over output per unit e + total windfall gains or losses over total output. In other words, they seem to be the clear and simple expression of inflation, 'money chasing goods'.

Thus, to control P, according to Keynes, is to control the money income or earnings of the community relative to the total output of goods as well as other ratios set out in his equations.

The equations distinguished between cost inflation representing the ratio of wage increases to productivity increases W/P, and demand inflation (aggregate demand) which will tend to raise prices if I' exceeds S and to depress them when S exceeds I'.

Total demand for goods and services springs from the propensity to invest and the propensity to consume. An increase in either propensity, when there is unemployment, results in increased activity, but with full employment it will be met by higher prices.[70]

If the total demand for goods and services is above the supply potential of the economy there will be inflationary pressure, and if it is below the supply potential there will be unemployment. This is the effect of the two propensities on the price level. The investment demand for goods and services is related to the total demand by the 'multiplier' which is the reciprocal of the propensity to save.

Keynes, therefore, though a firm believer in the importance of money in the economy as a whole, thought that its effect on the price-level 'was devious and had to operate indirectly through its effect on one or other of the terms in [his] fundamental equations'.[71] The equations, explains Harrod, have no reference to the quantity of money in specifying the determinants of the price-level. Keynes was not concerned mainly with the quantity of money, but with the level of efficiency wages, the amount of savings and the amount of investment.[72] Investment demand and consumer demand are two major forces operating directly on the price-level.[73]

To Keynes, a change in the quantity of money operated on prices through interest rates. The effect of such a change depended on the elasticity of the liquidity preference. Next comes the effect of a change in interest rates on investment, whose effect on the economy depends on the current value of the multiplier.[74]

In this regard, Hawtrey wondered whether one of Keynes' aims had been 'to devise a non-monetary theory of money'.[75] He added that savings, investments, consumption, non-available output, changes in relative prices and changes in prices relative to wages and costs, are all non-monetary concepts. This resulted in 'an explanation of monetary phenomena in terms of non-monetary concepts'.

This non-monetary theory of money seems natural since money, besides being in itself an asset, represents non-monetary assets. By definition, money is a measure of value, a store of value and a medium of exchange, etc., of any economic assets or goods and services. It cannot be isolated from these non-monetary assets or goods and services. A mutual influence operates between money and non-monetary assets and all are subject to policy decisions. Thus, it becomes simple logic to think in terms of a non-monetary theory of money.

In Lebanon, where inflation is higher than elsewhere at present, M must be controlled since M in this case affects prices. It is claimed in Lebanon that investment is not responsive to the rate of interest, especially in wartime. The demand for credit depends on the security situation rather than on interest rates. The Keynesian theory is said to be inappropriate here because it is held that Keynes did not care about inflation: his theory would be more appropriate to a period of recession. This is why monetarists turned back to the quantity theory, claiming that it is only monetary policy that works. And the trend today is more monetarist than Keynesian, due to substantial rates of inflation. Contrary to the thinking of the fifties in Britain there is now little scepticism as regards the power of monetary policy in the United States, Germany and Japan.[76]

Would the steering wheel today be safer in the hands of central banks rather than under the invisible hand of Adam Smith? Would the experience of the eighties warrant setting up a central economic institution instead of a central bank to operate on other economic variables, even those outside the monetary field?

Sayers holds that, as the economy is made up of people whose liquidity situation is subject to change, central bankers must exercise a discretionary influence upon the monetary situation which at present follows no set code of rules. Central banks have to adapt their ways to the shape of the community's constantly-changing financial habits.[77]

Monetary policy must aim for growth as well as targeting because growth and monetary policy are the two sides of the coin in fighting inflation. Thus, measures should be taken to increase productivity and real output which would lead eventually to price stability along with real growth. But such measures are outside the field of central banking, and other measures to remove bottlenecks and wasteful uses of resources are also not in the power of the central bank. Exports could be encouraged and plans for industry financed. Also, by providing information on markets or on investment possibilities obstacles can be removed on the supply side. Jacob Viner,[78] however, does not allow the central bank to maintain a growth objective, though others see it as an important factor in the fight against inflation and even in safeguarding the monetary unit.

Volcker lucidly recommends 'eliminating monetary excesses in order not to feed inflation', yet Sir Roy Harrod cites an example of a rise in prices (in Britain in 1968) without an increase in the money supply as high as the increase in *PT*, or in GNP.[79] According to Harrod, the price rise was due to wage increases in excess of increases in productivity. Consequently, Harrod adds, according to the quantity theory *V* must have been rising.[80] And here inflation was fed more by excessive wage increases than by an increase in *M*. Here Harrod seems to depart from the spirit of the quantity theory, confessing that he 'should disclaim being a quantity theorist'.[81]

The question put by Harrod was whether or not monetary policy can have an important influence on the course of events.[82] He felt that 'the whole liquidity position' is influenced by operating on the quantity of money. Also, what causes the 'diffused difficulty of borrowing' is the reduction in the money supply which is not secondary but more 'critical' than interest-rate policy.[83]

Modern monetarists, led by Milton Friedman, shared the quantity theorist's view in considering *V* and *K* relatively—but not completely—stable and predictable enough to enable monetary policy to regulate aggregate demand through controlling *M*.[84]

Money is like water to the land or blood to the body. The central banker must ensure a good circulatory system, helping such circulation to all parts of the body despite obstacles in the economic maze. Central banking, therefore, as a discretionary control on the monetary system, must extend its work to other relevant fields in the economy. The central banker should seek out not only 'the newly important sensitive spots' which have changed with the changing structure of the economic system, but all spots in order 'to keep the financial structure upon an even keel'.[85]

The concluding question is why, since the quantity theory has limitations, should not the authorities proceed from targeting to use the analysis of Keynes and Harrod, exploring all possibilities so as to work on the other economic variables besides money. In fact, it is impractical to isolate monetary from fiscal policy. 'Practical monetarism' seems to imply that pure monetarism is impractical.

Examining the workings of the monetary and banking system in Lebanon in a state of war, one wonders whether one can really be looking at Lebanon or another, more peaceful country. Banking regulations were imposed by the authorities, as was the case before the war, and the system has continued to function normally (except in periods of heavy fighting). It is fascinating indeed to find banking and central banking working regularly, respecting laws and regulations, and all within a state of anarchy.

A thorough macro-economic analysis of the financial aspects of the reconstruction plan was suggested for Lebanon in order that the monetary, balance of payments and price indications were adequately examined with a view to formulating policies to minimise pressures on available resources. The authorities welcomed IMF assistance to study the macro-economic implications of the plan and requested the services of an IMF staff member to promote policy co-ordination between the Ministry of Finance, the Bank of Lebanon and the Council for Development and Reconstruction.

The IMF noted with satisfaction that Lebanon continued to maintain its free foreign exchange system. It also believed that the measures taken by the Government to avoid a resurgence of inflationary pressures with various price, exchange rate and other policies, were 'well designed' and that with 'resolute implementation they should contribute to an improvement in the economic situation'.

Crowning the whole work was the appraisal of the IMF authorities in the Executive Board early in 1980. They expressed the view that the developments reflected 'the highly responsible fiscal, monetary, and exchange rate policies pursued by the authorities'. One representative said that in the circumstances the authorities had been able to manage the economy with 'an admirable degree of skill, courage, and imagination'; another said that 'the Lebanese economy had shown a high degree of resilience and that the economic policies pursued showed a willingness to react quickly to incipient inflationary pressures'. The United States representative expressed sympathy for the situation and deep appreciation for 'the sound economic policies pursued by the authorities in the very difficult circumstances'. He was particularly impressed with the relatively low inflation rate and the flexible exchange rate policy. The directors remarked that the authorities were subject to considerable stresses due to unsettled conditions in Lebanon, but that in the face of these stresses 'the economy had shown remarkable resilience and the authorities have managed a very difficult situation with admirable skill'.

NOTES

1. The price of petrol rose to twelve times its ordinary level in the western sector, and sometimes twenty-four times in the eastern sector.
2. *Arab Economist*, monthly periodical, Beirut, October 1978, p. 6.
3. Ibid., November 1978, p. 19.
4. Ibid., p. 20.
5. Ibid., p. 19.
6. Ibid., June 1979, pp. 16–17.
7. Ibid., December 1978, p. 12.
8. *An Nahar*, Beirut daily, 5 November 1979.
9. The Governor's speech, at the banquet of the Bankers' Association held in his honour, at the Bristol Hotel, on 22 October 1979.
10. Crowther, Geoffrey, *An Outline of Money*, p. 165.
11. Sayers, R. S., *Central Banking After Bagehot*, p. 3.
12. Chandler, Lester, V., *Benjamin Strong, Central Banker*, p. 99.
13. Chandler, *The Economics of Money and Banking*, p. 522.
14. Hawtrey, R. G., *The Art of Central Banking*, p. 268.
15. Hawtrey, R. G., *Economic Rebirth*, London, 1946, pp. 12 and 14.
16. Chandler, *The Economics of Money and Banking*, pp. 524–5.
17. Ibid., p. 528.
18. Ibid., p. 532.
19. Ibid., p. 528.
20. See Joint Development Group, *The Postwar Development of the Republic of Vietnam, Policies and Programs*.
21. Scigliano, Robert, *South Vietnam, Nation Under Stress*, p. viii.
22. The Gross Domestic Product or expenditure increased from LL7,105 million in 1973 to LL8,200 million in 1977. It is estimated for 1980 to be LL18.5 billion.
23. The real rate is the official rate deflated by an appropriate price index, normally the wholesale price index.
24. It was even impossible for both the author and the Director of the Ministry of National Economy to attend the meeting of the Central Council.
25. Because it belonged to ruined clients.
26. See Chapter 6, pp. 171–2.
27. Einzig, Paul, *Foreign Dollar Loans in Europe*, p. 49.
28. Demand deposits increased by LL496 million; time deposits increased by LL3,010 million and government deposits by LL71 million, while foreign liabilities decreased by LL249 million.
29. 1966 = base year.
30. The higher figure was given by the trade unions, using the average increase in 1980, for example, relative to the average increase in the previous year. The official figure, in contrast, uses the figures of December 1980 relative to the December figure of 1979.

31. Crowther, op. cit., p. 172.
32. Chandler, *The Economics of Money and Banking*, pp. 524–6.
33. Ibid.
34. Ibid.
35. Goldenweiser, *American Monetary Policy*, pp. 227–32.
36. The interesting historical example of the forced loan imposed in Czechoslovakia in 1919 was a crude device to correct the excess money. It was an emergency measure by which paper currency in circulation was reduced by one half at a single stroke. All paper money notes were cut in half. One half of each note retained one half of its face value. The other half entitled the holder to a bond participating in an interest-bearing government loan equivalent to half of the face value. Hawtrey, *Economic Rebirth*, pp. 47–8.
37. Chandler, *The Economics of Money and Banking*, pp. 255–6.
38. Viner, Jacob, *Problems of Monetary Control, Essays in International Finance, No. 45*, p. 35.
39. 'Reflexions on the conduct of monetary policy,' the First Mais Lecture, given by the Governor at the City University, London on 9 February 1978, *Bank of England Quarterly Bulletin*, March 1978, p. 34.
40. Chandler, *The Economics of Money and Banking*, p. 356.
41. Volcker, Paul A., 'Monetary Targets in an Age of Inflation', *Journal of Monetary Economics*, 1977.
42. Volcker, Paul A., 'A Broader Role for Monetary Targets', *Federal Reserve Bank of New York Quarterly Review*, Spring 1977, Vol. 2, p. 25.
43. Volcker, Paul A., 'Monetary Targets in an Age of Inflation', op. cit., p. 64.
44. *Federal Reserve Bulletin*, June 1975, p. 342.
45. Holmes, A. R., and Sternlight, P. D., 'The Implementation of Monetary Policy in 1976', *Federal Reserve Bank of New York Quarterly Review*, Spring 1977, p. 41.
46. Davies, Richard, 'The Federal Reserve's Use of Longer Term Targets for Monetary Growth', talk to the City University of London, 9 March 1978, p. 32.
47. *Bank of England Quarterly Bulletin*, December 1978, p. 499.
48. Ibid., p. 534.
49. *Bank of England Quarterly Bulletin*, 9 February 1978, p. 33.
50. Ibid.
51. This was tested in the research department of the Bank of Lebanon.
52. Lebanese M3 = Lebanese M2 + foreign exchange deposits of the private sector residents.
53. Keynes, John Maynard, *A Treatise on Money*, Vol. 2, p. 339.
54. Ibid., p. 340.
55. Keynes, *A Treatise on Money*, Vol. 1, p. 134.
56. Keynes, *A Treatise on Money*, Vol. 2, p. 343.
57. Ibid., p. 345.
58. Keynes, *A Treatise on Money*, Vol. 1, p. 146.
59. Keynes, *A Treatise on Money*, Vol. 2, pp. 345–446.
60. Ibid., pp. 339–446.
61. Ibid., pp. 211–12.
62. Ibid., p. 292.
63. Harrod, *Money*, p. 161.
64. Whittlesey and Wilson, *Essays in Money and Banking in Honour of R. S. Sayers*, p. 109.
65. Ibid., p. 109.
66. Harrod, op. cit., pp. 77–8.
67. Ibid., p. 162.
68. Ibid., p. 111.

69. Hawtrey, R. G., *The Art of Central Banking*, p. 34.
70. Harrod, op. cit., p. 167.
71. Ibid., p. 166.
72. Ibid., pp. 181–2.
73. Ibid., p. 168.
74. Ibid., p. 182.
75. Hawtrey, *The Art of Central Banking*, p. 359.
76. Harrod, Roy, 'Topical Comment', *Essays in Dynamic Economics Applied*, London, 1961, p. 249.
77. Sayers, R. S., *Central Banking After Bagehot*, p. 6.
78. See above, Chapter 3.
79. P = the price level and T = the level of transactions.
80. Harrod, *Money*, p. 160.
81. Ibid.
82. Harrod, 'Topical comment', pp. 241–2.
83. Ibid., p. 245–6.
84. Chandler, *The Economics of Money and Banking*, op. cit., p. 337. K (Marshallian) relates the total demands for money balances (L) to the level of income (Y).
85. Sayers, op. cit. p. 35.

Appendix I

THE FIRST LIST OF BANKS ISSUED BY THE BANK OF LEBANON, 1 SEPTEMBER 1965

Name of bank	Date of establishment or registration at the Ministry of National Economy
Société Centrale de Banque	25.3.26
Banco di Roma	25.10.26
Banque Misr-Liban	18.12.29
Banque Tohme	30.12.42
Arab Bank Limited	6.5.43
Banque Nationale pour le Commerce et l'Industrie (Afrique)	15.1.44
British Bank of the Middle East	22.6.46
Société Bancaire du Liban	28.10.46
Rafidain Bank	23.6.48
Compagnie Française de Crédit et de Banque	19.12.49
Banque Libanaise pour le Commerce	11.5.50
Banque Sabbagh	28.8.50
Banque G. Trad (Crédit Lyonnais)	10.3.51
Banque du Liban et d'Outre Mer	16.6.51
Banque Intra	17.12.51
Lebanese United Bank	3.3.52
Saudi National Commercial Bank	5.8.52
Banque Al-Ahli	27.3.53
Banque Belgo-Libanaise	17.8.53
Algameine Bank Nederland	2.3.54
Commercial Bank	30.11.54
Eastern Commercial Bank	6.6.55
Chase Manhattan Bank	8.7.55
First National City Bank	12.7.55
Eastern Bank Limited	4.11.55
Banque Chartouni	28.3.56
Banque Saradar	28.7.56

Banque Beyrouth et des Pays Arabes	10.11.56
Comptoir National d'Eip	19.3.57
Banque Joseph Lati & Fils	16.12.57
Banque Naayem	19.4.58
Banque Beyrouth Ryad	5.9.58
Banque S. Schoucair	15.9.58
Banque d'Epargne	16.9.58
Banque Pharaon & Chiha	6.1.59
Banque de Crédit National	8.6.59
Mebco Bank	25.7.59
Bank of Lebanon & the Middle East	25.11.59
Banque Byblos	10.12.59
Adcom Bank	24.12.59
Union National Bank	28.12.59
Banque Lombard-Liban	18.1.60
Arab Real Estate Bank	22.4.60
Banque des Activités Économiques	7.5.60
Banque Kabbabe	2.9.60
Lebanese Savings Bank	23.9.60
Banque de l'Économie Arabe	3.11.60
Banque de l'Industrie et du Travail	21.11.60
Jordan National Bank	22.12.60
Eastern Development Bank	3.4.61
Banque Libano-Bresilienne	28.4.61
Development Bank	5.5.61
Crédit Libanais	29.7.61
Banque Sogex-Liban	17.8.61
Banque Beyrouth Pour le Commerce	13.10.61
Banque Audi	3.2.62
Banque Nasr Libano-Africaine	8.2.62
Bank of Kuwait and the Arab World	26.5.62
International Arab Bank	15.8.62
Crédit Hypothecaire Libanais	2.10.62
Banque Joseph Geagea	4.10.62
Société Tunisienne de Banque	22.10.62
Kairouz Bank	29.10.62
Banque Al-Omrane	29.11.62
Banque de Crédit Populaire	20.12.62
Banque Emile Farrane	9.1.63
Banque Saderate Iran	15.1.63
Société Nouvelle de la BSL	2.3.63

Moscow Narodny Bank Ltd	30.3.63
Bank of America National Trust and Savings Association	1.6.63
Banque Majdalany	14.6.63
Banque de Crédit Professionnel	7.8.63
Rif Bank	14.8.63
Commercial Business Bank	8.8.63
Banque d'Affaires Immobilières	19.8.63
Banque Al-Arz	10.9.63
Prosperity Bank of Lebanon	17.10.63
Rabia Cooperative Bank	23.10.63
National Cooperative Bank	6.11.63
Investment Bank	23.11.63
Banque de l'Essor Économique Libanais	20.12.63
Beirut Universal Bank	6.1.64
Beirut National City Bank	12.2.64
Banque Libanaise des Émigrés	26.3.64
Federal Arab Bank	27.3.64
Habin Bank Overseas Ltd	9.4.64
Bank of Nova Scotia	8.5.56

Appendix II

ALTERNATIVE APPROACHES TO THE DETERMINATION OF CEILINGS ON CENTRAL BANK CREDIT

(i) United States

A study organised in 1968 by the Board of Governors of the Federal Reserve System on the discount mechanism proposed a 'Basic Borrowing Privilege', plus additional 'adjustment credit'.[1] The former is actually a re-discount ceiling determined as a proportion of a bank's capital stock and surplus. It is determined on a weekly average basis and is equal to between 20 and 40 per cent of a bank's capital and can go up to $1 million; between 10 and 20 per cent of its capital stock and reserves between $1 million and $10 million; and 10 per cent of capital stock and reserves in excess of $10 million. A bank, therefore, with $1 million of capital stock and reserves may borrow between $200,000 and $400,000 on each day of the seven-day reserve period or between $1,400,000 and $2,800,000 on one day during the period. Moreover, the bank cannot borrow in more than half the number of weeks in any quarter of the year, i.e., it can use this ceiling in at most twenty-five weeks in any one year. The additional adjustment credit was designed to provide for seasonal and emergency needs.

(ii) Austria

Under the Credit Control Agreement (revised in July 1966) credit ceilings were determined as fixed proportions of an institution's net worth and liabilities. They were equal to 70 per cent of liabilities, plus 75 per cent of net worth.[2]

(iii) France

Re-discount ceilings were introduce at the Banque de France in 1948. Originally, they were associated with each bank's discount current account at the Banque de France. They were, therefore, set at about the level of re-discounts outstanding on 30 September 1948. The global ceilings subsequently rose due to adjustments in the ceilings of individual banks. Afterwards, they were fixed on the basis of a complex formula, taking into consideration factors such as deposits, assets and capital accounts.[3]

(iv) Italy

Ceilings on collateralised advances are set at a certain percentage of the bank's total deposits, but are reviewed and revised from time to time. Commercial banks do not know what their ceilings are. There are no re-discount ceilings.[4]

(v) Federal Republic of Germany

Each credit institution in West Germany has access to the discount window on the basis of a re-discount quota established by the Central Bank. This quota depends basically on the type of credit institution and its equity capital. It is determined as a fixed multiple of an institution's net worth and is reviewed frequently. (The method for the computation of quotas has not been published. Any institution can ascertain the amount of its quota.)[5]

(vi) Japan

Ceilings for Central Bank credit (discounts and advances combined) were introduced in 1962. They were set at the level of total borrowing from the Bank of Japan at the time. In 1964 ceilings for individual banks were determined as a percentage of the total ceilings. The percentage depended on the Bank's capital, deposits and the amount of money borrowed by it in the call-money market. Later (August 1967), a more complex formula was adopted, based on capital funds (including reserves and undistributed profits). From this, the amount of borrowing in the call-money market and that from the Bank of Japan was subtracted. This new method gave an advantage to banks with large and increasing capital funds. The ceiling is revised every three months, and the duration of credit varies from two days to three months in the light of the asset needs of the individual bank.[6]

(vii) Belgium

Re-discount quotas are set for individual banks on the basis of their capital and reserves, separately for certified bills and others. In fact quota ceilings have been reached only in exceptional circumstances, and the National Bank has almost never refused to discount eligible bills.[7]

NOTES

1. 'Reappraisal of the Federal Reserve Discount Mechanism', *Federal Reserve Bulletin*, Board of Governors of the Federal Reserve System, July 1968, pp. 546–9.
2. Net worth is reduced here by the value of certain assets such as real estate, buildings and permanent investment in other enterprises. Garvy, George, 'Fundamental

Reappraisal of the Discount Mechanism, The Discount Mechanism in Leading Industrial Countries Since World War II' (Board of Governors of the Federal Reserve System), pp. 67–8.
3. Ibid., p. 108–9.
4. Ibid., p. 144.
5. Ibid., p. 130.
6. Ibid., pp. 160–1.
7. Ibid., p. 79.

Appendix III

LIST OF INTRA BANK PARTNERSHIPS

Banks

Beidas was Chairman and General Director of the following banks:

The Arab Real Estate Bank S.A.L.
The Bank of Kuwait and the Arab World S.A.L.
Intra Bank Geneva S.A.
Bank of the North Ltd
Bank of Liberia Ltd
Bank Intra Sao Paolo S.A.
Bank Intra Rio de Janeiro S.A.

Companies

Beidas was Chairman and General Director of the National Electricity Company S.A.L. and was also a member of the board of directors of the following companies:

International Traders
Radio-Orient
Libano-Suisse Société d'Assurances S.A.L.
Middle East Airlines, Air Liban S.A.L.
Mideast Aircraft Services Co. S.A.L.
Société des Eaux de Jal-El-Dib. S.A.L.
Les Constructions Modernes S. A. L.
Société Financière & Immobilière du Port de Beyrouth
Société de Gestion & d'Exploitation du Port de Beyrouth
Rabia Company S. A. L.
Chantiers Navals de la Coitat

Beidas was also founder and board member of the following:

Lebanese Dry Dock and Ship Building Repairing Company
Near East Resources S. A. L.
The Arab Tankers S. A. L.

Bibliography

OFFICIAL DOCUMENTS

Money and Credit Board: Conseil de la Monnaie et du Crédit (CMC). *Minutes of the Board Meeting*, 1961–1963.

The Central Council of the Bank of Lebanon, *Minutes of the meetings of the Central Council*, 1963–1972.

Banque de Syrie et du Liban: 'Rapport relatif aux propositions de revision de la loi fédérale du 23 décembre 1953 sur la Banque nationale Suisse' (extension des moyens d'action de la Banque d'émission), 16 May 1966.

Motta, Dr Ricardo, Vice President of the Board of Management of the Swiss National Bank, 'Some Aspects of the Swiss National Bank's Policy', lecture delivered on 16 June 1962 to the International Conference of Commercial Bank Economists in Hertenstein, Lucerne (in German).

Iklé, Dr M., member of the Direktorium of the Swiss National Bank, 'Switzerland's International Capital Relations', address delivered before the Statistical and Economic Society, Zurich, on 27 February 1967.

Hay, Alexandre, Vice-Président de la Direction Générale de la Banque Nationale Suisse, 'Les Moyens d'Action de la Banque Nationale Suisse et leur extension', conférence donnée de la réunion des cadres de la caisse d'épargne de Genéve et du Crédit foncier Vaudois à Territat, 21 octobre 1967.

'Fundamental Reappraisal of the Discount Mechanism', prepared for the Steering Committee for the Fundamental Reappraisal of the Discount Mechanism Appointed by the Board of Governors of the Federal Reserve System: 1961, 1962 and 1963 prepared by Khalil Salem: 1964 and 1965 prepared by George Chahine Medawar.

Ministry of Justice, *The Official Gazette*.

Bank of England: *The Bank of England Act, 1946, and the Charters of the Bank of England*; *The Bank of England Charters and Statutes, 1960*; *The Bank of England Internal Administration* (mimeographed), no date. *Bank of England Quarterly Bulletin.*

Her Majesty's Stationery Office, Committee on the Working of the Monetary System, *Report*, August 1959, Comnd 827, London, reprinted 1964.

Board of Governors of the Federal Reserve System: Federal Reserve Act (as amended through October 1, 1961), Washington, 1961; *The Federal*

Reserve System: Purposes and Functions, 4th edition, Washington DC, 1961; *Federal Reserve Bulletin* (Washington DC); Reappraisal of the Federal Reserve Discount Mechanism *Report on Research undertaken in Connection with a System Study*, August 1968. *Report of A System Committee*, July 1968.

Federal Reserve Bank of New York: Volcker, Paul A., President, *A Broader Role for Monetary Targets* 22 February 1977; Davis, Richard, Senior Economic Adviser, *Monetary Objectives and Monetary Policy*, 2 March 1977.

The Swiss National Bank, *The Swiss National Bank* (mimeographed) September 1965.

INTERNATIONAL DOCUMENTS

International Monetary Fund: *International Financial Statistics*; *Balance of Payments Yearbook, 1956-57*, Washington 1959; *Articles of Agreement of the International Monetary Fund*, Washington (4th printing) 1959.

PERIODICALS

The Economist
The Banker
Journal of Monetary Economics
Financial Times
Prospects, Business News Survey, Swiss Bank Corporation
Le Commerce du Levant
Mid-East Commerce
Businessmen
Almassaref (The Banks)
Al-Dalil Al-Iktissady (Economic Guide)
Lebanese and Arab Economy
Al-Iktissady (The Economist)
Al-Nahar, *Al-Anwar*, *Al-Hayat*, *Al-Moharrer* — Beirut daily newspapers

BOOKS

Ascheim, Joseph, *Techniques of Monetary Control*, Baltimore, Johns Hopkins University Press, 1961.

Aschinger, F. M., *Switzerland as a Financial Centre*, 50th Anniversary Commemorative Lecture (Cairo, National Bank of Egypt, 1960).

Bar, Hans, J., in collaboration with Ruesch, Ernest, *The Banking System of Switzerland*, revised 3rd edition, Zurich, 1964.

Clarke, W. M., *The City in the World Economy*, London, The Institute of Economic Affairs, 1966.

Chandler, Lester V., *Benjamin Strong, Central Banker*, Washington , D.C., Brookings Institution, 1958.

Chandler, Lester V., and Goldfeld, Stephen M., *The Economics of Money and Banking*, New York, Harper & Row, 1948.

Cobbold, Cameron Fromanteel, Baron, *Some Thoughts on Central Banking*, Stamp Memorial Lecture delivered before the University of London on 13 November 1962, London, Athlone Press, University of London, 1962.

Commission on Money and Credit, *Monetary Management*, Englewood Cliffs, N. J., Prentice-Hall, 1963.

Crowther, Geoffrey, *An Outline of Money*, London, Thomas Nelson and Sons, 1948 (revised edition).

De Kock, M. J., *Central Banking*, London, Staples Press, 1961.

De S. Gunasekera, H. E., *From Dependent Currency to Central Banking in Ceylon, An Analysis of Monetary Experience, 1825–1957*, London, London School of Economics, 1962.

Economic Research Institute, *Middle East Economics Papers*, Beirut, American University of Beirut, 1954–63.

Einzig, Paul, *Foreign Dollar Loans in Europe*, London, Macmillan, 1965. *The History of Foreign Exchange*, London, Macmillan, 1962.

Ellsworth, F. T., *The International Economy*, revised edition, New York, Macmillan, 1958.

European Economic Community, *Instruments of Monetary Policy in the Countries of the European Economic Community*, Brussels, EEC, 1962.

Fehrenbach, T. R., *The Gnomes of Zurich*, London, Leslie Frewin, 1966.

Friedman, Milton, and Roose, Robert V., *The Balance of Payments: Free Versus Fixed Exchange Rates*, Washington D.C., American Enterprise Institute for Public Policy Research, 1967.

Goldenweiser, E. A., *American Monetary Policy*, 1st edition, New York, McGraw-Hill, 1951.

Guenther, Harry F., 'Banking in Lebanon', *The Banker*, London, July 1964.

Hall, N. F., *The Exchange Equalisation Account*, London, Macmillan, 1935.

Harrod, Sir Roy, *International Economics*, Cambridge, Cambridge University Press, 1963.

Harrod, R. F., *Reforming the World's Money*, London, Macmillan, 1965.

Harrod, R. F., *Money*, London, Macmillan, 1969.

Hawtrey, R. G., *Economic Rebirth*, London, Longmans, Green, 1946.

Hawtrey, R. G., *The Art of Central Banking*, 2nd edition, London, Frank Cass, 1962.

Hawtrey, R. G. *The Gold Standard in Theory and Practice*, 5th edition, London, Longmans, Green, 1947.

Hoss, Salim, 'The roles of central banking in Lebanon', doctoral thesis, Indiana University, 1961.

Hourani, A. F., *Syria and Lebanon*, London, Oxford University Press, 1954.

Hutchison, T. W., *Positive Economics and Policy Objectives*, London, Allen and Unwin, 1964.

Iklé, Max, *Switzerland: An International Banking and Finance Centre*, Stroudsburg, Pa., Dowden, Hutchinson & Ross, 1972.

Irfed, *Liban—Situation Economique*, 1962, Rapport Préliminaire sur l'Economie du Liban (7 volumes).

Joint Development Group, *The Postwar Development of the Republic of Vietnam*, Policies and Programs, New York, Praeger, 1970.

Kamerschen, David R. and Klise, S. Eugene, *Money and Banking*, 2nd edition, Edmund, South Western American Publishing Company, 1963.

Kanaan, Daoud Khalil, *Beirut in History* (in Arabic), Beirut, 1963.

Kent, Raymond F., *Money and Banking*, 3rd edition, New York, Holt, Rinehart and Winston, Inc, 1957.

Keynes, John Maynard, *A Treatise on Money*, Vol. I and II, London, Macmillan, 1971.

Kindleberger, Charles F., *International Economics*, Richard D. Erwin, Homewood, Illinois, 1963.

Kisch, Sir Cecil and Elkin, W. A., *Central Banks, A Study of the Constitutions of Banks of Issue, with an Analysis of Representative Charters*, 4th edition, London, Macmillan, 1932.

Klat, P. J., *Lebanese Prosperity: Myth or Miracle*, Middle East Forum, February 1961.

Livingstone, J. M., *Britain and the World Economy*, Harmondsworth, Penguin Books, 1966.

Mahmassani, Yahya A., *A Central Bank for Lebanon* (American University of Beirut), 1961.

Marse, Dr Fouad, *Money and Banking in the Arab Countries*, Arab League Institute of Arab Higher Studies, Syria and Lebanon (in Arabic), 1958.

Meade, J. E., *The Theory of International Economic Policy*, Vol I, *The Balance of Payments*, Oxford, Oxford University Press, 1962.

Mikdashi, Zuhayr, 'The monetary system of Lebanon', MA thesis, American University of Beirut, Beirut, 1956.

Porter, Harvey, *The History of Beirut*, Syria, 1912. Originally reprinted from *Al-Kulliyah*, the journal of the Syrian Protestant College of Beirut, Syria.

Robinson, Roland I., Boehmler, Erwin W., Franc, June H., and Loring C. Farewell, eds., *Financial Institutions*, Richard D. Erwin, Homewood, Illinois, 1965.

Samuelson, Paul, A., *Economics*, 5th edition, New York, McGraw-Hill, 1961.

Sayers, R. S., *Banking in Western Europe*, Oxford, Clarendon Press, 1962.

Sayers, R. S., *Central Banking after Bagehot*, London, Oxford University Press, 1957.

Sayers, R. S., *Modern Banking*, 5th edition, Oxford, Clarendon Press, 1960.

Scammell, W. M., *International Monetary Policy*, 2nd edition, London, Macmillan, 1964.

Scigliano, Robert, *South Vietnam, Nation Under Stress*, Boston, Houghton Mifflin, 1964, p. viii.

Viner, Jacob, *Problems of Monetary Control*, Essays in International Finance, No. 45, May 1964, International Finance Section, Princeton, N.J., 1964.

Whittlesey, C. R., and Wilson, J. S. C., *Essays in Money and Banking: in Honour of R. S. Sayers*, Oxford, Clarendon Press, 1968.

Yaffi, Talha, 'The monetary and banking system of Lebanon with special reference to monetary reform', doctoral thesis, University of Wisconsin, 1958.